W9-CNS-702

BUSINESS REPLY CARD

FIRST CLASS   PERMIT NO. 33107   PHILADELPHIA, PA

POSTAGE WILL BE PAID BY ADDRESSEE

HANLEY & BELFUS, INC.
Medical Publishers
P.O. Box 1377
Philadelphia, PA 19105-9990

BUSINESS REPLY CARD

FIRST CLASS   PERMIT NO. 33107   PHILADELPHIA, PA

POSTAGE WILL BE PAID BY ADDRESSEE

HANLEY & BELFUS, INC.
Medical Publishers
P.O. Box 1377
Philadelphia, PA 19105-9990

STATE OF THE ART REVIEWS (STARs)

SUBJECT	FREQUENCY	PRICE (U.S.)	PRICE (Foreign)	PRICE (Single)
☐ CARDIAC SURGERY	Triannual	$88.00	$98.00	$38.00
☐ NEUROSURGERY	Biannual	$75.00	$84.00	$42.00
☐ OCCUPATIONAL MEDICINE	Quarterly	$68.00	$78.00	$29.00
☐ PHYSICAL MED & REHAB (PM&R)	Quarterly	$66.00	$76.00	$28.00
☐ SPINE	Triannual	$78.00	$88.00	$34.00

☐ 1989 subscription ☐ 1988 subscription   ☐ Single issue
Check subject title above.   Title _____

I enclose payment: ☐ Check ☐ Visa ☐ Master Card   Credit Card # _____ Exp. Date _____
Name _____   Signature _____
Title _____   Street Address _____
Company/Hospital _____   City/State/Zip _____

Send order to:
HANLEY & BELFUS, INC.
210 South 13th Street / Philadelphia, PA 19107 / 215-546-7293

STATE OF THE ART REVIEWS (STARs)

SUBJECT	FREQUENCY	PRICE (U.S.)	PRICE (Foreign)	PRICE (Single)
☐ CARDIAC SURGERY	Triannual	$88.00	$98.00	$38.00
☐ NEUROSURGERY	Biannual	$75.00	$84.00	$42.00
☐ OCCUPATIONAL MEDICINE	Quarterly	$68.00	$78.00	$29.00
☐ PHYSICAL MED & REHAB (PM&R)	Quarterly	$66.00	$76.00	$28.00
☐ SPINE	Triannual	$78.00	$88.00	$34.00

☐ 1989 subscription ☐ 1988 subscription   ☐ Single issue
Check subject title above.   Title _____

I enclose payment: ☐ Check ☐ Visa ☐ Master Card   Credit Card # _____ Exp. Date _____
Name _____   Signature _____
Title _____   Street Address _____
Company/Hospital _____   City/State/Zip _____

Send order to:
HANLEY & BELFUS, INC.
210 South 13th Street / Philadelphia, PA 19107 / 215-546-7293

Spine

Spinal Segmental Pain and Sensory Disturbance

Michael A. Wienir, M.D.
Editor

Volume 2 / Number 4 September 1988
HANLEY & BELFUS, INC.-Philadelphia

STATE OF THE ART REVIEWS

Publisher: HANLEY & BELFUS, INC.
210 South 13th Street
Philadelphia, PA 19107

SPINE: State of the Art Reviews
September 1988 Volume 2, Number 4

ISSN 0887-9869
ISBN 0-932883-69-9

SPINE: State of the Art Reviews is published triannually (three times per year) by Hanley & Belfus, Inc., 210 South 13th Street, Philadelphia, Pennsylvania 19107.

POSTMASTER: Send address changes to SPINE: State of the Art Reviews, Hanley & Belfus, Inc., 210 South 13th Street, Philadelphia, PA 19107

This issue is Volume 2, Number 4.

The Editor of this publication is Linda C. Belfus.

The subscription price is $78.00 per year U.S., $88.00 per year outside U.S. (add $30.00 for air mail). Single issues $34.00 U.S., $38.00 outside U.S. (add $10.00 for single issue air mail).

CONTENTS

subspecialties. The authors provide a comprehensive review of all the various subgroups of TOS, including a look at how each subgroup has fared over the last 30 years since the term was coined.

The author reviews the common entrapment neuropathies of the arm in terms of their pathogenesis, clinical features, electrodiagnostic localization, and treatment. Two frequently encountered entrapment syndromes, the carpal tunnel syndrome and ulnar nerve entrapment at the elbow, are discussed in detail. Some focal mononeuropathies that are secondary to external factors are also described.

Radicular leg pain associated with low back pain is a costly and ubiquitous problem. This article presents a rational and convenient classification of the causes of segmental sensory distribution and radicular pain in the lower extremity and outlines the salient clinical features.

The term RSD refers to a constellation of symptoms and signs following injury to bone, nerve, and soft tissue. The discussion focuses on RSD syndromes in the extremities, and addresses clinical features, pathophysiology of pain, diagnostic studies, and various treatment modalities. Two case reports are presented that illustrate principles in the management of RSD complicating trauma and orthopedic surgery.

Patients with focal nerve damage generally present with some combination of pain and neurologic deficit. Specific syndromes are discussed according to anatomic regions: posterior hip and thigh pain, lateral and anterior hip and knee pain, medial thigh and leg pain, anterior tibial pain, posterior calf pain, and heel and sole pain.

CONTRIBUTORS

Ulrich Batzdorf, M.D.
Professor of Neurosurgery, UCLA School of Medicine, Los Angeles, California

Said R. Beydoun, M.D.
Associate Professor of Neurology, University of Southern California, Los Angeles County–University of Southern California Medical Center, Los Angeles, California

William T. Couldwell, M.D.
Resident, Los Angeles County–University of Southern California Medical Center, Los Angeles, California

John J. Kelly, Jr., M.D.
Associate Professor, Department of Neurology, Tufts–New England Medical Center, Boston, Massachusetts

Phillip H. Omohundro, M.D.
Cincinnati Sportsmedicine and The Midwest Institute for Orthopedics, Cincinnati, Ohio

Richard Payne, M.D.
Associate Professor of Neurology, University of Cincinnati Medical Center, Cincinnati, Ohio

John M. Porter, M.D.
Professor of Surgery, and Head, Division of Vascular Surgery, Oregon Health Sciences University, Portland, Oregon

Austin J. Sumner, M.D.
Professor of Neurology, Hospital of the University of Pennsylvania, Philadelphia, Pennsylvania

Martin H. Weiss, M.D.
Professor and Chairman, Department of Neurosurgery, University of Southern California School of Medicine; Chief of Neurosurgery, Los Angeles County–University of Southern California Medical Center, Los Angeles, California

Michael A. Wienir, M.D.
Assistant Clinical Professor of Neurology, UCLA School of Medicine, Los Angeles, California

Asa J. Wilbourn, M.D.
Director, EMG Laboratory, Cleveland Clinic; Assistant Clinical Professor of Neurology, Case Western Reserve University School of Medicine, Cleveland, Ohio

PUBLISHED ISSUES 1986–1988

FUTURE ISSUES 1988–1989

Subscriptions and single issues available from the publisher—Hanley & Belfus, Inc., Medical Publishers, 210 South 13th Street, Philadelphia PA 19107 (215) 546-7293.

PREFACE

Physicians dealing with patients who have spinal disorders may encounter a number of bewildering patient complaints. Local and limb pain and limb sensory symptoms are the most common regardless of the underlying etiology or pathology.

This issue of **Spine: State of the Art Reviews** presents practical approaches to the diagnosis of patients presenting with local and limb symptoms of pain, numbness, paresthesia, and dysesthesia. The problems of diagnosis of local musculoskeletal, orthopedic, rheumatologic, and vascular conditions are not addressed but rather those entities affecting the neural structures are emphasized.

In the first chapter, I outline the symptoms, signs, and electrodiagnostic features of cervical and lumbosacral radiculopathy. Next, Dr. Ulrich Batzdorf discusses the differential diagnosis of lesions that may cause cervical radiculopathy. The next chapters focus on neurologic conditions that must be considered in the differential diagnosis of patients presenting with upper extremity pain and numbness: I discuss the anatomy and etiologic processes affecting the brachial plexus; Dr. Austin Sumner presents his views on idiopathic brachial neuritis; Dr. Asa Wilbourn and Dr. John Porter provide a comprehensive review of the literature on thoracic outlet syndromes; and Dr. Said Beydoun discusses focal entrapment neuropathies of the upper extremities. The subsequent chapters deal with lumbosacral pathology and neurologic problems that must be considered in the differential diagnosis of leg radicular symptoms: Dr. Martin Weiss and Dr. William Couldwell review the differential diagnosis of lesions that cause lumbar radiculopathy; entrapment neuropathies of the lower extremities, lumbar plexopathy, and diabetic amyotrophy are considered by Dr. John Kelly; and Dr. Richard Payne and Dr. Phillip Omohundro review concepts of reflex sympathetic dystrophy that may affect both the arm and the leg.

I am confident that this book will serve as a useful, helpful, and valuable guide to evaluating and managing patients with limb pain and sensory disturbance. I am most appreciative of the superb efforts of all the experts who authored chapters.

MICHAEL A. WIENIR, M.D.
GUEST EDITOR

MICHAEL A. WIENIR, MD

LIMB RADICULAR PAIN AND SENSORY DISTURBANCE

Assistant Clinical Professor of Neurology, UCLA School of Medicine, Los Angeles, California

Reprint requests to:
Michael A. Wienir, MD
San Fernando Valley Neurologic
  Medical Group, Inc.
18370 Burbank Blvd., Suite 107
Tarzana, CA 91356

With the exception of localized neck and low back pain, the most common complaint of patients with cervical or lumbar spine disease or injury is pain in the arm or leg. Radicular pain is more common in the leg than in the arm and least common in the thoracic region.[43] Sciatica or lumbar radiculopathy alone has a prevalence of 4.8% in men and 2.5% in women over the age of 35.[5] Sensory symptoms manifested as numbness, paresthesia, and dysesthesia extending into the extremity are also commonly noted. Patients with primary musculoskeletal pathology involving the muscle, ligaments, tendons, joints, discs, and bones of the neck or back almost invariably report localized neck or back pain, stiffness, and impaired range of motion. On occasion, however, patients without demonstrable intraspinal injury or nerve or nerve root pathology will report pain and even sensory symptoms extending down one or both arms or legs. This referred subjective discomfort represents a sclerotomal reference pattern and does not absolutely indicate primary neural pathology. Some of the referred limb pain may be secondary to facet joint changes affecting small branches of posterior primary rami of nerve roots, but this is not associated with evidence of intraspinal pathology. In addition, leg pain may be secondary to retroperitoneal or pelvic processes, and arm pain may be a manifestation of cardiac or chest disease.

The most important cause of limb pain and sensory disturbance is encroachment on, irritation of, or injury to nerve roots. It is the onset, persistence, and evolution of nerve root symptoms and signs which mandate awareness of possible significant spinal pathology and generate the need for appropriate diagnostic and

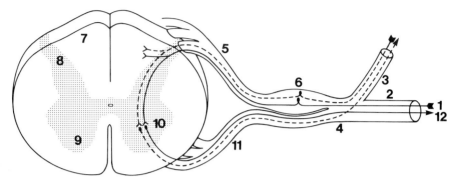

FIGURE 1.   Cross-section of spinal cord segment.
   1: Sensory (afferent) fiber (axon) from muscle
   2: Anterior primary ramus of spinal nerve
   3: Posterior primary ramus of spinal nerve
   4: Spinal nerve
   5: Dorsal sensory nerve root
   6: Dorsal root ganglion (cell bodies of sensory axons)
   7: Spinal cord white matter fiber tracts
   8: Spinal cord gray matter—dorsal (sensory) horn
   9: Spinal cord gray matter—ventral (motor) horn
  10: Site of monosynaptic connection of reflex arc
  11: Ventral motor nerve root
  12: Motor (efferent) fiber (axon) to neuromuscular junction

therapeutic intervention. The identification of spinal root lesions, radiculopathy, is frequently challenging. Confusion can arise in patients with pain but without classic sensory, motor, and reflex findings on clinical examination. Difficulty with diagnosis also occurs in patients who have sensory and motor symptoms and signs but do not have pain. In a recent review of the surgical results in lumbar disc disease, Rish[77] reported 64% of surgical patients with a satisfactory response, 24% with a poor response, and 12% who were frank failures. A review of 1500 surgical cases in the literature found 50% excellent responses, 80% improved or bettered, 20% continued with symptoms, 10% had recurrence, a 3% chance of infection and a 1% mortality. Successful conservative care of sciatica in myelographically proven lumbar disc disease varies from study to study.[5,77] I believe that the more accurate the diagnosis and the more intelligent the treatment plan, the better the results. A clear understanding of the nature of radiculopathy is essential in dealing with patients with limb pain and sensory disturbance to avoid unnecessary, useless, and harmful treatment and to guide the physician toward appropriate action.

ANATOMY OF THE REFLEX ARC

To understand the nature of radiculopathy, one has to consider and remember the basic nature of the reflex arc (Fig. 1).[37,38,44,76] Sensory nerve fibers in the peripheral nerves carry pain and position information from peripheral receptors in skin, muscle, and other structures back toward the spinal cord. These sensory fibers then separate from the nerve and enter the dorsal root or sensory root. Here they are not associated with motor fibers as they are in the

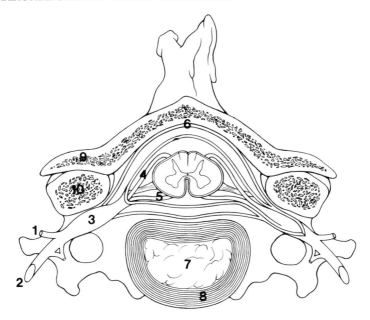

FIGURE 2.   Cross-section of spinal cord with relation of neural structures to bone, disc, and dura at neural foramina.

    1: Dorsal primary ramus
    2: Ventral primary ramus
    3: Dorsal root ganglion
    4: Dorsal root
    5: Ventral root
    6: Dura
    7: Disc—nucleus pulposus
    8: Disc—annulus fibrosis
    9: Inferior articular facet of rostral vertebra
  10: Superior articular facet of caudal vertebra

peripheral nerve. The nerve cell body of the sensory nerves is located in the spinal or dorsal root ganglion. Sensory fibers then continue on into the spinal cord where some fibers course up and down the cord and other fibers continue down to the ventral gray matter of the cord where they synapse with connections of the cell bodies of motor nerves. The motor nerve fibers then exit the cord and travel in the ventral or motor root independent of sensory fibers. Finally, the ventral root joins the dorsal root to form the peripheral spinal nerve.

The spinal cord and the dorsal and ventral roots are located within the spinal canal (Fig. 2). These structures come together to form the spinal nerve just outside the dura in the region of the neural foramina where the spinal nerve roots exit from the confines of the spinal canal. A dorsal primary ramus extends to the paraspinous region and a ventral primary ramus continues toward the limb, combining with other ventral rami to form the structures of the brachial plexus and from there the peripheral nerves. The symptoms and signs seen in the patient with radiculopathy depend on which of these structures is affected rather than on the nature of the underlying pathology.

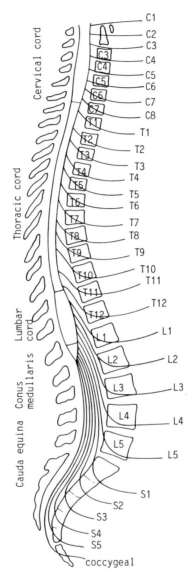

FIGURE 3. Segmental organization of spinal cord and spinal nerves and relationship to vertebral bodies.

SEGMENTAL NATURE OF NERVE ROOTS

The spinal nerves and nerve roots are arranged in a rigorous formal segmental fashion.[17,18,44,45] Individual spinal nerves and nerve roots can be numbered in a consistent and stereotyped fashion, corresponding to the segment of origin in the spinal cord and the subsequent point of exit through neural foramina. There are eight cervical segments, although C1 has no sensory representation. There are twelve thoracic roots and segments, five lumbar roots, and five sacral roots (Fig. 3).

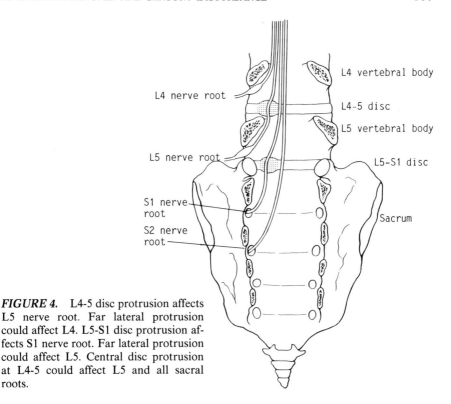

FIGURE 4. L4-5 disc protrusion affects L5 nerve root. Far lateral protrusion could affect L4. L5-S1 disc protrusion affects S1 nerve root. Far lateral protrusion could affect L5. Central disc protrusion at L4-5 could affect L5 and all sacral roots.

In the cervical area, the nerve roots exit the spinal canal through foramina or openings above the vertebral bodies of the same number. For example, the C6 nerve root exits through the C5-6 foramina and the C7 nerve root exits through the C6-7 opening. A C5-6 disc herniation generally results in a C6 radiculopathy and a C6-7 disc protrusion results in a C7 radiculopathy. The C8 nerve root exits through the C7–T1 foramina, and the subsequent thoracic roots exit below the vertebral body of the same number. Therefore, the T10 nerve root exits through the T10–T11 foramina.

In the lumbar region, the nerve roots also exit below the vertebral body of the same number. For example, the L5 nerve root exits through the L5–S1 foramina (Fig. 4). However, disc herniation at this level generally spares the L5 nerve root, which actually exits above the area of the disc. L5–S1 disc herniation usually catches the S1 nerve root as it passes downward toward the next neural foramina. L4–5 disc lesions tend to spare the L4 nerve root and result in L5 radiculopathy. A far lateral disc protrusion or spondylotic process may of course result in irritation of the root exiting at that level. Thus, a lateral L4-5 lesion would cause an L4 radiculopathy, and a lateral L5–S1 lesion would cause an L5 radiculopathy.

Sensory fibers consistently innervate relatively specific areas of skin and underlying tissue, and a pattern of pain and sensory disturbance emerges with injury or damage to a given nerve root or spinal nerve. The areas of skin innervated by specific spinal segments or sensory roots are called dermatomes (Figs. 5 and 6).

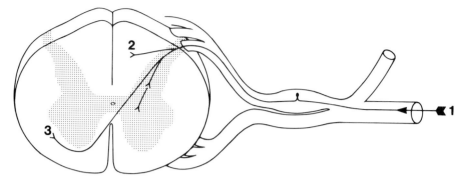

FIGURE 5.   Cross-section of spinal cord.
 1: Sensory (afferent) fiber (axon) from dermatomal skin receptors
 2: Large fibers bring position/vibratory sense information to spinal cord
 3: Small fibers bring pain/temperature sense information to spinal cord

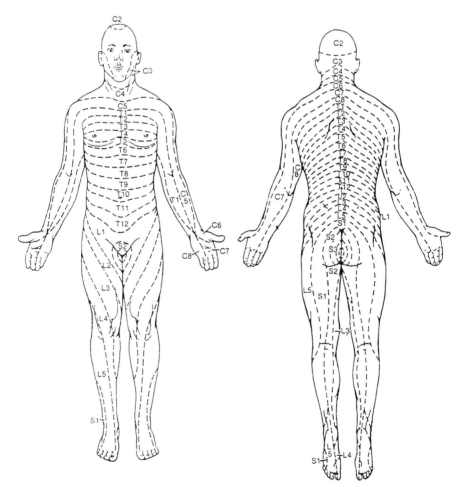

FIGURE 6.   Sensory charts showing anterior and posterior aspects of the body.

In addition, there is a consistent stereotyped innervation of limb muscles by motor fibers in the ventral roots and spinal nerves. Therefore, a radicular lesion involving motor fibers will be associated with a characteristic pattern of motor disturbance.

The deep tendon reflexes represent a clinical way to examine the integrity of the spinal reflex arc, which is also organized in a segmental fashion. Tapping a tendon with a hammer shortens the tendon and stretches the muscle, resulting in stimulation of sensory nerve fibers. Electrical information then follows the path of the reflex arc. Segmental motor fibers are activated and the result is an observable twich or contraction of a specific muscle or muscle group.

By ascertaining the distribution of subjective sensory symptoms and pain and by correlating this with specific motor, sensory, and reflex findings, the physician can often determine which spinal nerve or nerve root is involved. Electrodiagnostic studies are also frequently utilized to objectively document abnormalities in a specific nerve root distribution and to extend the sensitivity of the clinical examination.

SENSORY RADICULAR SYMPTOMS AND SIGNS

When pain fibers in the sensory nerve roots or the spinal nerves are irritated, the result is pain in the distribution of the root involved. The pain may, however, often be poorly localized. With subjective symptoms alone and without definitive neurologic or physiologic findings, it is impossible to accurately localize the site of the abnormality.[70] The discomfort is described in a variety of ways.[34] Often sharp, it is frequently lancinating or shooting or radiating but may be described as a persistent, vague, dull aching or agonizing pain of variable intensity. Often the pain is described as burning, searing, tearing, cutting, hot, or boring. The pain may be continuous and unrelenting or intermittent and at times is associated with muscle cramping. Depending on the underlying etiology, the pain may be dependent on position or movement. In lumbosacral radiculopathy, pain is often precipitated or worsened by positions or activities that increase intra-disc pressure.[72] Valsalva maneuvers associated with coughing, sneezing, or bowel movement, and forward flexion frequently increase pain. Pain is often increased by sitting and lifting. Although the pain may be in the distribution of the nerve root, the pain may be referred to only a portion of the nerve root distribution.

The nature of the pain description depends on the education and communication skills of the patient. In addition, there is a congenital variability in the ability to perceive pain. The patient's personality is important in determining the response to pain. Some individuals are stoic whereas others are hypochondriacal or exaggerate the nature of the pain. Anxiety, depression, and sleep deprivation may enhance the response to pain. Individuals with manipulative passive-aggressive personalities often exaggerate the nature of the pain.

Pain is frequently, although not invariably, associated with other sensory complaints or perversions in the distribution of the root affected. Patients note numbness or a reduction in the perception of sensory stimuli, although total absence of sensation or anesthesia is unusual. They report paresthesia in the form of formication, pins and needles, or a "Novocaine"-like sensation. They also note a painful distortion of sensation or dysesthesia when the appropriate skin is stimulated. Clinical examination frequently reveals an alteration in the perception of pinprick, light touch, and/or temperature in the appropriate distribution. Patients may report intolerance to heat or cold in the distribution of the affected nerve root. When pain or tactile perception is reduced, the term hypalgesia is used. In increased sensory perception, the term hyperesthesia is appropriate. The term anesthesia is used to describe absence of sensation.

The sensory dermatomal distribution that is most often quoted and reproduced and that most consistently correlates with clinical experience is based on the work of Keegan and Garrett, which was published in 1948.[57] The data were obtained by documenting altered sensation in individuals with compression or injury to single nerve roots. The determination of dermatomal distribution has evolved from the original work of Sherington in 1894 and the observations in patients with herpes zoster radiculitis by Head at the turn of the century.[76] Foerster's contribution to the understanding of dermatomal patterns evolved from his extensive neurosurgical practice and the concept of "remaining sensibilities," and his chart differs somewhat from that of Keegan and Garrett.[32] Lewis, in 1942, determined yet another map by injecting hypertonic saline as an irritant into intraspinal ligaments and selected muscles.[63]

There is considerable overlap between one dermatome and the next and, in general, absolute anesthesia does not result from injury to a single isolated nerve root. However, irritation of a single nerve root does result in very focal and isolated dermatomal pain, paresthesia, dysesthesia, and altered sensation. When a sensory nerve root is irritated, the brain mistakes the source of the incoming pain or sensory impulses; consequently the pain or sensation is perceived to be coming from the dermatomal distribution of the nerve root rather than from the actual area of pathology and irritation.

DISTRIBUTION OF PAIN AND SENSORY DISTURBANCE IN CERVICAL RADICULOPATHY

There is no C1 sensory root but C2, 3, and 4 innervate the skin of the back of the head and the front of the neck. The C5, 6, 7, and 8 and T1 nerve roots innervate the arm. Cervical spinal diseases or injuries that comprise nerve roots result in pain and sensory symptoms and signs in specific patterns. Again, signs and symptoms frequently affect only a part of the involved root distribution.

The C5 distribution extends from the lower anterior neck and chest, over the anterior shoulder, and along the upper arm over the biceps (Fig. 7). The pattern then extends down the middle of the volar aspect of the forearm to the wrist. There is no extension into the hand or to the dorsum of the wrist.

The C6 distribution (Fig. 8) spreads from the top of the shoulder anteriorly and the back of the neck posteriorly. It then encompasses the entire median aspect of the arm down to include the dorsal and ventral aspect of the thumb.

C7 anteriorly involves the palm of the hand extending to the index and middle fingers (Fig. 9). Posteriorly or dorsally the nerve root innervates the skin from the back of the neck and courses over the posterior shoulder, the posterolateral upper arm, and then down the mid-dorsal forearm to the dorsum of the index and middle finger.

C8 extends from the back of the neck down the ulnar aspect of the upper arm and forearm (Fig. 10). The distribution encompasses the dorsal and ventral aspect of the index and little finger but there is very little involvement of the volar forearm.

The T1 nerve root distribution begins on the upper anterior chest just under the C5 region (Fig. 11). C6, 7, and 8 are not reflected on the anterior trunk. T1 then extends down the anterior, volar, ulnar aspect of the upper arm and forearm, but this root is not represented in the hand. T1 also has representation

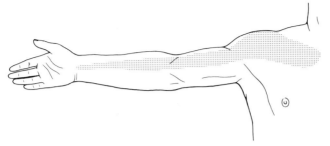

FIGURE 7. C5 dermatome.

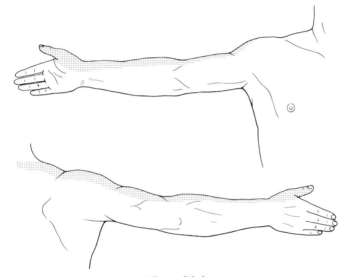

FIGURE 8. C6 dermatome.

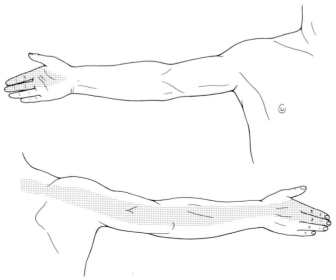

FIGURE 9. C7 dermatome.

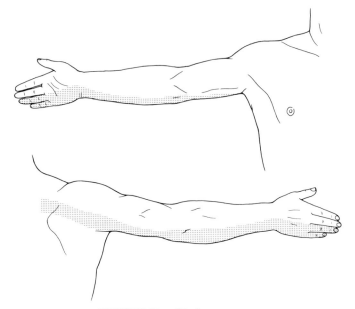

FIGURE 10. C8 dermatome.

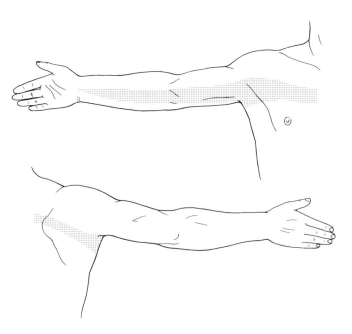

FIGURE 11. T1 dermatome.

over the upper back region. The complexity of segmental innervation is primarily due to the migration of limb buds during embryologic development.

In a series of 846 surgical patients with cervical radiculopathy secondary to cervical spondylosis and or disc disease, Henderson et al.[47] found arm pain to be present in 99.4%. Neck pain was present in 79.7%, scapular pain was present in 52.5%, anterior chest pain (which may mimic angina) was present in 17.8%, and headache was present in 9.7%. The overwhelming proportion of patients, 98.7%, had C6 or C7 radiculopathy, but the distribution of pain and paresthesia was not always specific: 45.5% reported diffuse non-dermatomal symptoms, 24.8% had C6 symptoms, and 25.5% had C7 symptoms. Objective sensory loss was present in a C6 distribution in 50.1% and in a C7 distribution in 32.5% but absent in 14.8%. The consistency of sensory findings in cervical radiculopathy varies from study to study.[71,93] In Henderson's patients with C6 lesions, 80% had sensory changes in this distribution, 12% had C7 changes, and 7% had no changes. With C7 lesions, 59.7% had objective C7 findings, 24.5% ahd C6 changes, and 14% had no objective sensory changes.

DISTRIBUTION OF PAIN AND SENSORY DISTURBANCE IN LUMBAR RADICULOPATHY

In the lower extremities, intraspinal pathology most commonly involves the L4, L5, and S1 nerve roots.[73] The L1, L2, L3 dermatomes are less often involved.[39] The sensory pattern of these upper lumbar nerve roots begins in the low back and then extends diagonally in a laminated fashion, down onto the anterior medial aspect of the thigh, paralleling the direction of the inguinal ligament. L3 extends to the medial aspect of the knee.

The L4 nerve root distribution (Fig. 12) extends from the back over the lateral dorsal thigh. The dermatome then angles over the knee and extends over the medial pretibial region to the medial malleolus. The dermatome generally extends onto the medial aspect of the foot and may affect the great toe.

The L5 nerve root pattern (Fig. 13) extends from the back down over the lateral hip and down the lateral aspect of the thigh. The pattern then extends over the lateral aspect of the knee and down over the middle and lateral aspect of the pretibial area. The dermatome courses over the anterior ankle to involve the second, third, and fourth toes both dorsally and ventrally, with involvement of the middle portion of the sole and the lateral heel. The great toe may also be involved.

The S1 dermatome extends from the low back and buttocks and passes down over the lateral posterior thigh and the lateral posterior calf. It involves the lateral malleolus, the lateral foot, and the little toe (Fig. 14).

The S2 dermatome includes a perirectal distribution and then extends distally down the medial posterior thigh and the medial calf down to the heel. The S3, S4, and S5 dermatomes are perirectal and do not extend down to the leg.

SENSORY DIFFERENTIAL DIAGNOSIS

It should be remembered that although the pattern of distribution of sensory root innervation is specific, there is an independent pattern of peripheral nerve sensory innervation. The distribution of nerve root and peripheral nerve symptoms and signs is usually such that a clear determination of the site of neural involvement can be made. However, at times this may be quite difficult. This problem is discussed in detail in the sections on plexus and nerve injury.

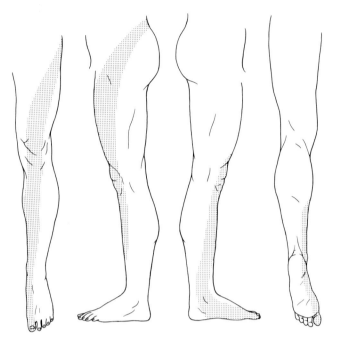

FIGURE 12.   L4 dermatome.

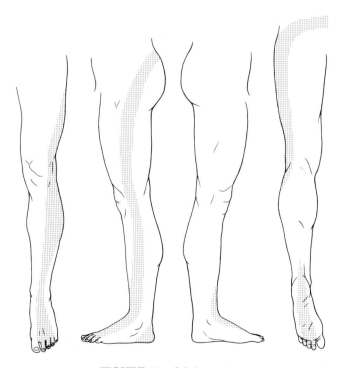

FIGURE 13.   L5 dermatome.

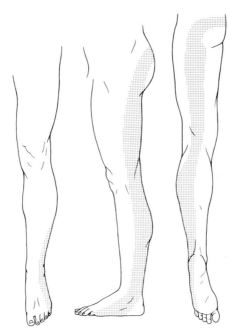

FIGURE 14. S1 dermatome.

MOTOR SIGNS AND SYMPTOMS OF RADICULOPATHY

Injury or damage to the lower motor neuron fibers results in characteristic alterations in the muscles innervated by those fibers. The changes in the muscle and in muscle function are in general the same regardless of where the lesion is located in the lower motor neuron. Whether the pathologic process involves the anterior or motor horn cells in the spinal cord, the nerve roots, or the peripheral nerves themselves, the changes in the individual muscles will be the same. Weakness of the muscle is the hallmark of lower motor neuron disturbance. If the process continues, the result may be wasting and atrophy of the muscle. At times spontaneous twitching of the muscle or fasciculations may be seen or felt.

Muscle weakness is quantitated in the clinical examination by using the Medical Research Council scale:[1] No contraction or power is MRC 0; a flicker of contraction and minimal movement is MRC 1; active but not antigravity movement is MRC 2; antigravity strength is MRC 3; active movement against resistance is MRC 4; and normal strength is MRC 5. The examiner should not only grade muscle strength, but should observe and feel the contraction of the muscle being tested and comment on any spasm that might be present.

Although the motor examination is considered an objective part of the neurologic examination, the skill, objectivity, experience, and training of the examiner are critical in obtaining reproducible and accurate findings. There are marked individual differences in overall strength between patients. Patient co-operation with the testing can be affected by a lack of will or ability to cooperate because of pain, malingering, or conversion reactions associated with unconscious psychiatric phenomena. Motivational, educational, social, monetary and intellectual factors may affect the motor as well as the sensory examination. The physician must consider all of these factors when confronted by possible clinical reduction of strength.

Just as there is a stereotyped sensory distribution of the nerve root and peripheral nerves, so there is a characteristic pattern of motor innervation. A given muscle may show weakness, wasting, atrophy, and fasciculation because of injury to the anterior horn cell, nerve root, nerve plexus, or peripheral nerve itself. It is the pattern of the muscles affected which helps to determine exactly where the lesion is located.

The problems of localization are somewhat complicated by the fact that many muscles have dual root innervation. Further confusion can arise because of individual variation with regard to motor nerve innervation of muscles. For example, Young et al.,[95] in 1983, studied L5 and S1 muscle innervation. The tibialis anterior muscle was predominantly L5 in 90%, the extensor digitorum brevis was predominantly L5 in 74%, the lateral gastrocnemius was L5-innervated 60% of the time, and the medial gastrocnemius was predominantly L5 8% of the time. The extensor hallucis longus was predominantly L5 10% of the time. The S1 nerve root was dominant in the medial gastrocnemius 82%, the lateral gastrocnemius 20%, and the extensor hallucis longus 80% of the time. L5 and S1 provided equal innervation to the lateral gastrocnemius 20% of the time.

However, in many clear radiculopathies, a distinct pattern of motor disturbance can be outlined. Although detailed clinical motor examination is essential for evaluation, a clear determination of the extent of motor involvement frequently requires the additional diagnostic sensitivity of electromyography.

In general, the pattern of motor involvement will be different with a given nerve injury or a nerve root process. For example, an axillary nerve injury will result in weakness, atrophy, and denervation of the deltoid and the teres minor muscle. A C5 radiculopathy will involve the deltoid and teres minor along with the supraspinatus, infraspinatus, biceps, and brachioradialis muscles. These latter muscles are clearly out of the distribution of the axillary nerve.

The following tables list the major muscles and muscle functions innervated by specific cervical nerve roots. The muscles are grouped by their dominant root innervation, and additional root supply is noted in parentheses. There is some disagreement among various investigators but the following represents a consensus that is clinically useful.[1,12,21,36,38,44] Peripheral nerve innervation is also noted in parentheses.

MOTOR FINDINGS IN CERVICAL RADICULOPATHY

C5 Radiculopathy

Muscle (Nerve)	Function
1. Deltoid (axillary)	Shoulder abduction (C6)
2. Teres minor (axillary)	Shoulder external rotation
3. Supraspinatus (suprascapular)	Shoulder abduction
4. Infraspinatus (suprascapular)	Shoulder external rotation (C6)
5. Biceps (musculocutaneous)	Elbow flexion (major C6)
6. Brachioradialis (radial)	Elbow flexion (major C6)
7. Rhomboids (dorsal scapular)	Scapular stabilization with shoulder flexion, extension, abduction (C4)
8. Levator scapulae (dorsal scapular)	Scapular elevation (C3/4)
9. Serratus anterior (long thoracic)	Scapular stabilization (C6/7)

The nerve supply to the rhomboids and the levator scapulae comes directly from the C5 nerve root. Denervation or abnormality in these muscles is indicative of a primary radiculopathy proximal to the upper trunk of the brachial plexus.

C6 Radiculopathy

Muscle (Nerve)	Function
1. Biceps (musculocutaneous)	Elbow flexion (C5)
2. Brachioradialis (radial)	Elbow flexion (C5)
3. Extensor carpi radiali (radial)	Wrist extension (C7)
4. Supinator (radial)	Elbow supination (C5/7)
5. Pronator teres (median)	Elbow pronation (C7)
6. Flexor carpi radialis (median)	Wrist flexion (C7/8)
7. Teres major (lower subscapular)	Scapular stabilization with shoulder extension, adduction, internal rotation
8. Pectoralis major-clavicular (pectoral)	Shoulder adduction, flexion (C5/7/8)

C7 Radiculopathy

Muscle (Nerve)	Function
1. Triceps (radial)	Elbow extension (C8)
2. Anconeus (radial)	Elbow extension (C6/8)
3. Extensor carpi radialis (radial)	Wrist extension (C6/8)
4. Extensor digitorum (radial)	Finger extension (C6/8)
5. Extensor carpi ulnaris (radial)	Wrist extension (C6/8)
6. Flexor carpi radialis (median)	Wrist flexion (C6/8)
7. Palmaris longus (median)	Wrist flexion (C6/8)
8. Latissimus dorsi (thoracodorsal)	Shoulder extension, adduction (C6/C8)
9. Pectoralis major–sternocostal (pectoral)	Shoulder adduction, flexion (C6/8/T1)

C8 Radiculopathy

Muscle (Nerve)	Function
1. Triceps (radial)	Elbow (major C7)
2. Extensor carpi ulnaris (radial)	Wrist extension (C6/7)
3. Extensor indicis proprius (radial)	Finger extension–Index (C7)
4. Extensor pollicis (radial)	Thumb extension (C7)
5. Abductor pollicis longus (radial)	Thumb abduction (C7)
6. Flexor carpi ulnaris (median)	Wrist flexion (C7/T1)
7. Flexor digitorum superficialis (median)	Finger flexion–proximal (C7/T1)
8. Flexor pollicis longus (median)	Thumb flexion–distal (T1)
9. Flexor digitorum profundus (median/ulnar)	Finger flexion–distal (T1)
10. Pronator quadratus (median)	Wrist pronation (C7/T1)
11. Flexor pollicis brevis (median)	Thumb flexion (T1)
12. Abductor, flexor, opponens digiti quinti (ulnar)	Little finger movements (T1)

C8 and T1 radiculopathy are uncommon but are often confused with ulnar nerve compromise at the elbow. Clinical or EMG involvement of muscles such as the extensor carpi ulnaris documents root involvement out of the distribution of the ulnar nerve.

T1 Radiculopathy

Muscle (Nerve)	Function
1. Flexor pollicis longus (median)	Thumb flexion–distal (C8)
2. Flexor digitorum profundus (median/ulnar)	Finger flexion–distal (C8)
3. Pronator quadratus (median)	Elbow pronation (C8)
4. Opponens, adductor, flexor pollicis, abductor pollicis brevis (median)	Thumb movements (C8)
5. Abductor, flexor, opponens digiti quinti (ulnar)	Little finger movements (C8)
6. Interossei (ulnar)	Finger abduction, adduction (C8)
7. Lumbricals (median/ulnar)	Finger proximal flexion and distal extension (C8)

In Henderson's extensive study of surgical cervical radiculopathy,[47] C6 radiculopathy was associated with objective biceps weakness in 39%. Triceps weakness was present in 16.6%, deltoid weakness was present in 1.9%, and 43.3% had no objective weakness. With C7 lesions, 57.4% had triceps weakness, 7.8% biceps weakness, and 32.8% had no weakness.

MOTOR FINDINGS IN LUMBOSACRAL RADICULOPATHY

The following table lists the major muscles and muscle functions innervated by the most commonly affected lumbar and sacral nerve roots.

L4 Radiculopathy

Muscle (Nerve)	Function
1. Quadriceps (femoral)	Knee extension (L3)
2. Adductors (obturator)	Hip adduction (L2/L3)
3. Gracilis (obturator)	Knee flexion (L3)
4. Tibialis anterior (deep peroneal)	Ankle dorsiflexion (L5)
5. Tibialis posterior (posterior tibial)	Ankle plantar flexion and inversion (L4/S1)

L5 Radiculopathy

Muscle (Nerve)	Function
1. Tibialis anterior (deep peroneal)	Ankle dorsiflexion (L4)
2. Extensor digitorum longus (deep peroneal)	Toe extension–Distal (L4/S1)
3. Extensor hallucis longus (deep peroneal)	Great toe extension (L4/S1)
4. Extensor digitorum brevis (deep peroneal)	Toe extension–Proximal (S1)
5. Peroneus longus and brevis (superficial peroneal)	Ankle plantar flexion and eversion (S1)
6. Gastocnemius–lateral/soleus (posterior tibial)	Ankle plantar flexion (S1)
7. Tibialis posterior (posterior tibial)	Ankle plantar flexion and inversion (L4/S1)
8. Hamstrings–medial (sciatic) semimembranosus/semitendinosus	Knee flexion (L4/S1)
9. Gluteus maximus (inferior gluteal)	Hip extension (S1)
10. Gluteus medius (superior gluteal)	Hip abduction and internal rotation (S1)
11. Tensor fasciae latae (superior gluteal)	Hip abduction (S1)

One of the most common diagnostic problems is differentiating L5 radiculopathy from peroneal nerve injury in patients with foot drop. Documentation of involvement of the tibialis posterior,[46] tensor fasciae latae, and gluteus medius[13] serves to clearly implicate an L5 disturbance, as these muscles are not innervated by the peroneal nerve.

A word of caution must also be expressed with regard to isolated abnormalities in the extensor digitorum brevis. In people over the age of 40, this muscle frequently shows morphologic and histologic changes in the absence of clinical symptoms.[53,90]

S1 Radiculopathy

Muscle (Nerve)	Function
1. Gastrocnemius–medial/soleus (posterior tibial)	Ankle plantar flexion (L5)
2. Tibialis posterior (posterior tibial)	Ankle plantar flexion and inversion (L5)
3. Intrinsic foot muscles (posterior tibial)	Toe abduction and adduction (L5/S2)
4. Flexor hallucis/digitorum (posterior tibial)	Toe flexion (S2)
5. Peroneus longus and brevis (superficial peroneal)	Ankle plantar flexion and eversion (L5)
6. Extensor digitum brevis (deep peroneal)	Toe extension–proximal (L5)
7. Hamstrings–lateral/biceps femoris (sciatic)	Knee flexion (L5)
8. Gluteus maximus (inferior gluteal)	Hip extension (L5)
9. Gluteus medius (superior gluteal)	Hip abduction and internal rotation (L5)

S1 radiculopathy prominently affects the medial gastrocnemius, lateral hamstring (biceps femoris), and the gluteus maximus.[13] L5 nerve root injury tends to preferentially affect the lateral gastrocnemius, medial hamstrings (semimembranosus, semitendinosus), gluteus medius, and tensor fasciae latae.

REFLEX RADICULAR SIGNS

A number of deep tendon reflexes can be reduced or completely lost because of cervical or lumbosacral radiculopathy.[17,18,44] Injury to either sensory or motor fibers can alter the reflex. At times the reflex may be reduced without any objective clinical evidence of sensory loss or muscle weakness. However, the presense of an altered reflex does not necessarily indicate an active radiculopathy. Once the reflex has been reduced it is not uncommon for the asymmetry to persist even after the patient has become totally asymptomatic either as a consequence of treatment or the natural healing processes.

In the upper extremities, the bicep, triceps, and brachioradialis reflexes are most commonly elicited but the pectoral reflex can also have diagnostic utility.

Reflex	Nerve Root
Biceps	C6 (C5)
Triceps	C7 (C6/C8)
Brachioradialis	C6 (C7)
Pectoral	C5

In Henderson's surgical patients with C5 radiculopathy, the biceps reflex was reduced in 66.7% and no reflex abnormality was found in 33.3%.[47] In C6 lesions, the biceps reflex was reduced in 59%, the triceps reflex was reduced in 14.2%, and no reflex change was found in 26.7%. In C7 radiculopathy, the triceps reflex was reduced in 63.4%, the biceps reflex was reduced in 12.5%, and 24% had no reflex changes. In C8 lesions, the biceps reflex was reduced in 19%, the triceps reflex was reduced in 47.6%, and 33.3% had no reflex change.

In the lower extremities, the knee and ankle jerk are most commonly elicited, but the great toe reflex can have diagnostic utility.[86]

Reflex	Nerve Root
Knee	L4 (L5)
Ankle	S1
Great Toe	L5

Asymmetric loss or reduction in one of these reflexes is an important observation in the diagnosis of radiculopathy. Care must be taken in obtaining reflexes. A breach in technique of examination can result in spurious results.

NECK AND BACK EXAMINATION

Examination of the patient with possible cervical and or lumbosacral radiculopathy clearly requires examination of the spinal region in question. In the paraspinous muscles, tenderness and spasm may be seen in association with impaired range of motion and flattening of the normal cervical and lumbar lordosis. These findings may be related to local musculoskeletal factors and are not directly a manifestation of nerve root compromise.

In the neck, the patient's subjective radicular symptoms can at times be reproduced by changes in neck position. Spurling's maneuver with oblique extension of the neck and vertical compression of the head is a particularly important finding if the patient's symptoms are specifically reproduced. Cervical intraspinal pathology may also compress the spinal cord and its vascular supply. In this situation, forward flexion of the neck will result in Lhermitte's sign,[10] manifested by an electric-like sensation extending into the trunk or limbs. Patients with cord involvement often have other evidence of myelopathy such as leg spasticity, weakness, and sensory disturbance. Some may have sphincter symptoms and arm spasticity, weakness, atrophy, and fasciculations. Sensory complaints such as burning paresthesias and dysesthesias may also be encountered.[15]

In the leg, L5 and S1 radicular pain can often be reproduced by the straight leg raising (SLR) test.[22,30,33,91] During this test, called Lasègue's maneuver, the knee is kept extended and the leg is slowly lifted to cause flexion of the hip. During the first 20-30° of hip flexion, there is generally no movement or traction of the sciatic nerve or nerve roots. However, after 30°, there is traction on the nerve roots as they pass through the neural foramina. This is usually maximum when the hip is flexed to 60-90°. Maximum stretching and movement occur at the L5 and S1 nerve root level, and a positive test results when the patient reports radicular type pain extending down the leg during the appropriate part of the procedure. The SLR test can also be performed by extending the knee with the patient sitting on the edge of an examining table. Knutsson[60] has stated that the SLR test is of "decisive importance" for the diagnosis of radiculopathy associated with lumbar disc herniation. However, although almost all patients under age 30 with L5 or S1 radiculopathy secondary to disc disease will have a true positive SLR test, many patients with limb pain on SLR do not have disc herniations. In addition, older patients with confirmed radiculopathy and patients with root lesions above L5 frequently have a negative SLR test.[78]

The extent of the nerve root irritated, not the severity of the compression, is said to determine the extent of the distribution of the pain elicited by the procedure (Fig. 15). When a small portion of the root is irritated, straight leg raising may produce only pain localized to the buttock. Greater involvement of the length of the root results in pain being perceived to extend all the way down the leg in a complete dermatomal distribution.[11]

Pain is often worsened by dorsiflexing the ankle at the point of maximum hip flexion. Pain can also be increased by neck flexion at the point of maximum tolerable hip flexion.[55] This procedure is called the confirmatory Lasègue's maneuver. Low back pain elicited with straight leg raising and pain elicited before the hip is flexed 20-30° is not truly indicative of nerve root irritation and should not be recorded as a "positive" test of nerve root irritation. Hamstring muscle tightness elicited during the test is common and is not indicative of true radiculopathy.

When there is marked L5 or S1 radiculopathy, a crossed SLR test may

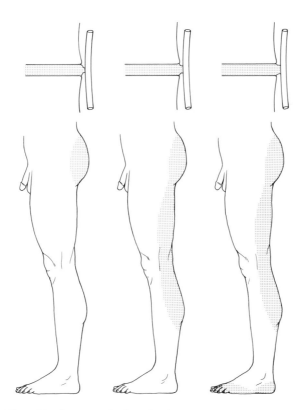

FIGURE 15. The subjective area of referred pain tends to be proportionate to the extent of spinal nerve contact rather than the amount of pressure applied.

elicit marked radicular pain. In this situation, pain is elicited on the side of the lesion with standard straight leg raising. Raising the opposite leg also causes radicular pain on the involved side. This is a rather dramatic test and almost always is indicative of significant nerve root pathology.

Although there may be some movement of the L4 nerve root upon straight leg raising, often patients with L4 radiculopathy do not have pain with this test. The L1, L2, and L3 nerve roots move relatively little with straight leg raising and almost never are associated with pain during this maneuver, even when significant nerve root irritation exists at these levels. The reverse SLR test, also called the femoral stretch test, often precipitates radicular pain under these circumstances. The test is performed with the patient lying prone; the hip is then extended, resulting in reproduction of the patient's subjective complaints.

Further information can also be obtained during the back examination by palpating the sciatic nerve as it passes through the sciatic notch in the buttock. Patients with L5 and S1 radiculopathy have local tenderness upon palpation. At times, true radicular dermatomal pain can be reproduced in this way.

ELECTRODIAGNOSTIC TECHNIQUES

The diagnosis, confirmation, and documentation of radiculopathy often require more information than can be obtained by even the most detailed neurologic examination. Electromyography, nerve conduction studies, F-wave determinations, H reflexes and the newer techniques of dermatomal evoked responses can greatly expand the information available to the physician.[24,37,40] These techniques can identify and clearly define the presence and extent of a radiculopathy even when the clinical examination is inconclusive.[64] In addition, patients often have neurologic limb symptoms that are caused by more than one pathologic process. The presence of cervical radiculopathy in association with an independent focal nerve entrapment such as a carpal tunnel syndrome or cubital tunnel syndrome is relatively common. Proper evaluation and treatment of this "double crush" syndrome require appropriate electrodiagnostic testing.

Electrodiagnostic testing is often crucial in formulating a diagnosis, in determining the prognosis, and in planning appropriate medical or surgical intervention. Patients may be candidates for surgical intervention because of severe intractable radicular limb pain. Clinical examination may fail to convincingly delineate the root or roots involved. Neuroimaging techniques may identify abnormalities at several levels but the mere presence of a benign anatomic intraspinal abnormality such as a disc bulge or herniation or spondylotic changes with foraminal narrowing does not mean that these anatomic abnormalities are related to the patient's symptoms.

CT and MRI of the spine, as well as myelograms, show abnormalities that increase exponentially with age and often do not correlate to nerve root dysfunction or clinical symptoms. Large anatomic defects can be seen on images in patients without clinical symptoms or signs.[19,48,66,67] These anatomic changes in the discs, bones, and joints are then clinically irrelevant and have no causal relationship to the clinical picture. In a 1984 study, Weisel et al.[89] found that over 35% of asymptomatic individuals had abnormal lumbar CT scans. Over 19% of those under the age of 40 had a herniated nucleus pulposus, whereas 50% of the patients over the age of 50 had abnormalities, including canal stenosis and facet joint arthropathy. McRae[66,67] also pointed out that asymptomatic cervical and lumbar disc protrusions are common. Disc protrusions were diagnosed by postmortem dissection, radiography, and myelography. In 60% of patients over 30, multiple anterior and lateral disc protrusions were demonstrated. In 40% of these cases, multiple posterior disc protrusions were noted. In the neck, disc thinning and osteophyte formation were present at C5–6 and C6–7 in more than 50% of the spines of patients over age 40. There was no statistical difference between symptomatic and asymptomatic patients. Other studies[62,75] also demonstrated that at autopsy, 15 to 30% of lumbar spines have herniated discs and that degenerative changes in the posterior elements or motion segments are noted in virtually all individuals over 60 years of age. Determining a causal relationship between a given episode of back or leg pain and a specific radiologic abnormality requires careful logical clinical and electrodiagnostic analysis. Furthermore, noncompressive radiculopathy such as radicular infarcts in diabetes mellitus are not visualized on anatomic tests.[3,85] Lumbar radiculopathy may be associated with a normal myelogram. The presence of EMG changes in this setting may be due to lateral entrapments from lateral disc herniations, lateral recess stenosis, or foraminal stenosis.[65,87,92]

Electrodiagnostic techniques provide insight into which nerve or nerve root is physiologically injured. Electrodiagnostic testing can show whether anatomic changes on imaging studies have clinical significance and can help to determine the significance of confusing clinical symptoms and signs. These tests can serve as a basis for rational therapeutic intervention.

The "accuracy" of electrodiagnostic studies in radiculopathy is difficult to define.[55,59,64,84] An "accurate" diagnosis really must take into account symptoms, clinical signs, neuroimaging (CT, MRI, myelogram) findings, electrodiagnostic findings, and probably surgical findings and response to surgery. In "true" radiculopathy, not all patients have abnormalities in all clinical and test parameters. The diagnosis of true radiculopathy still comes down to the judgment of experienced and well-trained clinicians, who consider all the data. Accuracies of EMG in radiculopathy have been reported as high as 85% by Lane,[61] 77% by Knutsson,[60] and 70% by Fisher.[30] In clinical spinal stenosis, Jacobson[52] found abnormalities bilaterally in 33% of patients with only unilateral symptoms and Seppalainer[82] found bilateral abnormalities in 36 of 37 patients. Hall[41] found EMG more helpful than clinical examination. In Eisen's 1983 series,[24] 46% of patients with cervical root pain and 65% of patients with lumbar root pain were said to have had objective motor or sensory deficits on clinical examination. Of those patients with objective findings, confirmatory electrodiagnostic abnormalities were found with somatosensory evoked potentials in 70%, with F-wave determinations in 50%, with EMG in 79%, and with myelography in 82%. However, there was no mention of how many patients without objective neurologic findings on clinical examination had abnormalities on electrodiagnostic testing. Khatri et al.,[59] in a 1984 study, were able to show that although CT and EMG were often in accordance in a given patient, an abnormal EMG correlated better with the demonstrated course of the radiculopathy than did the CT findings. The false-negative EMG studies might be explained by the observations of Fisher[30] in 1978 and Montcastle[69] in 1974. These authors have suggested that pain in radicular syndromes may be related to injury or abnormality of the small afferent pain fibers. Changes in these fibers will not be reflected in the clinical electrophysiologic studies to be described.

ELECTROMYOGRAPHY

Electromyography is a technique that enables trained physicians to observe electrophysiologic phenomena in the resting and actively working muscle.[4,6,37,79,83] EMG is a physician-performed extension of the clinical neurologic examination and should not be considered simply a laboratory test. The EMG examination requires skill, training, knowledge, objectivity, and judgment. A small needle electrode is inserted through the skin into the substance of the muscle. Although the procedure does involve a small amount of local discomfort, it is very well tolerated by almost all patients. Needle insertion may occasionally result in local bruising, and there is also the small potential for needle-induced infection or injury to underlying structures, as there is with any needle puncture, but the procedure is otherwise risk free and should be considered noninvasive. The technique can employ either a small monopolar electrode referenced to a distant surface electrode or a larger coaxial needle electrode. The former is generally much better tolerated and its large pick-up area makes for easier recognition of abnormal spontaneous activity. In my practice the monopolar technique is utilized almost exclusively.

The electrode explores electrical potential activity in the muscle. This information is then fed into an EMG machine, which amplifies the potentials and then allows for their display on a cathode ray oscilloscope. In addition the visual display, an auditory response is heard through a loud speaker. The electromyographer observes the auditory and visual responses and determines whether or not there are abnormalities in the muscle being studied. Strip recorders are available to record these electrical potentials but they are rarely used in clinical practice.

Electromyographic abnormalities in a given muscle can be broadly categorized as myopathic or neuropathic. Myopathic changes occur in certain primary diseases of the muscle such as muscular dystrophy or inflammatory myopathy. Neurogenic abnormalities may result from lesions of the anterior horn motor cell, the motor root, the spinal nerve root, the brachial or lumbar plexus, or the peripheral nerves themselves. The neurogenic changes are essentially the same regardless of the site of injury in the lower motor neuron. Determination of which nerve structure is involved depends on abnormal muscle patterns. Therefore, a number of muscles in a given limb must be sampled, and the physician performing the procedure must be knowledgeable of root and nerve innervation patterns. This technique looks at the response of the muscle to damage, injury, or irritation of motor nerve fibers innervating muscles. If a pathologic process involves only the dorsal root or sensory fibers, the EMG will remain normal even in the face of classical pain, objective sensory changes, and reflex alterations.

SPONTANEOUS EMG ACTIVITY AT REST

Insertion of the needle electrode into a muscle is associated with a brief electrical discharge that lasts only a little longer than the movement of the muscle. Although this is a normal phenomenon, in early and late neurogenic lesions there may be an exaggeration, increase, or prolongation of this response.

At rest, the normal muscle is electrically silent. In lower motor neuron processes and in some myopathic conditions, abnormal electrical discharges indicative of muscle membrane irritability can be seen. Fibrillation potentials are the smallest potentials observed in electromyography.[7] They cannot be visualized by the clinician and are recognized only by EMG (Fig. 16). They are not seen until 10 to 14 days after an acute injury to a nerve structure. These potentials are positive then negative, diphasic or triphasic, 1.0 to 5.0 milliseconds in duration, and 20 to 300 microvolts in amplitude. They often occur rhythmically at 2 to 15 per second but may occur 30 per second and with irregularity. They produce a characteristic sound of grease on a griddle, rain on a tin roof, or the crinkling of tissue paper.

All muscle membranes are said to have a degree of oscillation in their baseline membrane electrical potentials. This is, however, below a threshold level for electrical discharge in normal non-denervated muscle fibers. Neurogenic injury results in the lowering of that threshold of discharge so that the individual muscle fibers discharge spontaneously when the oscillating membrane potential reaches the lowered threshold level. Denervation hypersensitivity of the individual muscle fibers may also have a causal role in the generation of fibrillation potentials.

Positive sharp waves are another form of abnormal spontaneous electrical activity seen on EMG (Fig. 17). They have the same significance as fibrillation potentials and probably represent fibrillation potentials that arrive at a damaged region of muscle. This results in the blocking of the propagation of the potential. Positive sharp waves have a sharp initial positivity and then a slower negative decay. They may be rhythmic or irregular, last up to 10 milliseconds, and have amplitudes that average 150 microvolts. They can occur 2 to 100 per second but are usually seen with a frequency of around 10 per second.

The third type of abnormal discharge seen at rest is the bizarre high frequency run. This is a nonspecific sign of neuromuscular irritability and can be seen in normal individuals as well as in those with neuropathic and myopathic processes.

Fasciculations are a fourth type of spontaneous discharge. They represent discharges of a group of muscle fibers or an entire motor unit. These potentials may be generated in the anterior horn cell or its axon. They may constitute evidence of a root lesion but are rarely seen in this context.[14] Fasciculations can also be seen in normal asymptomatic individuals.

MOTOR UNIT ACTION POTENTIALS

Muscle contraction is initiated by discharge of individual motor units. The motor unit is the smallest unit that can be activated by voluntary effort. The motor consists of one anterior horn cell, its axon or nerve fiber, the neuromuscular junction, and all the muscle fibers innervated by branches of that axon. The number of muscle fibers innervated by one nerve fiber varies from 30 in the small muscles controlling eye movements, to 1700 in the large proximal limb muscles. These muscles are distributed randomly through the muscle, although they do fire off synchronously. The EMG needle electrode may record as many as 10 to 20 motor units at a time. The individual motor units are usually diphasic or triphasic: that is, their potentials cross the baseline two or three times. In normal muscle, less than 15% of the motor units have a polyphasic wave form. The amplitude of the motor unit is generally between 300 microvolts to 2 millivolts and the duration is usually between 4 and 15 milliseconds with an average of 8 to 10 milliseconds. The size of the motor unit varies with the muscle being studied and the age of the patient. The size of the motor unit on the oscilloscope is also a consequence of the relationship of the recording electrode to the motor unit.

In neurogenic processes, the motor unit becomes polyphasic and the potential crosses the baseline multiple times. In addition, the duration and sometimes the amplitude of the motor unit potential are increased. This can occur early on because conduction along the terminal branches of the nerve fiber is variably slowed, leading to desynchronization and prolongation of the potential. Later, sprouting of terminal branches of nerve fibers occur in an attempt to reinnervate normal muscle fibers denervated by disease or injury in the adjacent motor units.

In muscle disease, the individual muscle fibers are affected and they drop out of the motor units. The motor units then become polyphasic and in addition have reduced duration and amplitude. (Fig. 18).

INTERFERENCE PATTERN

The electromyographer must also observe the overall pattern of motor unit activity. At rest, the normal muscle is electrically silent and no motor units are seen. With weak voluntary contraction, only a few motor units may be seen discharging in the region of the recording electrode. The individual motor units will typically be seen to discharge at 5 to 10 times per second. With an increase in effort on the part of the patient, the motor units will begin to fire more frequently. In addition, more motor units will be recruited into the picture. Each new motor unit will be firing off rhythmically and independently. As the strength of the voluntary contraction is further increased to maximum, the oscilloscope screen is filled with frequently firing and overlapping motor unit action potentials forming an interference pattern (Fig. 19).

With a neuropathic process, the number of motor units is reduced and it is more difficult to recruit additional motor units for contraction. The interference pattern is reduced often to a point where the individual motor units can be easily recognized. In myopathic disease, the number of motor units is unaffected. Therefore, the interference pattern remains full even when there is clinical weakness. The amplitude of the interference pattern is, however, reduced in myopathic disease.

EMG IN RADICULOPATHY

The presence of a reduced interference pattern and an increased number of long duration complex polyphasic motor unit action potentials in muscles in a nerve root distribution is the electrophysiologic hallmark of a chronic or subacute radiculopathy. Acute radiculopathy results in fibrillation potentials and positive sharp waves as early as 7 to 14 days after the onset of nerve root compromise.[24,30,56] These potentials may be seen first in the paraspinous musculature but often paraspinous abnormalities are absent and changes are seen only in the distribution of the anterior primary rami of the nerve. Denervation may also be limited to the paraspinous musculature when only the posterior rami of the nerve roots are affected and the anterior rami are spared.[29] These findings of acute denervation may evolve over a 2 to 6 week period, with distal muscles being affected after proximal muscles. The abnormal discharges may continue for 30 to 180 days after correction of the root irritation and may be seen for more than 2 years following laminectomy.[54] In 5 to 15% of unoperated spines, paraspinous denervation may be the only electrophysiologic manifestation of radiculopathy.[24,30,56] There is a great deal of segmental overlap in the cervical and superficial lumbar paraspinous musculature. There is less overlap in the deep lumbar paraspinous muscles, but a clear-cut isolated root level cannot be

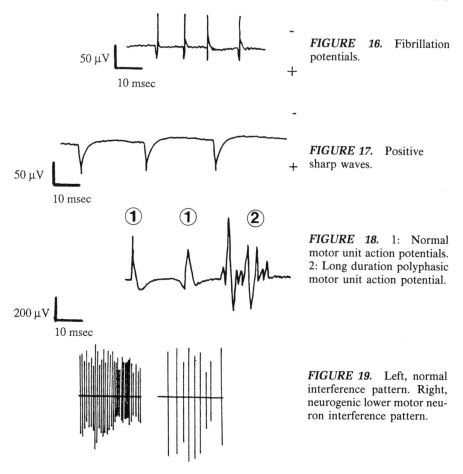

FIGURE 16. Fibrillation potentials.

FIGURE 17. Positive sharp waves.

FIGURE 18. 1: Normal motor unit action potentials. 2: Long duration polyphasic motor unit action potential.

FIGURE 19. Left, normal interference pattern. Right, neurogenic lower motor neuron interference pattern.

delineated with isolated paraspinous change with any degree of certainty. Paraspinous fibrillations and positive sharp waves are common after surgery and their presence does not definitely indicate a recurrence of radiculopathy.[54,81] However, localized paraspinous denervation in the deep lumbar muscles may be indicative of recurrent radiculopathy if the findings are at least 3 cm lateral to the surgical scar.

Alteration in recruitment pattern and reduction of the interference pattern can be seen almost immediately and may persist indefinitely. Small polyphasic potentials can also often be seen within 14 to 21 days after onset. Large complex polyphasic motor units representing reinnervation and sprouting often require 2 to 3 months for evolution.[24] Polyphasic changes may be the only finding on EMG in subacute or chronic disease.[16,24,50,56]

NERVE CONDUCTION STUDIES

Nerve conduction tests are entirely noninvasive and without risk to the patient. The procedure involves electrical stimulation of nerves by surface electrodes. Recording is obtained by surface electrodes placed over muscles in the case of motor nerve conduction studies and over the nerves themselves in the

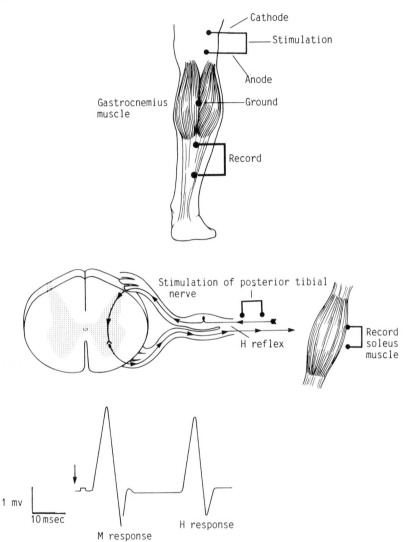

FIGURE 20. H-reflexes.

case of sensory conduction studies. Nerve conduction studies are essential for determining the integrity of peripheral nerve function and are discussed in detail in the section dealing with these specific problems. Motor and sensory nerve conduction studies are usually normal in radiculopathies unless compression of the nerve root is severe enough to cause wallerian degeneration. This results in a reduction in the amplitude of the motor action potential and possible slowing of conduction. There are, however, several related techniques that are of particular help in specifically diagnosing radiculopathies.

H-REFLEXES (Fig. 20)

The H-reflex is the physiologic manifestation of the S1 reflex arc and is a true monosynaptic reflex, unlike the F-wave, which is discussed later.[8,9,24,42,55]

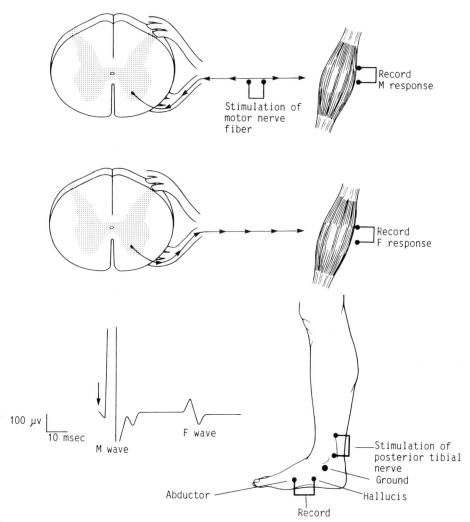

100 µv

10 msec

M wave

F wave

Stimulation of
posterior tibial
nerve

Ground

Abductor

Hallucis

Record

FIGURE 21. F-wave responses.

Abnormalities of the H-reflex can be the earliest clinical or physiologic finding in an S1 radiculopathy. The test is performed by placing surface recording electrodes over the skin above the soleus muscle. The posterior tibial nerve is then percutaneously stimulated in the popliteal fossa behind the knee. After stimulation, the first potential recorded is the orthgrade M response secondary to stimulation of the motor fibers leading to the muscle. Electrical potentials then pass back to the cord along sensory fibers corresponding to the sensory fibers of the S1 reflex. These fibers enter the spinal cord and synapse with the S1 motor cells, and electrical activity then passes down the S1 motor fibers to the soleus muscle. With interruption of the S1 pathway, the H reflex is delayed or abolished. In my laboratory, the upper limit of normal is 33 milliseconds. There should not be more than 1.5 millisecond difference in latency or a 50% difference in amplitude between right and left.

F-WAVES (Fig. 21)

Stimulation of motor nerves results not only in orthograde conduction down to the appropriate muscle, but also in backfiring or antegrade conduction back to the anterior horn cell of origin of that particular motor fiber.[24,31,42,68,95] The motor cell is then stimulated and another electrical potential is conducted orthograde back down to the muscle. The first response is then the usual M response but a somewhat variable F-wave can also be noted as a second delayed potential. Because the F-wave requires the integrity of the spinal nerve and motor nerve root, it can be delayed in motor radiculopathies. Often, however, the nerve being stimulated emanates from more than one nerve root so that even with a prominent root injury, an F response may be normal because of the integrity of the adjacent nerve root. F-waves are of rather low amplitude, averaging only 1% of M wave amplitude.[25] Furthermore, F-waves tend to be variable and 5 or 10 stimulations may be necessary before the F-wave of the shortest latency can be accurately documented. These potentials represent conduction along the largest diameter and fastest conducting motor fibers, and conduction along different fibers explains the variability seen in practice.[24]

In the lower extremities, stimulation of the posterior tibial and peroneal nerves generates F-waves from the L5 and S1 nerve roots. There may be an S2 component with the former nerve stimulation. An absolute prolongation of the F-waves beyond 33 milliseconds in the arms and 55 milliseconds in the legs with stimulation of nerves at the wrist and ankle, respectively, or a right-left asymmetry of 2 milliseconds is felt to be significant.[24-27] Eisen[24] found F-waves to be abnormal in 14 to 47% of radiculopathies. On rare occasions, an F-wave abnormality may be the only electrophysiologic manifestation of radiculopathy.

DERMATOMAL SOMATOSENSORY EVOKED POTENTIALS (Fig. 22)

The newest technique available to study radiculopathies involves stimulation of sensory fibers in individual dermatomes and recording evoked responses over the appropriate scalp region with surface or small needle electrodes.[20,23,24,35,40,74,80] Although there remains some controversy with regard to the efficacy and usefulness of this technique,[2] my experience supports the enthusiasm of most investigators.[20,24,80] With this risk-free and noninvasive technique, the skin in a specific area of a dermatome is repetitively stimulated with a small electrical current. The stimulus is stereotyped and repetitive and results in or evokes a small stereotyped electrical response in the sensory cortex of the brain. These evoked responses are of such small magnitude that they are obscured by other randomly occurring electrical potentials in the brain, heart, muscles, and other extraneural structures. Although the evoked responses are of extremely low amplitude, they are consistent and occur in a specific relationship to the presented stimulus. The other potentials are random in relation to the stimulus. Therefore, the electrical potentials to a large number of stimuli can be electronically averaged together. The random activity will be averaged and cancelled out. The stereotyped time-locked responses will stand out and can be measured and examined. The latency and amplitude of the evoked potentials can be compared against absolute values.[24] In addition, right to left latency differences of 2 milliseconds and amplitude differences of 50% are significant. Dvonch,[20] using this technique to study lumbar radiculopathy, found 86% correlation with myelographic defects

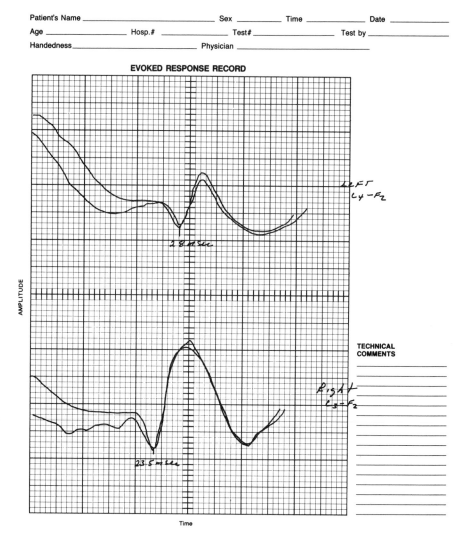

Patient's Name _____ Sex _____ Time _____ Date _____

Age _____ Hosp.# _____ Test# _____ Test by _____

Handedness_____ Physician _____

FIGURE 22. Evoked response record. Left C7 radiculopathy with latency delay and amplitude reduction.

in 70 patients and an 88% surgical correlation. Scarff[80] found abnormalities in 90% of patients considered to have lumbar radiculopathy.

This technique complements electromyography. In clinical radiculopathy, either motor or sensory fibers are preferentially involved at the site of primary irritation.[40] EMG looks at the motor fibers of the ventral root and does not identify abnormalities in purely sensory radiculopathies. Patients with severe radicular pain and sensory symptoms can have a normal electromyogram. Dermatomal evoked responses look at the sensory fibers of the dorsal root and would be expected to document abnormalities in this group of patients. The combined use of this technique with EMG enhances our ability to document and diagnose both cervical and lumbar radiculopathies.

REFERENCES

1. Aids to the Investigation of Peripheral Nerve Injuries. Medical Research Council of Great Britain (revised 2nd ed.). Her Majesty's Stationary Office, London, 1965.
2. Aminoff MJ, Goodin DS, Barbara NM, et al Dermatomal somatosensory evoked potentials in unilateral lumbosacral radiculopathy. Ann Neurol 17:171–176, 1985.
3. Asbury AK: Proximal diabetic neuropathy. J Neurol 2:179–180, 1977.
4. Bastron JA, Lambert EH: The clinical value of electromyography and electrical stimulation of nerves. Med Clin North Am 1025–1036, 1960.
5. Bell GR, Rothman RH: The conservative treatment of sciatica. Spine 9:54–56, 1984.
6. Buchthal F: The electromyogram. World Neurol 1962, pp 16–29.
7. Buchthal F, Rosenfalck P: Spontaneous electrical activity of human muscle. Electroenceph Clin Neurophysiol 20:321–336, 1966.
8. Braddom RL, Johnson EW: Standardization of H reflex and diagnostic use in S1 radiculopathy. Arch Phys Med Rehabil 55:161–166, 1974.
9. Braddom RL, Johnson EW: H reflex: Review and classification with suggested clinical uses. Arch Phys Med Rehabil 55:412–417, 1974.
10. Brody IA, Wilkins RH: L'Hermitte's sign. Arch Neurol 21:338–340, 1969.
11. Cailliet R: The Low Back Syndrome, 3rd ed. Philadelphia, FA Davis Co., 1982, p 159.
12. Chusid JG, McDonald JJ: Correlative Neuroanatomy and Functional Neurology, 9th ed. Los Altos, CA, Lange Medical Publishers, 1958.
13. Conrad B, Benecke R: Electromyographic examination of gluteal muscles in the differential diagnosis of lumbar herniated discs. Arch Psychiatry Neurol 277:333–339, 1979.
14. Conradi S, Grimby L, Lundeno G: Pathophysiology of fasciculations in ALS as studied by electromyography of single motor units. Muscle Nerve 5:202–208, 1982.
15. Crandell PM, Batzdorf R: Cervical spondylotic myelopathy. J Neurosurg 31:57–66, 1966.
16. Crane CR, Krusen EM: Significance of polyphasic potentials in the diagnosis of cervical root involvement. Arch Phys Med Rehabil 49:403–406, 1968.
17. DeMyer W: Anatomy and clinical neurology of the spinal cord. In Baker AB, Joynt RJ (eds): Clinical Neurology. Philadelphia, Harper and Row, 1986.
18. De Jong RN: Case taking and the neurologic examination. In Baker AB, Joynt RJ (eds): Clinical Neurology, Philadelphia, Harper and Row, 1986.
19. Dively RL, Oglevir RR: Preemployment examination of the low back. JAMA 160:856–858, 1956.
20. Dvonch V, Scharff T, Bunch W, et al: Dermatomal SSEP: Their use in lumbar radiculopathy. Spine 9:291–293, 1984.
21. Dyck PJ, Low PA, Stevens JC: Diseases of peripheral nerves. In Baker AB, Joynt RJ (eds): Clinical Neurology. Philadelphia, Harper and Row, 1986.
22. Edgar MA, Park WM: Induced pain patterns in straight-leg raising in lumbar disc protrusions. J Bone Joint Surg 56B4:658–667, 1974.
23. Eisen A, Elleker G: Sensory nerve stimulation and evoked cerebral potentials. Neurology 30:1097–1105, 1980.
24. Eisen A, Hoirch RT: The electrodiagnostic evaluation of spinal root lesions. Spine 8:98–106, 1983.
25. Eisen A, Odusote K: Amplitude of the F-wave: A potential means of documenting spasticity. Neurology 29:1306–1309, 1979.
26. Eisen A, Schomer D, Melmed C: The application of F-wave measurements in the differentiation of proximal and distal upper limb entrapments. Neurology 27:662–688, 1977.
27. Eisen A, Schomer D, Melmud C: An electrophysiologic method for examining lumbosacral root compression. Can J Neurol Sci 4:117–123, 1977.
28. Feinstein B: Referred pain from paravertebral structures. In Buerger AA, Tobis JS (eds): Approaches to the Validation of Manipulation Therapy. Springfield, IL, Charles C. Thomas, 1977.
29. Fisher MA, Kaur D, Houchins J: Electrodiagnostic examination, back pain, and entrapment of posterior rami. Electromyogr Clin Neurophysiol 25:183–189, 1985.
30. Fisher MA, Shivde AJ, Teixera C, et al: Clinical and electrophysiological appraisal of the significance of radicular injury in back pain. J Neurol Neurosurg Psychiatry 41:303–306, 1978.
31. Fisher MA, Shivde AJ, Teixera C, et al: The F-response: a clinically useful physiologic parameter for evaluation of radicular injury. Electromyogr Clin Neurophysiol 19:65–75, 1979.
32. Foerster O: The dermatomes in man. Brain 56:1–39, 1933.
33. Goddard MD, Reid JD: Movements induced by straight-leg raising in the lumbosacral roots, nerves, and plexus, and in intra pelvic section of the sciatic nerve. J Neurol Neurosurg Psychiatry 28:12–18, 1965.

34. Goldner JL: Pain: extremities and spine—evaluation and differential diagnosis. In Omer GE, Spinner M (eds): Management of Peripheral Nerve Problems. Philadelphia, WB Saunders, 1980.
35. Gonzalez EG, Hayden M, Bruno R, et al: Lumbar spinal stenosis: analysis of pre- and post-operative somatosensory evoked potentials. Arch Phys Med Rehabil 66:11–14, 1985.
36. Goodgold J: Anatomical Correlates of Clinical Electromyography. Baltimore, Williams and Wilkins, 1980.
37. Goodgold J, Eberstein A: Electrodiagnosis of Neuromuscular Diseases. Baltimore, Williams and Wilkins, 1973.
38. Gray H: Anatomy of the Human Body. Philadelphia, Lea and Febiger, 1956.
39. Gutterman P, Shenkin H: Syndromes associated with protrusion of upper intervertebral discs. J Neurosurg 38:499–503, 1973.
40. Haldeman S: The electrodiagnostic evaluation of nerve root function. Spine 9:42–45, 1984.
41. Hall S, Bartleson JD, Onofrio BM, et al: Lumbar spinal stenosis. Ann Intern Med 103:271–275, 1985.
42. Hammer K: Nerve Conduction Studies. Springfield, IL, Charles C Thomas, 1982.
43. Harner RN, Wienir MA: Differential diagnosis of spinal disorders. In Rothman RH, Simeone FA (eds). The Spine, 2nd ed. Philadelphia, WB Saunders, 1982.
44. Haymaker W: Bing's Local Diagnosis in Neurological Disease, 15th ed, St. Louis, CV Mosby, 1969.
45. Haymaker W, Woodhall B: Peripheral Nerve Injuries. Philadelphia, WB Saunders, 1956.
46. Heffernam LPM: Electromyographic value of the tibialis posterior muscle. Arch Phys Med Rehabil 60:170–174, 1974.
47. Henderson CM, Hennessy RG, Shuey HM: Posterior-lateral foramenotomy as an exclusive operative technique for cervical radiculopathy: A review of 846 consecutively operated cases. Neurosurgery 13:504–512, 1983.
48. Hitselbeyer WE, Willen RM: Abnormal myelogram in asymptomatic patients. J Neurosurg 28:204–206.
49. Honet JC, Jebsen RH: Electrodiagnosis I: Electromyography. Medical Times 95::678–692, 1967.
50. Hoover BB, Caldwell JW, Krusen EM, et al: Value of polyphasic potentials in diagnosis of lumbar root lesions. Arch Phys Med Rehabil 51:546–548, 1970.
51. Inman VT, Saunders JB: J Nerve Ment Dis 99:660–667, 1944.
52. Jacobson RE: Lumbar Stenosis. An electromyographic evaluation. Clin Orthop 115:68–71, 1976.
53. Jennekens FGI, Tomlinson BC, Waldon JN: Extensor digitorum brevis: histological and his-tochemical aspects. J Neurol Neurosurg Psychiatry 35:124–132, 1972.
54. Johnson EW, Burkhart JA, Earl WC: Electromyography in post laminectomy patients. Arch Phys Med Rehabil 53:239–241, 1972.
55. Johnson EW, Fletcher FR: Lumbosacral radiculopathy: Review of 100 consecutive cases. Arch Phys Med Rehabil 62:321–3, 1981.
56. Johnson EW, Melvin JL. Value of electromyography in lumbar radiculopathy. Arch Phys Med Rehabil 52:239–249, 1971.
57. Keegan JJ, Garrett FD: The segmental distribution of the cutaneous nerves in the limbs of man. Anat Res 102:409–438, 1948.
58. Kellgren JH, Lewis T: Observations related to referred pain, visceromotor reflexes, and other associated phenomena. Clin Sci 4:47, 1949.
59. Khatri BO, Baruah J, McQuillen MP. Correlation of electromyography with computed to-mography in evaluation of lower back pain. Arch Neurol 41:594–7, 1984.
60. Knutsson B: Comparative value of electromyographic, myelographic, and clinical-neurological examination in the diagnosis of lumbar root compression syndrome. Acta Orthop Scand 49(Suppl):1–135, 1961.
61. Lane MD, Tamhanker MN, Demopoulos JT: Discogenic radiculopathy in multidisciplinary management. NY State J Med 32:36, 1978.
62. Lawrence JS: Disc degeneration—its frequency and relation to symptoms. Ann Rheum Dis 28:121–127, 1969.
63. Lewis T: Pain. MacMillan, 1942.
64. Leyshon A, Kirman EO, Parry CB: Electrical studies in the diagnosis of compression of the lumbar root. J Bone Joint Surg 63B:71–75, 1981.
65. McNab L: Negative disc exploration. J Bone Joint Surg 53A:891–903, 1971.
66. McRae DL: Asymptomatic disc protrusions. Acta Radiol 46:9–27, 1956.
67. McRae DL: The significance of abnormalities of the cervical spine. Am J Roentgenol 84:3–25, 1960.
68. Mayer RF, Feldman RG: Observations on the nature of the F-wave in man. Neurology 17:147–156, 1967.

69. Montcastle VB: Pain and temperature sensibilities. In Montcastle VB (ed): Medical Physiology. St. Louis, CV Mosby, 1979.

70. Mooney V, Robertson J: The facet syndrome. Clin Orthop 115:149–156, 1976.

71. Murphy F, Simmons JC, Brunson B: Surgical treatment of laterally ruptured cervical disc. J Neurosurg 38:679–683, 1973.

72. Nachemson AL: The lumbar spine, an orthopedic challenge. Spine 1:59–71, 1976.

73. Paine KWE, Haung PWH: The lumbar disc syndrome. J. Neurosurg 37:75–82, 1972.

74. Perlik S, Fisher MA, Patel DV, et al: On the usefulness of somatosensory evoked responses for the evaluation of lower back pain. Arch Neurol 43:907–913, 1986.

75. Pope M, Wilder D, Boothe J: The biomechanics of low back pain. In White AA, Gordon SL (eds): Symposium on Idiopathic Low Back Pain. St. Louis, CV Mosby, 1982, pp 252–295.

76. Ranson SW, Clark SL: The Anatomy of the Nervous System. Philadelphia, WB Saunders, 1956.

77. Rish BL: A critique of the surgical management of lumbar disc disease in a private neurosurgical practice. Spine 9:500–504, 1984.

78. Rothman RH, Simeone FA, Bernini PM: Lumbar disc disease. In Rothman RH, Simeone FA (eds): The Spine, 2nd ed. Philadelphia, WB Saunders 1982, pp 508–645.

79. Samaha FG: Electrodiagnostic studies in neuromuscular disease. N Engl J Med 285:1244–1249, 1971.

80. Scarff TB, Dollman DE, Bunch WH: Deermatomal somatosensory evoked responses in the diagnosis of lumbar root entrapment. Surg Forum 32:489–491, 1981.

81. See JH, Kraft GH: Electromyography in paraspinal muscles following surgery for root compression. Arch Phys Med Rehabil 56:50–53, 1975.

82. Seppalainer AM, Alaranta H, Saini J: Electromyography in the diagnosis of lumbar spinal stenosis. Electmyogr Clin Neurophysiol 21:55–66, 1981.

83. Shahani BT, Young RH: Clinical electromyography. In Baker AB, Joint RJ (eds): Clinical Neurology. Philadelphia, Harper and Row, 1986.

84. Stein B: Lumbar disc diagnosis. Arch Neurol 41:593, 1984.

85. Sun SF, Stroib EW: Diabetic thoraco-abdominal neuropathy. Ann Neurol 9:75–79, 1981.

86. Taylor TKF, Wienir MA: The great toe extensor reflexes in the diagnosis of lumbar disc disorder. Br Med J 2:487–489, 1969.

87. Tonzola RJ, Ackel AA, Shahani BT, et al: Usefulness of electrophysiologic studies in the diagnosis of lumbrosacral root disease. Ann Neurol 9:305–308, 1981.

88. Waylonis GW: Electromyographic findings in chronic cervical radicular syndromes. Arch Phys Med Rehabil 49:407–412, 1968.

89. Wiesel SW, Nicholas T, Feffer HL: A study of computer assisted tomography. The incidence of positive CAT scans in an asymptomatic group of patients. Spine 9:549–556, 1984.

90. Wilchers D, Guyton JD, Johnson EW: Electromyographic findings in extensor digitorum brevis in normal population. Arch Phys Med Rehabil 57:84–85, 1976.

91. Wilkins RH, Brody IA: Lasêgue's sign. Arch Neurol 21:219–221, 1969.

92. Wiltse RD, Guyer CW, Spencer CW, et al: Alar transverse process impingement of the L5 spinal nerve. Spine 9:31–41, 1984.

93. Yoss RE, Corbin FB, MacCarty CS, et al: Significance of symptoms and signs in localization of involved roots in cervical disc protrusion. Neurol 7:673–683, 1957.

94. Young R, Getty J, Jackson A, et al: Variation in pattern of muscle innervation by the L5 and S1 nerve roots. Spine 8:616–624, 1983.

95. Young RR, Shahani BT: Clinical value and limitation of F-wave determination. Muscle Nerve 13:248–249, 1978.

ULRICH BATZDORF, MD

DIFFERENTIAL DIAGNOSIS OF ARM AND THORACIC RADICULAR PAIN AND SENSORY DISTURBANCE

Professor of Neurosurgery, UCLA School of Medicine, Los Angeles, California

Reprint requests to:
Ulrich Batzdorf, MD
Division of Neurosurgery
UCLA Medical Center
Los Angeles, CA 90024

It is important first to seek clues pointing to the possibility that the local problem of pain and sensory disturbance is the result of widespread systemic disease, such as infection, inflammatory disease, or a metastatic neoplastic process rather than a strictly local process. These conditions are discussed under their appropriate subheadings.

Table 1 represents an overview of pathologic conditions of spinal and intraspinal origin which must be considered in patients presenting with radicular pain and sensory disturbances (see also Fig. 1). Acute traumatic conditions such as spinal fractures and penetrating injuries have of course been omitted since the immediacy of the injury will be evident.

SYMPTOMS

Pain Patterns and Referred Pain

Radicular pain has characteristic features: it is often described as sharp, searing, toothache-like; it is distributed in the general pattern of the nerve root cutaneous innervation. Pain of muscular origin, by contrast, tends to be described as dull and aching. Radicular pain may be aggravated by coughing or by stretching the root. Since the neuroforamen may become somewhat narrowed during neck extension, radicular pain of disc or osteophyte origin may increase in this position. Certain occupations, such as hod carriers or painters, require the neck to be maintained in extension for many hours each day. This not only aggravates radicular pain, but may also lead to accelerated disc degeneration and osteophyte formation. Similarly, individuals who wear bifocal glasses

TABLE 1. Differential Diagnosis of Arm and Thoracic Radicular Pain and Sensory Disturbance

A. Disc and Joint Degeneration
 1. Acute Disc Protrusion
 2. Spondylosis
      Interspace, Facet Joint Degeneration
      Secondary Subluxation and Shingling
      Ligamentous Ossification of Posterior or Anterior Longitudinal Ligaments

B. Post-traumatic/Post-surgical
 Bone/Disc/Ligaments
 1. Facet Fracture
 2. Ligamentous Instability
 3. Incomplete Surgical Fusion
 4. Swan-neck Deformity

 Cord/Root/Investment
 1. Arachnoid Cysts and Pouches
 2. Arachnoid Scarring
 3. Stretch Injuries of Root

C. Infectious/Inflammatory
 Bone/Disc/Ligaments
 1. Osteomyelitis
 2. Disc Space Infection
 3. Rheumatoid Arthritis/Spondylitis

D. Developmental
 Bone/Disc/Ligaments
 1. Klippel-Feil Deformity
 2. Hemivertebra with Scoliosis
 3. Congenitally Small Canal/Foramina

 Cord/Root/Investment
 1. Arachnoid Cyst, Extra- or Intradural

E. Vascular
 Bone/Disc/Ligaments
 (See tumors)

 Cord/Root/Investment
 1. Arteriovenous and Other Vascular Malformations

F. Neoplastic
 Bone/Disc/Ligaments
 1. Bone Tumors
      Aneurysmal Bone Cysts
      Hemangiomas
      Osteoid Osteoma
 2. Metastatic Tumors

 Cord/Root/Investment
 1. Benign Nerve Sheath Tumors
 2. Meningiomas
 3. Metastatic Tumors

G. Referred Pain

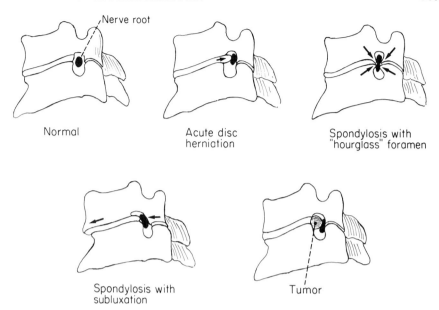

FIGURE 1. Relationship of cervical nerve root to various types of pathology.

and wear those to look at vertically-positioned material (for example, computer screens, music on music stands, or museum displays) may aggravate radicular pain by extending their necks to look through the lower part of the lens. Pain due to mechanical root compression at the neuroforamen may be increased in the upright position and reduced when the patient is recumbent. Slight flexion sometimes, but not always, helps to relieve such mechanical pain by "opening" the foramen. When the spondylotic process is associated with an element of subluxation, such postural maneuvers may have the reverse effect or no effect because subluxation is increased in flexion. Pain and dysesthesias associated with disease processes not directly related to foraminal narrowing or mechanical loading of the spine, such as intradural tumors, would not be expected to be affected as clearly by positional changes.

Although referred pain is itself a complex subject, it is known that visceral stimuli can bring about pain and sometimes paresthesias in radicular or near-radicular distribution. Stimuli arising from diaphragmatic irritation, heart, pericardium, and gallbladder are the best known examples of such referred pain. It is not uncommon to encounter patients who have undergone a complete emergency room cardiologic workup for pain that turns out to be of radicular origin.

Radicular pain and sensory changes in dermatomal distribution, when attributable to a single nerve root level, unilaterally or bilaterally, make more diffuse pathologic entities such as arachnoidal scarring ("arachnoiditis"), syringomyelia or vascular malformations of the cord unlikely. Tumors, on the other hand, both intradural and extradural, as well as arachnoid cysts, can be very focal and may give rise to very localized radicular symptoms.

EXAMINATION

Local Neck Findings

Mobility   Most patients with cervical spondylosis exhibit some restriction in neck mobility, particularly extension and lateral flexion of the cervical spine. In acute or subacute conditions, the extremes of neck motion are often accompanied by neck pain. Patients with rheumatoid disease and spondylitis often hold their heads and necks in a characteristically stiff posture. Extensive ossification of the posterior longitudinal ligament or anterior longitudinal ligament also may result in significant reduction in mobility, although rotatory motion at C1-2 is not affected in the same manner by these conditions as it is in rheumatoid arthritis. In situations in which extensive pathologic fusion has developed, attempted motion often is not associated with pain. Commonly, however, one sees patients with arm pain and dysesthesias accompanied by reduced neck mobility, where neck pain is the factor limiting mobility. Neck pain in this situation may result from neck muscle spasm or posterior primary division root irritation, or may originate from the facet joints, disc annulus or ligamentous structures. Palpation of the neck often confirms the presence of muscle spasm, and sometimes a tender hypertrophied facet joint can be felt. The patient usually has no difficulty in telling the examiner that a source of point tenderness has been identified. In the author's experience, facet joint disease alone may cause arm pain and dysesthesias (Fig. 2), and both symptoms may respond favorably to a diagnostic injection of local anesthetic into the facet joint under fluoroscopic control. The ability to block pain by peripheral injection, however, cannot always be used to exclude reliably a more central (i.e., root) source of the pain. Multiple injections, including placebo injections, sometimes are necessary to localize a source of pain.

Vertical compression of the cervical spine by the examiner (Spurling's maneuver) will aggravate or precipitate root pain and dysesthesias in the upper extremities when the neuroforamen is narrowed by disc and/or osteophyte. Such a maneuver also places stress on the facet joint and thus may also aggravate pain due to facet joint disease.

In extreme cases of anterior osteophyte formation, a patient may experience dysphagia and hoarseness.

Neurologic Examination

The presence of radicular pain and dysesthesias does not necessarily mean that there will be associated "objective" findings, such as reflex changes, motor weakness or atrophy, or a demonstrable and reproducible sensory deficit. Conversely, the absence of such findings does not speak against the organic nature of the patient's complaints. The presence of motor symptoms or signs and of sensory deficit, when accompanying radicular pain and dysesthesias, generally reflects more severe compression of the nerve root than when such motor manifestations are absent. Coexistence of long tract signs, notably increased lower extremity tone, ankle clonus and extensor plantar responses, immediately focuses attention on an intraspinal process compressing the spinal cord, which additionally has produced root symptoms.

Patterns of Radicular Pain

See Table 2.

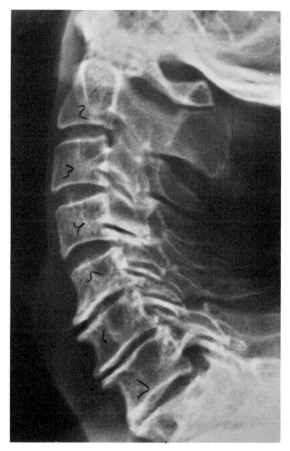

FIGURE 2. Cervical spine radiograph showing significant facet arthropathy at C4-5, the cause of this patient's arm pain.

Radiology and Imaging

Techniques for evaluation of the cervical spine and its contents have improved remarkably over the last decade. Listed below are the most useful techniques in practice today. The diagnostic procedures particularly useful in specific conditions are discussed under the appropriate subheadings.

1. Radiologic
   a. Plain films, including anterior-posterior and lateral projections, oblique views, open-mouth view of C1-2
   b. Lateral views in flexion, neutral and extension
   c. Polytomography (planography)
2. Myelography (water-soluble contrast material)
3. Computerized tomographic scanning (soft tissue and bone window settings)
   a. Without contrast
   b. With contrast
4. Magnetic resonance imaging
5. Isotope bone scans

TABLE 2. Patterns of Radicular Pain

Nerve Root	Disc Level	Symptoms	Findings
C3	C2–C3	Pain and numbness in posterior cervical area, mastoid area, sometimes ear	No detectable weakness or reflex change; EMG may be abnormal.
C4	C3–C4	Pain and numbness in posterior cervical area radiating to top of shoulder; occasional chest pain	Weakness difficult to detect; no reflex changes. EMG may be abnormal.
C5	C4–C5	Pain in lateral cervical area radiating to top of shoulder; numbness over deltoid and biceps area	Weakness of shoulder abduction; deltoid atrophy. EMG may be abnormal.
C6	C5–C6	Pain radiating to arm and forearm, often to thumb and index fingers; paresthesias/numbness in thumb and index finger.	Weakness and/or atrophy of biceps muscle; biceps reflex depressed or absent. EMG may be abnormal.
C7	C6–C7	Pain radiating to forearm, often to middle finger, sometimes to adjacent fingers; paresthesias/numbness in same fingers	Weakness and/or atrophy of triceps muscle; triceps reflex depressed or absent. EMG may be abnormal.
C8	C7–T1	Pain down into medial forearm to ring and little finger; paresthesias/numbness in same fingers	Weakness and/or atrophy of triceps and small muscles of the hand; no reflex change.

ACUTE CERVICAL DISC PROTRUSION

Acute protrusion of a cervical disc is most commonly the result of a specific acute injury. This injury may be caused by lifting or straining activity, or may be the result of a motor vehicle or sports injury. Neck pain usually is almost immediate in onset, together with arm pain and sensory symptoms. As protective muscle spasm develops in the axial musculature over the first few days after injury, headache and more diffuse cervical pain radiating to the shoulders will often develop. Although acute disc protrusions may occur at almost any level of the cervical spine, they are most common at the levels of the neck where mobility is greatest, that is, at C4-5, C5-6 and C6-7. The pattern of pain, corresponding to the root involved, is as described in Table 2. Arm pain was present in over 99% of Henderson's [12] patients, neck pain in 80%, and scapular pain in approximately 50% of patients, with chest pain and headache being less common. Direct vertical blows to the top of the head, such as may occur when an individual in an automobile is propelled against the roof of the vehicle, may result in rather symmetric disc protrusion with bilateral symptoms. Whether symptoms of arm pain and sensory disturbance remit, persist, or are followed by development of more deficit including motor deficit, presumably depends on the local relationships of the nerve root and its vasculature to the protruded disc and the bony foramen. A congenitally small foramen will not accommodate even a small disc protrusion without symptoms; conversely, a protrusion of significant size may be tolerated without symptoms in a person with a capacious neuroforamen. Such disc protrusions may, however, harden in time and can become the focal point of later osteophyte development. Whether disc protrusions really retract is debatable. Symptomatic improvement may be the result of a combination of decreased root swelling, some degree of accommodation of the stretched nerve root to the narrowed foramen, as well as possibly some retraction of the disc protrusion. High-velocity injuries may produce such severe disruption of the intervertebral disc that no significant repair or accommodation can take place. The radicular pain associated with acute disc protrusion is often extremely severe and difficult to control without narcotic medication.

Diagnostic Techniques

The most accurate methods of diagnosing cervical disc protrusion with root compression are computerized axial tomography (CT) (Fig. 3), magnetic resonance imaging (MRI) and myelography.[6,15] Cross-sectional views of the two imaging techniques provide excellent demonstration of the neuroforamina and any encroaching disc. Sagittal MR images are particularly helpful in identifying indentations of cord and subarachnoid space by the disc. For many physicians, myelography is still the diagnostic procedure they feel most secure with, although it is of course invasive. If myelography is performed with water-soluble contrast, as is now the common practice, a few CT images at the level of a demonstrated myelographic abnormality will often provide useful additional information regarding the anatomical relationships. Plain films should be obtained to rule out other disease processes but seldom show abnormalities with acute disc protrusions except for changes in the curvature of the spine due to muscle spasm and perhaps slight interspace narrowing.

Electrodiagnostic studies are useful after the second or third week. These are discussed in the first chapter of this monograph.

CHRONIC CERVICAL DISC DISEASE AND SPONDYLOSIS

Subacute and chronic radicular pain with or without upper extremity sensory disturbances is among the most common of complaints encountered in clinical medicine. Although an acute event, such as an upper extremity movement requiring significant effort or a motor vehicle accident, may stand out as the initiating event, many patients have radicular symptoms without such signal episodes. Because the pathologic changes that narrow the neuroforamen, i.e., osteophyte and/or facet joint disease or degeneration of Luschka's joint, precede the development of symptoms, even minor trauma, such as stretching the arm in a particular position, sleeping in an awkward posture, or a movement that might previously have been carried out without symptoms, may now give rise to pain and dysesthesias.

Chronic degenerative changes in the cervical disc, with loss of height, water content and elasticity of the intervertebral disc, favor the buildup of osteophytes at the vertebral end-plates, which then encroach on the neuroforamen. Similar changes may take place at the true intervertebral joints, resulting in the typical "hourglass" appearance of the neuroforamen on oblique views of the cervical spine. With minor trauma, the nerve root may become edematous in this situation in a manner similar to that described for acute disc herniation, and the combination of a swollen nerve root coursing through a narrowed foramen having roughened edges serves to perpetuate the pain and accompanying neurologic symptoms. Once the root is swollen, relatively trivial additional provocation,

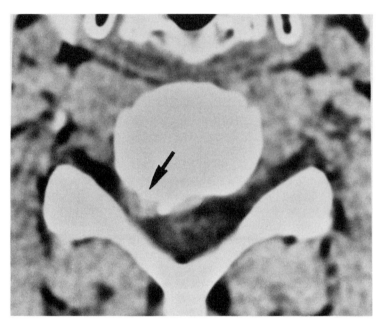

FIGURE 3. CT scan showing right C5-6 disc protrusion, projecting into neuroforamen. There also is some osteophyte formation at this site.

such as traveling in a moving vehicle, often aggravates symptoms. Reduction of root edema with rest and immobilization may restore the relationships of root, osteophyte and foramen to the status quo prior to the onset of symptoms, in which the root was able to exist comfortably; often, however, the ordinary activities of life aggravate the root symptoms repeatedly, medication and physical therapy fail, and the patient ultimately requires surgical therapy. Local neck pain and reduced mobility of the neck are common symptoms, present in 80% of patients with radiculopathy; sensory changes and motor changes are present in 50–60% of patients coming to surgery.[10]

Diagnostic Techniques

Plain radiographs of the spine will provide a clue to the level or levels of spine disease which may be responsible for the radicular syndrome in cervical spondylosis. High-quality CT scans are extremely helpful in assessing the size of the neuroforamen. Several cautions must be observed in their interpretation. Since neuroforamina are approximately 5–8 mm in vertical diameter, scanners that generate scans at too great a slice interval may not show the neuroforamen at its widest diameter and may therefore give rise to a mistaken notion of foraminal narrowing; the physician should insist on seeing bone windows, since soft tissue scans, highlighting disc and ligaments, also tend to show the foramen to be narrower than it really is. Reconstructions in the parasagittal plane show the foramen in profile and should be an integral part of the evaluation.

High-quality MR scans have found increasing applicability to the diagnosis of chronic disc and osteophytic disease. Since MR scans do not show bone per se as well, the author has found cross-sectional MR scans less useful than cross-sectional CT scans; mid-sagittal or para-sagittal MR scans are, however, of great value in assessing compression of the anterior subarachnoid space and the spinal cord. For many, however, water-soluble contrast myelography, in combination with CT scanning, remains the most secure way of defining root sleeve pathology. It must be pointed out, however, that myelography often does not define the more lateral component of neuroforaminal encroachment well, since the subarachnoid space does not extend out to the full extent of the neuroforamen.

It is not uncommon for a middle-aged or elderly patient with cervical radiculopathy to have several levels of abnormality by radiologic and imaging criteria. The clinical syndrome may have sufficient dermatomal overlap to make it difficult to decide which of two adjacent interspace levels is responsible for the patient's pain syndrome. In such instances, the author has found the injection of local anesthetic into the disc interspace under fluoroscopic control, as recommended by Roth,[22] helpful in analyzing the pain syndrome. When there is significant facet joint arthropathy, local anesthetic injections of the facet joint may similarly be very useful in localizing the pain syndrome. It is, of course, also possible that disease at more than one interspace is responsible for a patient's pain syndrome.

A diagnostic (and therapeutic) trial of cervical traction may be of help. Traction, however, is often misapplied, usually by placing the patient's head and neck at an angle not optimal for his or her particular problem, and the sought-for clue, that "opening up" of the foramen has relieved pain, may instead be a statement by the patient that the traction was abandoned after the first attempt because the pain became more severe. Thus, the patient must be provided with careful instructions if a trial of cervical traction at home is to be employed.

DEGENERATIVE CHANGES WITH SUBLUXATION

The process of cervical spondylosis involves not only the disc, with osteophyte formation at the adjacent end-plates; involvement of the facet joints and joints of Luschka often is also present and has already been mentioned. In some patients, the major aspect of the disease process appears to be a relaxation of ligamentous structures, both at the vertebral bodies (annular ligament) and at the joints (capsular ligaments), permitting significant subluxation of the vertebral bodies when forward flexion is carried out. This forward movement is capable of deforming the neuroforamen, thereby producing root symptoms that are relieved when the spine is restored to normal alignment. Similarly, telescoping of vertebrae, sometimes termed shingling, can result from a combination of disc and joint disease, and can narrow the neuroforamen.

Static films of the spine and imaging scans, which are all obtained with the patient in horizontal position, do not necessarily reflect subluxation or shingling, and it is important to obtain flexion and extension films of the cervical spine in the true lateral projection for complete assessment of the disease process.

ADDITIONAL FACTORS THAT MAY CONTRIBUTE TO SPONDYLOTIC DISEASE

Spinal Deformity.   Patients with severe thoracolumbar scoliotic deformities of the spine may have a compensatory curvature in the cervical region which can result in compression or stretch radiculopathy. Because scoliotic deformities may increase in degree with age, it is possible for a patient with

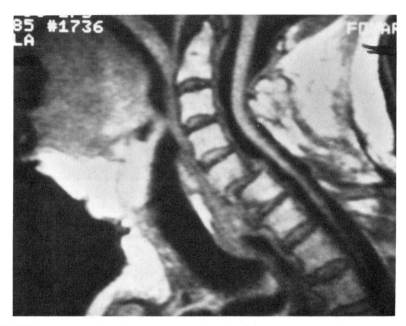

FIGURE 4.   Severe hyperlordotic neck deformity in spondylosis in a 70-year-old man. Such deformities may give rise to local neck and radicular pain.

long-standing scoliosis to develop radicular symptoms in later life. Hemi-vertebrae are not uncommon in the thoracic spine and may be related to the development of scoliosis. Deformities of the thoracic spine often occur in older people, particularly in women who have developed osteoporosis. While these deformities most often result in local pain of spinal origin, severe thoracic kyphosis may produce an exaggerated cervical lordosis with resulting radiculopathy[3] (Fig. 4). Osteoporosis also can result in demineralization of the cervical vertebrae with resultant loss in height and the potential of nerve root compression.

   Ligamentous Calcification.   While focal degenerative calcification of the posterior longitudinal ligament is not uncommonly seen, particularly on cross-sectional CT scans, there has been greater interest in a rarer condition in which there is extensive calcification of the posterior longitudinal ligament in a rostro-caudal direction, spanning multiple vertebral levels. Ossification of the posterior longitudinal ligament primarily produces compression of the spinal cord within the spinal canal, causing a myelopathy;[11] since motion of the cervical spine is often severely restricted, radicular symptoms are relatively less common in this condition. Harsh et al. encountered arm pain in 30% of patients, but upper extremity weakness was present in 85% and sensory symptoms in 80%. The same considerations apply to the even rarer condition of extensive calcification and ossification of the anterior longitudinal ligament (Forestier's disease) (Fig. 5).

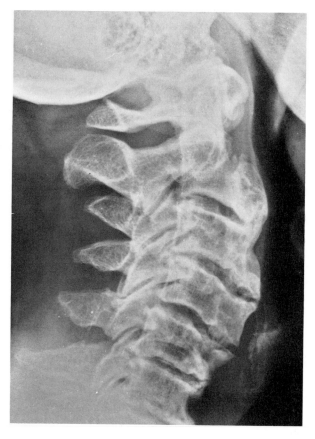

FIGURE 5. Extensive ossification of the anterior longitudinal ligament, causing radicular and local neck pain, as well as dysphagia, in a 69-year-old woman.

POST-TRAUMATIC / POST-SURGICAL RADICULAR PAIN

Delayed post-traumatic changes of the cervical spine and its associated ligaments can occur and may give rise to radicular symptoms. Such injuries most commonly involve either the facet joints or ligaments supporting the spine. Unrecognized small facet joint fractures may result in pressure on nerve roots from gradual displacement of a fracture fragment or from callus formation. Stretching of ligamentous structures, particularly the interspinous ligament in flexion injuries, or capsular ligaments can result in the development of gradual root compression because of ligamentous instability. The changes resulting from ligamentous instability may not be evident on films taken immediately after the injury has occurred, but may become apparent after days or weeks.

Trauma can also produce pathologic changes in the spinal roots and their coverings, and in the spinal cord. High-velocity injuries, particularly motorcycle injuries, sometimes result in cervical nerve root avulsions, with extensive motor and sensory deficits. Arachnoid pouches often form at the site of avulsed roots.

Less severe stretch injuries undoubtedly occur by a similar mechanism. Extensive arachnoid scarring, which may enmesh some of the roots, can develop following trauma. This condition is difficult to diagnose, except by myelography and MRI.

While intramedullary cysts may develop as a sequel to severe or moderate spinal cord injury, symptoms produced by such cysts are primarily those of myelopathy rather than radiculopathy.

Post-surgical changes of the spine also may be the cause of delayed radiculopathy. The most severe type of change is the so-called swan neck deformity,[24] which results when facet joint instability follows an extensive laminectomy. Often such deformities are the sequel of wide laminectomy and bone removal performed in the course of operations for excision of benign tumors, such as meningiomas. Spinal deformity often becomes progressive when the gravitational axis of the spine is disturbed.

Failure of fusion following an anterior arthrodesis of the cervical spine, itself performed for radicular symptoms or myelopathy, can lead to persistent radicular pain and dysesthesias, with or without motor deficit. Symptoms are obviously aggravated by the abnormal motion at the interspace, which is transmitted to the neuroforamina. Posterior spinal operations, which include excision of the strong interspinous ligament perhaps in conjunction with partial facet joint removal, may result in delayed and symptomatic deformity as described above, particularly when other predisposing factors, such as altered posture, are also present.

INFECTION OR INFLAMMATION OF THE SPINE

Infections of the spine are most commonly hematogenous in origin, and may be a sequel to bacteremia from a remote source. Osteomyelitis of the cervical spine has been seen following dental procedures and in conjunction with scalp infections and other nearby infections, spread being postulated by either a venous or lymphatic route.[8] The causative organisms are most frequently staphylococci, although the literature reports an increasing number of gram-negative infections. When nerve root symptoms and neck pain develop, there usually is already some degree of vertebral destruction, so that mechanical compression of the root may be the underlying mechanism. Significant soft tissue edema, which may include the contiguous anterior and posterior spinal ligaments, is often seen; inflammatory changes also may occur in the root and its coverings, contributing to the root swelling. Systemic manifestations of sepsis are not infrequently present, although they may be masked by prior administration of antibiotics.

Intervertebral disc space infections, as distinct from osteomyelitis, may result from injections into the disc interspace. Pyogenic disc infections are relatively rare, and while tuberculosis is less common in this country today, it must still be considered a potential cause of disc space infections. Osteomyelitis and disc space infections may appear days or weeks following the original inoculating infection, and the clinical presentation may be subacute and even chronic. Back and neck pain with radiation into the extremities is often an associated symptom in 85% of patients.[21] In early stages, plain lateral radiographs of the cervical spine may show significant prevertebral soft tissue swelling with elimination of the "fatty stripe"; bone changes may not be seen until several weeks later. The gallium bone scan is one of the most valuable diagnostic aids, particularly in suspected inflammatory disease of the spine.[18] MRI is an excellent diagnostic tool for inflammatory disease of the spine.[16] In disc space infections, the disc space becomes progressively more narrow and prevertebral soft tissue swelling will also develop.

The sedimentation rate and white blood cell count often are elevated, but blood cultures are not consistently positive. Positive blood cultures or cultures of biopsy material have been obtained in only half of patients in one study.[27] MRI has become a very valuable tool in the diagnosis of these infections, which show as a characteristic bright signal on T1 images. In some patients, a confirmatory bacteriologic diagnosis can be obtained by aspiration of the disc space or of the area of bone erosion under fluoroscopic control, using surgically aseptic technique.

The most common form of non-infectious inflammatory pathology of the spine is that associated with rheumatoid arthritis. Although atlanto-axial subluxation is the most common type of spinal problem associated with rheumatoid arthritis, dislocations may occur at multiple levels of the spine and can cause root symptoms, often associated with motor weakness. The latter may be particularly difficult to assess because of coexisting resorptive changes in the hands. When extensive spontaneous fusion of the spine has occurred, the spine becomes quite brittle and trivial trauma may result in fractures with myelopathic or root symptoms.[19] Obviously this diagnosis must be considered even when the other skeletal manifestations of rheumatoid arthritis are mild. Rarely, inflammatory changes of the cervical spine with radiculopathy are seen in association with psoriasis.

DEVELOPMENTAL ABNORMALITIES

Root symptoms may be the presenting manifestation of developmental abnormalities of either the spine or its neural contents. Klippel-Feil deformities, with formation of block vertebrae, may be associated with root symptoms because of the accelerated spondylotic degenerative changes that occur between adjacent block vertebrae (Fig. 6).[23] Hemi-vertebrae are seen in the thoracic spine and are frequently associated with scoliotic deformities of the spine.

Root symptoms are more likely to develop when the neuroforamina are congenitally small; sometimes this is seen in association with a congenitally narrow spinal canal (Fig. 7). Even small disc or osteophyte protrusions may be symptomatic when the canal or foramina are congenitally narrow.

Arachnoid cysts may be either extradural or intradural in location. They are rare in the cervical region[5] and are generally manifested as myelopathy rather than radiculopathy. Extradural cysts may have a greater tendency to be symptomatic; intradural cysts or arachnoid diverticuli are often encountered as incidental findings on myelography but occasionally they present with pain or sensory loss in radicular distribution.[13] By contrast, in our experience upper extremity symptoms associated with syringomyelia have been primarily in the form of dysesthesias, with or without accompanying hand atrophy or weakness and myelopathy.

VASCULAR MALFORMATIONS

Radicular pain was present in 23% of patients as an early manifestation of vascular malformations of the spinal cord,[1] although many patients also show myelopathic symptoms or even symptoms of central pain in the early stages of clinical presentation. Root symptoms could readily be produced by a distended blood vessel, such as a feeding artery or large draining vein, compressing a nerve

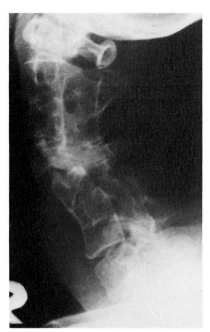
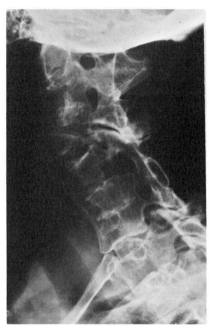

FIGURE 6. Klippel-Feil anomaly of the cervical spine with subluxation at C4-5, the only mobile interspace between two block vertebrae.

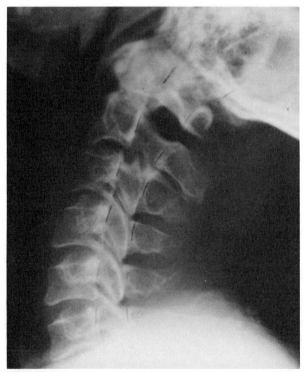

FIGURE 7. Congenitally narrow spinal canal. The facet joints project posteriorly to the level of the laminae.

root in the neuroforamen. Involvement of the dorsal root entry zone in the malformation also may produce radicular symptoms. Dural arteriovenous malformations seem to occur almost exclusively in the thoracic and lumbar regions.[25]

MRI has become a useful means of demonstrating vascular malformations of the spinal cord, a flow void pattern being recognized. Myelography will show a tortuous vascular pattern in the subarachnoid compartment, with distended vessels showing more prominently. Spinal angiography is essential to define the lesion fully and to allow consideration of all potential therapeutic options, including embolization.

NEOPLASMS

Bone tumors and aneurysmal bone cysts occur in the cervical spine.[26] They expand and thin out the vertebral bone, so that ultimately pain may develop or symptoms may follow relatively minor neck trauma in the course of which the thinned-out vertebral bone may collapse. Plain films of the cervical spine, particularly CT scans, are helpful in making the diagnosis (Fig. 8).

Other benign bone tumors, including osteoid osteoma, may be manifested as radiculopathy of the upper extremity or upper thoracic region.[9] Plain films may or may not be diagnostic. Isotope bone scans are very useful in localizing the disease process. CT and MRI techniques are helpful in further defining an osteoid osteoma.

Rarer benign and malignant primary bone tumors must also be considered: these generally show up as changes on plain films.

Tumors metastatic to the spine deserve special attention, since it is not uncommon for some malignancies to become manifest initially as metastatic disease.[20] Different pathologic processes can involve the cervical region: (1) direct extension of a malignant tumor to the cervical spine from adjacent tumor, as may be seen with thyroid malignancies; (2) disseminated metastasis to the bone, not uncommon with breast carcinoma (Fig. 9); and (3) epidural metastatic tumor, seen in association with a variety of malignant neoplasms including bronchogenic carcinoma and melanoma. Intramedullary metastasis and meningeal carcinomatosis are mentioned in connection with intraspinal neoplasms.

MRI has been found most helpful in establishing the diagnosis of disseminated focal spinal metastasis, with a characteristic low signal seen in the bony spine at multiple sites of involvement.

Neoplasms of Intraspinal Contents

Tumors of the intraspinal contents (i.e., the spinal cord, roots and their coverings) are perhaps the most significant consideration in the differential diagnosis of upper extremity pain and sensory disturbances aside from the more common problems of disc disease and spondylosis. Since spondylotic spine changes may be present in the same patient and erosive changes due to tumor may not be visible on plain films, there is danger that the initial plain films of the spine will lead to false emphasis on coexisting spondylosis. The importance of considering these tumors is that, if left untreated, they may enlarge to produce cord compression and symptoms of myelopathy. Larger tumors also are more difficult to remove surgically than smaller ones.

These tumors may be classified from several different points of view: (1) the compartment they are in: extradural, intradural, extramedullary or intramedullary; (2) the spinal level they are at: foramen magnum, upper cervical and lower cervical spine, thoracic spine, etc.; and (3) histology—meningioma

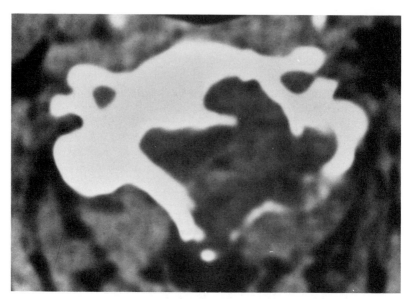

FIGURE 8.   Extensive bone destruction of C4 due to giant cell tumor. Patient presented with left-sided radicular shoulder pain.

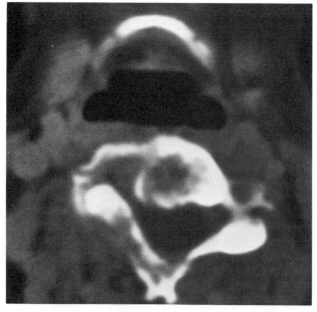

FIGURE 9.   CT scan showing extensive destructive changes of the C4 vertebra due to metastatic breast carcinoma.

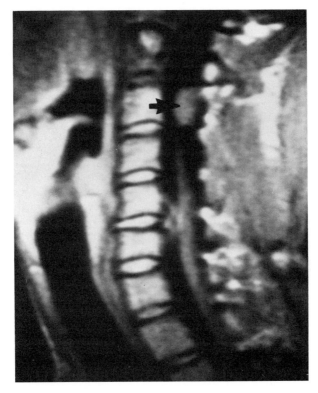

FIGURE 10. MR scan of cervical spine showing intraspinal extramedullary tumor (arrow) at C3, as well as osteophyte at C5-6.

and benign nerve sheath tumors are the most common primary tumor types, particularly in patients presenting with radicular symptoms.[17] Tumors of glial origin are intramedullary in location and rarely, if ever, manifest primarily as radiculopathy. Hemangioblastomas may occur in the spinal cord as rather focal intramedullary tumors, often associated with a cyst;[4] radicular pain and posterior column deficit often are presenting features. Metastatic tumors have also been considered among tumors of the bony spine; epidural metastasis is a common mode of metastatic spread from a variety of common malignant neoplasms, including those arising from lung, breast, kidney and the lymphoid system; they often present with radicular symptoms.[28] Pancoast tumors are notorious in this regard.[2] Intramedullary metastatic tumors are rare.

Clinical Symptoms. The clinical presentation of benign intraspinal tumors is generally gradual, progressive and unremitting.[17] There is no known relationship to trauma, but the jarring effect of head and neck trauma conceivably can slightly alter the relative position of an existing tumor to the cord and roots, so that symptoms seemingly date to the time of an injury. Root pain, often sharply demarcated, and paresthesias may precede other symptoms.[14] Local neck pain is not uncommon; motor weakness in the distribution of the involved nerve root may be an early or later manifestation. The spinal cord typically may be displaced to a significant degree in the absence of clinical features of the myelopathy until the tumor reaches a critical size. Coughing, sneezing and straining may alter the position of tumor to root sufficiently that such maneuvers can cause a transient increase in radicular symptoms. An increase in pain with bedrest has been associated with thoracic meningiomas and is postulated to be based on venous distention in the supine position.

Examination. There is nothing specific about the neurologic examination per se which favors the diagnosis of intraspinal tumor. If the general examination shows evidence of neurofibromatosis, the suspicion that there may be an intraspinal neurofibroma is increased. No cutaneous abnormalities are consistently associated with spinal meningioma. Reduced neck mobility is associated with local neck pain; focal motor weakness, atrophy and even fasciculations as well as sensory deficit in dermatomal pattern may all be seen in various combinations.

Diagnostic Evaluation. MR scanning has become a most valuable tool in the diagnosis of spinal cord tumors (Fig. 10).[7] The tumor mass is generally well seen within the subarachnoid space, displacing the nerve roots or spinal cord. The obvious advantage of MR scanning over myelography is that it is not invasive and the cerebrospinal fluid dynamics are therefore not altered by the diagnostic examination. Thus, there is no risk of shifting a somewhat mobile tumor mass in such manner as to allow it to become impacted against the spinal cord, with the possibility of acute neurologic worsening. The diagnosis of metastatic tumors has been noted above. If there is a suspicion of carcinomatous meningitis, this diagnosis can be confirmed by lumbar puncture and cytologic analysis of the cerebrospinal fluid.

REFERENCES

1. Aminoff MJ, Logue V: Clinical features of spinal vascular malformations. Brain 97:197–210, 1974.
2. Batzdorf U, Brechner VL: Management of pain associated with the Pancoast syndrome. Am J Surg 137:638–646, 1979.
3. Batzdorf U, Batzdorff A: Analysis of cervical spine curvature in patients with cervical spondylosis. Neurosurgery 22:827–836, 1988.
4. Browne TR, Adams RD, Roberson GH: Hemangioblastomas of the spinal cord. Arch Neurol 33:435–441, 1976.
5. Cloward RB: Congenital spinal extradural cysts. Ann Surg 168:851–864, 1968.
6. Coin CG, Coin JT: Computed tomography of cervical disk disease. J Comput Assist Tomogr 5:275–280, 1981.
7. DiChiro G, Doppman JL, Dwyer AJ, et al: Tumors and arteriovenous malformations of the spinal cord: assessment using MR. Radiology 156:689–697, 1985.
8. Feigenbaum JA, Stern WE: Infections of cervical disc space after dental extractions. J Neurol Neurosurg Psychiatry 37:1361–1365, 1974.
9. Goldstein GS, Dawson EG, Batzdorf U: Cervical osteoid osteoma: a cause of chronic upper back pain. Clin Orthop 129:177–180, 1977.
10. Gregorius FK, Estrin T, Crandall PH: Cervical spondylotic radiculopathy and myelopathy. Arch Neurol 33:618–625, 1976.
11. Harsh GR, Sypert GW, Weinstein PR, et al: Cervical spine stenosis secondary to ossification of the posterior longitudinal ligament. J Neurosurg 67:349–357, 1987.
12. Henderson CM, Hennessy RG, Shuey HM Jr, Shackelford EG: Posterior-lateral foraminotomy as an exclusive operative technique for cervical radiculopathy: a review of 846 consecutively operated cases. Neurosurgery 13:504–512, 1983.
13. Kendall BE, Valentine AR, Keis B: Spinal arachnoid cysts: clinical and radiological correlation with prognosis. Neuroradiology 22:225–234, 1982.
14. Long DM: Tumors Involving the cervical spine. In: The Cervical Spine Research Society (eds): The Cervical Spine. Philadelphia, JB Lippincott Co., 1983.
15. Masaryk TJ, Modic MT, Geisinger MA, et al: Cervical myelopathy: a comparison of magnetic resonance and myelography. J Comput Assist Tomogr 10:184–194, 1986.

16. Modic MT, Feiglan DH, Piraino BW, et al: Vertebral osteomyelitis: assessment using MR. Radiol 157:157–166, 1985.
17. Onofrio BM: Intradural extramedullary spinal cord tumors. *In* Clinical Neurosurgery 25. Baltimore, Williams & Wilkins Co., 1977.
18. Onofrio BM: Intervertebral discitis: incidence, diagnosis, and management. *In* Clinical Neurosurgery 27. Baltimore, Williams and Wilkins Co., 1980.
19. Rand RW, Stern WE: Cervical fractures of the ankylosed rheumatoid spine. Neurochir 4:137–148, 1961.
20. Raycroft J, Hockman R, Southwick W: Metastatic tumors involving the cervical vertebrae: surgical palliation. J Bone Joint Surg 60A:763–768, 1978.
21. Ross PM, Fleming JL: Vertebral body osteomyelitis. Clin Orthop 118:190–198, 1976.
22. Roth DA: Cervical analgesic discography: a new test for the definitive diagnosis of the painful-disk syndrome. JAMA 235:1713–1714, 1976.
23. Shoul MI, Ritvo M: Clinical and roentgenological manifestations of the Klippel-Feil syndrome (congenital fusion of the cervical vertebrae, brevicollis): report of eight additional cases and review of the literature. Am J Roentgenol 68:369–385, 1952.
24. Sim FH, Svien HJ, Bickel WH, et al: Swan-neck deformity following extensive cervical laminectomy: a review of 21 cases. J Bone Joint Surg 56A:564–580, 1974.
25. Symon L, Kuyama H, Kendall B: Dural arteriovenous malformations of the spine. J Neurosurg 60:238–247, 1984.
26. Verbiest H: Tumors involving the cervical spine. *In:* The Cervical Spine Research Society (eds): The Cervical Spine. Philadelphia, JB Lippincott Co., 1983.
27. Wenger DR, Bobechko WP, Gilday DL: The spectrum of intervertebral disc-space infection in children. J Bone Joint Surg 60A:100–108, 1978.
28. Young RF, Post EM, King GA: Treatment of spinal epidural metastases. J Neurosurg 53:741–748, 1980.

MICHAEL A. WIENIR, MD

UPPER EXTREMITY PAIN AND SENSORY DISTURBANCE

A. Brachial Plexopathy

Assistant Clinical Professor of Neurology, UCLA School of Medicine, Los Angeles, California

Reprint requests to:
Michael A. Wienir, MD
San Fernando Valley Neurologic Medical Group, Inc.
18370 Burbank Blvd., Suite 107
Tarzana, CA 91356

ANATOMY

The diagnosis of upper extremity pain and sensory disturbance requires consideration of the entire neural pathway from the nerve roots to the peripheral nerves themselves. The brachial plexus is formed by the C5, 6, 7, 8, and T1 spinal nerves after these structures have exited the neural foramina of the cervical spine (Fig. 1).[14,15] There can be individual variation of the plexus. In the pre-fixed plexus, there is a large contribution of the C4 spinal nerve and little T1. In the post-fixed plexus, there is no C4 contribution and branches of the T2 nerve may be included.

Prior to the formation of the first main divisions of the plexus, two important nerves are given off. The dorsal scapular nerve emanates from the C4 and C3 spinal nerves and innervates the levator scapulae muscle, which elevates the scapula, and the rhomboid muscle, which adducts and elevates the scapula. The long thoracic nerve branches from the C5, 6, and 7 nerve fibers and supplies the serratus anterior muscle. Involvement of this nerve results in prominent winging of the scapula but no sensory disturbance.

The first main divisions of the brachial plexus are the upper trunk formed by C5 and C6 fibers, the middle trunk formed from C7 fibers, and the lower trunk from C8 and T1 fibers. These trunks traverse the supraclavicular fossa. The upper trunk gives rise to the suprascapular nerve, which innervates the supraspinatus and infraspinatus muscles. The supraspinatus muscle provides initial abduction

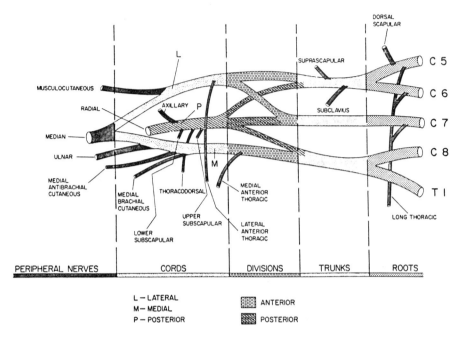

FIGURE 1. Anatomy of the brachial plexus. (Reproduced with permission from Good-gold J: Anatomic Correlates of Clinical Electromyography. Baltimore, Williams and Wilkins, 1980, p 56).

of the shoulder, and the infraspinatus muscle is important in external rotation of the shoulder. The subclavius nerve branch of the upper trunk has little clinical significance.

The trunks then divide and coalesce to form the anterior and posterior divisions and then the lateral, medial, and posterior cords. The cords are located at the border of the first rib and the major peripheral nerves that emanate from the cords arise in the axilla. The lateral cord is formed by branches of the upper and middle trunks. This cord forms the musculocutaneous nerve and joins with fibers of the lower trunk to form the median nerve. The posterior cord receives fibers from all three trunks and the branches to form the radial, axillary, and thoracodorsal nerves as well as the upper and lower subscapular nerves. The medial cord is an extension of the lower trunk. Fibers branch to form the median nerve after joining with the fibers of the lateral cord. In addition, the medial cord branches to form the ulnar nerve, the medial antebrachial cutaneous nerves, and the medial brachial cutaneous sensory nerves, which supply sensation to the medial aspect of the upper arm and the forearm. Fibers from both the lateral and medial cords form the medial and lateral pectoral or thoracic nerves and supply the pectoralis major and minor muscles.

Injury or disease affecting the structures of the brachial plexus can result in a complex pattern of pain and sensory, motor, and reflex abnormalities, depending on which structures are involved. Figure 2 shows the main sensory distribution of the branches of the brachial plexus. The specific motor innervation of muscles innervated by the branches of the brachial plexus is considered in detail in the chapter on specific nerve injuries.

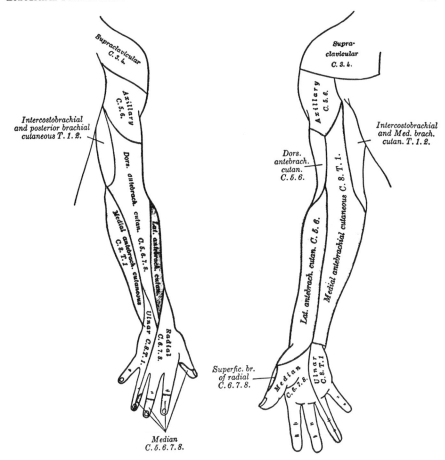

FIGURE 2. Posterior (left) and anterior (right) view of the segmental distribution of the cutaneous nerves of the right upper extremity. (Reproduced with permission from Clemente CD: Gray's Anatomy of the Human Body, 30th American ed. Philadelphia, Lea & Febiger, 1985, with permission.)

CLINICAL PRESENTATION

A patient may present with moderate to severe pain beginning in the proximal shoulder girdle and radiating or extending down the arm to the hand. Movement of the arm and shoulder may increase the pain. Although the pain may be described as a deep ache, it may also have a sharp lancinating radicular quality and may be associated with a sense of burning, paresthesia, dysesthesia, heat, coldness, and altered sensation in the arm. Examination may show weakness of shoulder abduction by the deltoid muscle. The deltoid muscle is innervated by C5 and C6 radicular fibers via the upper trunk, posterior division, and posterior cord of the plexus, and finally through the axillary nerve. Proximal radicular injury may result in clinical or electromyographic changes in the paraspinous muscles, the rhomboids, levator scapulae, and the serratus anterior muscle. These muscles are innervated by nerve structures proximal to the plexus and they will be spared by upper trunk or more distal lesions. Other C5 or C6 innervated muscles will of course be expected to show changes with proximal injury. As the injury is more distal, the muscles involved will have a different pattern. Axillary nerve injury involves only the deltoid and teres minor muscles. Posterior cord lesions also involve muscles innervated by the axillary, radial and thoracodorsal nerves, with sparing of more proximally innervated muscles. With upper trunk lesions, muscles innervated by the suprascapular, axillary, musculocutaneous, radial, and median nerves will be affected, with sparing of the more proximal innervated muscles.

Electrodiagnostic tests in the form of EMG, sensory and motor nerve conduction studies, F-wave determinations, and somatosensory evoked potentials (as described in the first chapter), are often essential to clearly delineate the pattern and extent of brachial plexus abnormalities.[8,10,37] Electrodiagnostic studies can be particularly useful in evaluating the severity of the lesion and in determining the prognosis. With severe avulsion injuries to preganglionic structures of the brachial plexus, the arm will be anesthetic and yet the sensory nerve action potentials and conduction velocities will be normal, as the damage occurs proximal to the dorsal root ganglion and the sensory fibers are not disconnected from their nerve cell bodies. Motor fibers are, however, completely disrupted. Wallerian degeneration takes place and these fibers become completely inexcitable. EMG shows denervation in the distribution of the nerve fibers affected. With proximal avulsion injuries, the posterior primary rami are often involved and denervation may be seen in the paraspinous cervical musculature. Myelography, CT, and MRI may also show traumatic meningoceles in these preganglionic lesions. In addition, the intradermal injection of histamine will result in a normal wheal and flare response, with preganglionic lesions indicative of the preservation of the integrity of the sensory nerve fibers. With serious trauma, there may be evidence of both pre- and post-ganglionic plexopathy.

ETIOLOGY

Plexus Stretching and Contusion

Of the pathologic processes affecting the brachial plexus, probably the most common involves stretching or contusion of the plexus.[19] This can occur after automobile or motorcycle accidents, falls from bicycles or horses, or trauma associated with football, skiing, sledding, wrestling, gymnastics, or even golf.[10,19,25] Soldiers or hikers with heavy rucksacks[7,39] and individuals who shoot weapons that recoil[38] can develop plexopathy. With falls, injury occurs on impact when the head and body are forcefully separated. When the arm is abducted at the time of the fall, the lower trunk and roots tend to be involved. When the arm is adducted, the upper trunk and roots are more likely to be involved. Dislocation of the humeral head commonly causes injury to the cords or terminal branches of the plexus such as the axillary nerve.[24,27] Callus from clavicular fractures or false aneurysms from associated axillary or subclavian arterial injury can be associated with late-onset plexopathy.[10] Brachial plexus injuries after birth trauma have long been recognized.[11-13] Upper trunk (C5-C6) injury is called Erb-Duchenne palsy and is most common. Klumpke-Dejerine palsy involves the lower trunk (C8-T1) fibers.

Kline, Hackett, and Happel[19] point out that until recently a conservative nonsurgical approach to stretch and contusion lesions of the plexus was advocated. Many of these patients suffer a local demyelinating block in neural conduction and recover in several months.[37] When the lesion is mild, incomplete, and infraclavicular or relatively distal the prognosis is good.[24,29] However, with severe lesions the degree of spontaneous return of function is often poor and the results of conservative care is often disappointing.[1,2,36,41] With new surgical techniques some authors are more aggressively considering operative intervention.[26,30,31] Kline and Judice[18] have advocated the need to determine clinically and electrophysiologically the status of each neural element involved. The determination of a complete or incomplete injury to each structure in the plexus is reevaluated over a four- or five-month period prior to consideration of operation.

Plexus Gunshot Wounds and Lacerations

Gunshot wounds of the plexus do not result in diagnostic dilemmas, although the extent and severity of the neural injury clearly require detailed clinical and electrodiagnostic evaluation. Surgical intervention is now advocated when there is complete loss in the distribution of one or more neural elements lasting at least two months.[19] Acute surgical intervention may be necessary for repair of associated vascular structures. The plexus can also be lacerated by sharp objects such as a knife, fragment of glass, or other sharp piece of metal. Neural structures can be transected or only contused. The timing and/or necessity of surgery requires considerable clinical judgment.

Plexus Injury After Medical Procedures

The list of procedures resulting in postoperative brachial plexopathy is extensive.[20,32,33] Plexopathy occurs after stretching of the neural elements during sternal splitting procedures for coronary bypass or after removal of thoracic neoplasms.[17,24,34] In Lederman's 1982 review,[22] 13% of 421 patients undergoing coronary artery bypass surgery had peripheral nervous system complications. Of the 55 injuries, 23 were brachioradiculoplexopathies and 21 of the 23 involved the lower trunk or the medial cord. In 17 there appeared to be a correlation to the site of jugular vein cannulation. Stretching of nerve fibers was felt to be the etiologic factor in the other affected patients.

The plexus can be injured during transaxillary first rib resection for thoracic outlet syndrome (see the chapter on Thoracic Outlet Syndromes). Transection of the plexus has occurred during radical mastectomy and the plexus may be cut with lymph node biopsy procedures in the neck or axilla. Axillary angiography can result in blood clots or aneurysms that compromise the plexus.[9,28]

Generally a conservative therapeutic approach is advocated in these cases. However, Kline[19] advocates consideration of surgery if there is complete deficit in the distribution of one or more elements that does not improve after several months.

Benign Tumors of the Plexus

Benign tumors of the brachial plexus are unusual.[5,6,16,40] Schwannomas or neurofibromas are most common. The latter may be associated with neurofibromatosis or von Recklinghausen's disease and may be multifocal. Rarely, malignant sarcomatous transformation occurs in these tumors.

Benign tumors are generally slow growing and present with insidious symptoms and signs, depending on the exact location within the plexus. Schwannomas can often be successfully removed surgically, as the tumor may be dissected away from nerve fibers. Neurofibromas are associated with substantial operative morbidity, as nerve fibers are more difficult to spare during tumor dissection.

Metastatic Tumors of the Brachial Plexus

By far, the majority of tumors that metastasize to the brachial plexus emanate from lung and breast malignancies.[21,23] Lymphoma and melanoma are much less common and metastasis from other tumors is rare. In up to 30% of cases, brachial plexopathy may be the first manifestation of underlying malignancy and often is the only site of metastatic disease, even when a primary neoplasm is known. Moderate to severe shoulder girdle and arm pain exacerbated by shoulder movement is the presenting complaint in 75 to 90% of patients. Paresthesias, dysesthesias, and hypersensitivity of the arm are the presenting symptoms in 10 to 25% of the patients. Many of these patients are misdiagnosed as having bursitis, arthritis, myofascial pain, or radiculopathy before the correct diagnosis is made.

On examination, the majority of patients (72% in one study[21]) have weakness, atrophy, and sensory changes in the lower trunk (C8-T1) distribution. Involvement of the entire plexus is less common, and isolated involvement of the upper trunk (C5-C6) is unusual. Horner's syndrome with ipsilateral ptosis and meiosis is seen in more than half of these patients, and lymphedema and swelling of the arm may be present because of involvement of venous and lymphatic structures. Imaging studies of the cervical spinal cord often show associated epidural metastatic disease, and MRI and CT imaging of the plexus may demonstrate the tumor,[3] but surgical exploration of the plexus is often required for definitive diagnosis.

Radiation Plexopathy

Radiation therapy to the neck, supraclavicular area, and axilla is often utilized for treatment of local and metastatic neoplasms. The radiation itself may result in a brachial plexopathy that is frequently difficult to distinguish from recurrence of neoplasm.[3,21,23] However, there are several statistical differences between radiation injury and recurrence of malignancy. Whereas pain is the most common presenting symptom with malignancy, 80% of patients with radiation injury have no pain initially. The majority of patients (78%) with radiation plexopathy have weakness and sensory changes and paresthesias in the upper trunk (C5-C6) distribution, while tumor affects more distal parts of the plexus. Horner's syndrome is rare with radiation plexopathy, whereas lymphedema is frequently seen.

The latency from the last dose of radiation to the first symptom of plexopathy can vary from 3 months to 26 years, although most commonly the latency is 1.5 to 5.5 years. If symptoms occurred within one year of termination of radiation therapy, patients with radiation plexopathy have almost invariably had more than 6000 R. If patients have had a lesser dose in the first year and symptoms develop, tumor is the most likely diagnosis. After one year, the dose of radiation does not help to distinguish patients with radiation changes from those with recurrent tumor.

Electrodiagnostic studies may also help differentiate radiation changes from tumor.[23] Myokymia and fasciculations are particularly common in EMG studies of patients with radiation plexopathy. In addition, EMGs may show progressive reduction in the amplitude of median nerve sensory action potentials with normal median and ulnar nerve motor responses.

Surgical intervention generally is to be avoided when a diagnosis of radiation plexopathy has been made. CT scanning of the plexus frequently shows distortion of normal anatomy, but clear differentiation of tumor from radiation fibrosis is often not possible. Exploration may still be required to identify tumor particularly when a neoplasm in this area may be the only evidence of active disease.

Idiopathic Brachial Neuritis

This entity is addressed in Part B of this chapter.

REFERENCES

1. Barnes R: Traction injuries of the brachial plexus in adults. J Bone Joint Surg 31B:10–16, 1949.
2. Bonney G: Prognosis in traction lesions of the brachial plexus. J Bone Joint Surg 41B:14–35, 1959.
3. Cascino TL, Kori S, Krol G, et al: CT of the brachial plexus in patients with cancer. Neurology 33:1553–1557, 1983.
4. Clancy WG, Brand RL, Bergfield JA: Upper trunk brachial plexus injuries in contact sports. Am J Sports Med 5:209, 1977.
5. Dart L, MacCarty CS, Love JG, et al: Neoplasms of the brachial plexus. Minn Med 53:959–964, 1970.
6. DasGupta T: Tumors of the peripheral nervous system. Clin Neurosurg 25:574–590, 1978.
7. Daube J: Rucksack paralysis. JAMA 208:2447, 1969.
8. Davis DH, Onofrio BM, MacCarty CS: Brachial plexus injuries. Mayo Clin Proc 53:799, 1978.
9. Dudrick S, Masland W, Mishkin M: Brachial plexus injury following axillary artery puncture. Further comments on management. Radiology 88:271–273, 1967.
10. Dyck PJ, Low PA, Stevens JC: Diseases of Peripheral Nerves. In Baker AB, Joynt RJ (eds): Clinical Neurology. Philadelphia, Harper and Row, 1986, p 51.
11. Eng GD: Brachial plexus palsy in newborn infants. Pediatrics 48:18, 1971.
12. Gilbert A, Khouri N, Carlizz H: Birth palsy of the brachial plexus: Surgical exploration and attempted repair in 21 cases. Rev Chir Orthop 66:33–42, 1980.
13. Gordon M, Rich H, Deutschberger J, et al: The immediate and long term outcome of obstetric birth trauma: Brachial plexus paralysis. Am J Obstet Gynecol 117:41, 1973.
14. Goodgold J: Anatomic Correlates of Clinical Electromyography. Baltimore, Williams and Wilkins, 1980.
15. Gray H: Anatomy of the Human Body. Philadelphia, Lea and Febiger, 1956.
16. Handler SD, Canalis RF, Jenkins HA: Arch Otolaryngol 103:653–657, 1977.
17. Hanson MR, Brewer AC, Furland AJ et al: Brachial plexus lesions following open heart surgery: A prospective analysis and possible new mechanism of injury. Neurology 30:441, 1980.
18. Kline DG, Judice DJ: Operative management of selective brachial plexus lesions. J Neurosurg 58:631–649, 1983.
19. Kline DG, Hackett ER, Happel LH: Surgery for lesions of the brachial plexus. Arch Neurol 43:170–181, 1986.
20. Kline DG, Hudson AR: Complications of nerve injury and nerve repair. In Greenfield L (ed): Complications in Surgery and Trauma. Philadelphia, JB Lippincott Co., 1984.
21. Kori SH, Foley KM, Posner JB: Brachial plexus lesions in patients with cancer: 100 cases. Neurology 31:45–50, 1981.
22. Lederman RJ, Breuer AC, Hanson MR, et al: Peripheral nervous system complications of coronary artery bypass graft surgery. Ann Neurol 12:297–301, 1982.
23. Lederman RJ, Wilbourn AJ: Brachial plexopathy: Recurrent cancer or radiation. Neurology 34:1331–1335, 1984.
24. Leffert R, Seddon H: Infraclavicular brachial plexus injuries. J Bone Joint Surg 47B:9–22, 1965.
25. Lusk M, Kline DG: Management of athletic brachial plexus injuries. In Schneider RC, Kennedy JC, Plant ML (eds): Sports Injuries: Mechanisms, Prevention and Treatment. Baltimore, Williams and Wilkins, 1985.
26. Lusskin R, Campbell JB, Thompson WAL: Post-traumatic lesions of the brachial plexus: Treatment of transclavicular exploration and neurolysis of autograft. J Bone Joint Surg 55A:1159–1176, 1973.
27. Mcgee KR, DeJong RN: Paralytic brachial neuritis. JAMA 174:1258, 1960.
28. Molner W, Paul DJ: Complications of axillary arteriotomies: An analysis of 1,762 consecutive studies. Radiology 104:269–276, 1972.

29. Nagano A: Brachial plexus injuries: Progress of postganglionic type. Orthop Surg 30:1534–1536, 1979.
30. Narakas A: The surgical treatment of traumatic brachial plexus injuries. Int Surg 65:521–527, 1980.
31. Narakas A: Surgical treatment of traction injuries of the brachial plexus. Clin Orthop 133:71–90, 1978.
32. Parks B: Postoperative peripheral neuropathies. Surgery 74:348–357, 1973.
33. Po BT, Hansen HR: Iatrogenic brachial plexus injury: A survey of the literature and of pertinent cases. Anesth Analg 48:915, 1969.
34. Stevens JW: Neurologic sequelae of congenital heart surgery. Arch Neurol 7:450–459, 1963.
35. Sunderland S: Mechanisms of cervical nerve avulsion injuries of the neck and shoulder. J. Neurosurg 41:705, 1974.
36. Taylor PE: Traumatic intradural avulsion of the nerve roots of the brachial plexus. Brain 85:579–602, 1962.
37. Trojaborg W: Electrophysiological findings in pressure palsy of the brachial plexus. J Neurol Neurosurg Psychiatry 40:1160, 1977.
38. Wanamaker WM: Firearm recoil palsy. Arch Neurol 31:308, 1974.
39. White HH: Pack paralysis: a neurologic complication of scouting. Pediatrics 41:1001, 1968.
40. Woodhall B: Peripheral nerve tumors. Surg Clin North Am 34:1167–1172, 1954.
41. Wynn-Parry CB: The management of traction lesions of the brachial plexus and peripheral nerve injuries to the upper limb: A study in teamwork. Injury 11:265–285, 1980.

AUSTIN J. SUMNER, MD

UPPER EXTREMITY PAIN AND SENSORY DISTURBANCE

B. Idiopathic Brachial Neuritis

Professor of Neurology
Hospital of the University
of Pennsylvania, Philadelphia,
Pennsylvania

Reprint requests to:
Austin J. Sumner, MD
Department of Neurology
HUP
3400 Spruce Street
Philadelphia, PA 19104

Idiopathic brachial neuritis has several synonyms, reflecting much confusion about the nature and pathogenesis of the disorder. These include multiple neuritis of the shoulder girdle, acute brachial radiculitis, neuralgic amyotrophy, acute paralytic brachial neuritis, Parsonage-Turner syndrome, cryptogenic brachial plexus neuropathy, and others. Although these terms all imply that the disease is painful and associated with acute paralysis of upper extremity muscles, there is no knowledge of the nature of the peripheral nerve pathology or of whether the lesions are located in roots, brachial plexus, or within major nerve branches of the plexus. In many instances the classical syndrome is associated with isolated nerve lesions in the forearm. The importance of the disease in clinical practice is to distinguish it from cervical radiculopathy, malignant infiltration of cervical roots or brachial plexus, and thoracic outlet and entrapment syndromes, all of which call for very different therapeutic approaches.

CLINICAL FEATURES

The onset of the disorder is typically heralded by unilateral neck and shoulder pain of a severe, deep, aching quality. Sometimes pain is also localized about the elbow. The localization of pain may give an indication as to the sites of the nerve lesions. Movements of the arm exacerbate pain, and in the most severe cases, the arm is maintained in a position of adduction at the shoulder and flexion at the elbow. Occasional patients are seen in the paralytic phase who admit to trivial or no pain at onset, but this accounts for only about 2% of cases. In two-thirds of cases, weakness is established within two weeks of the onset of pain. In a few there is virtually simultaneous onset of pain and weakness, but more typically, neurologic findings are not present until several days after the onset of pain. In about one-third of cases weakness is not recognized until up to one month after the onset of neuralgic pain. Severe pain only persists for a few days and then disappears, but in a significant proportion it may persist in mild form for many weeks. Muscle weakness does not progress after its onset. It is fully established at the time of initial examination, and barring the exceptional circumstance of a recurrent acute attack, progression in the neurologic findings should suggest an alternate diagnosis.

This author favors the hypothesis that individual nerve branches arising from the brachial plexus are the sites of attack in this disease. The axillary, suprascapular and long thoracic nerves are most commonly involved. Less frequently, lesions involve the musculocutaneous, radial, and median nerves. Only rarely is the ulnar nerve affected. Curiously, other nerve branches of these more major trunks show a special susceptibility. These include the anterior interosseous and the nerve to pronator teres from the median, and the medial antebrachial cutaneous extension of the musculocutaneous nerve. This pattern of involvement has lead to the speculation that the vulnerability of nerve branches from major trunks arising near joint crossings seems to be a factor in determining the distribution of nerve lesions, perhaps related to the vascular supply to nerves at these locations. Most patients have unilateral involvement. A significant number, however, have frank clinical or EMG evidence of more restricted bilateral disease. Classical proximal involvement on one side may be accompanied by an isolated distal mononeuropathy on the contralateral side. Phrenic nerve lesions leading to diaphragmatic paralysis and recurrent laryngeal nerve lesions leading to vocal cord paralysis are occasionally encountered in a setting of classical brachial neuritis. These observations suggest that the commonly encountered isolated mononeuropathies of long thoracic, anterior interosseous, phrenic, and recurrent laryngeal nerves may be fragmentary manifestations of brachial neuritis.

Motor findings predominate over sensory findings. The latter, when present, are usually distributed within the axillary or lateral antebrachial cutaneous territories. Fragmentary involvement within the palmar distribution of the median nerve is sometimes seen. The disease is usually encountered in otherwise healthy adults of either sex. Children are rarely affected. The so-called familial cases of recurrent "brachial neuritis" are clinically and electromyographically distinct with evidence of proximal demyelination and tomaculous changes in nerve biopsy. They should be regarded as a separate disorder, more closely related to cases of familial liability to pressure palsies than to idiopathic brachial neuritis.

INVESTIGATIONS

Electrodiagnostic studies are most useful in establishing the diagnosis, particularly by documenting the distribution of involvement. Nerve conduction studies indicate the nerve lesions are axonal rather than demyelinative. Conduction velocities within involved nerve is normal or reduced in proportion to the degree of axonal loss. Marked slowing in the acute phase, or conduction block and dispersion so typical of acute inflammatory demyelinative lesions are not seen. Spinal fluid is normal. Radiologic studies are indicated to rule out structural disease, but are normal in this disorder. High resolution MR and CT imaging may successfully demonstrate nerve trunk lesions in the near future.

ETIOLOGY AND PATHOGENESIS

The condition was first recognized among British servicemen in the Western desert during the Second World War. Therefore, factors associated with military service, especially vaccination and the carrying of heavy backpacks, came under suspicion as etiologic factors. It was also recognized early that the neuritis following serum sickness is quite similar to idiopathic brachial neuritis, and there is a strong suspicion that immune complex deposition within blood vessels may be responsible for the nerve lesions. Occurrence of brachial neuritis has been described after typhus, variola, diphtheria, and influenza, as well as after the administration of the triple vaccine and tetanus toxoid. It has also been associated with infectious mononucleosis, lupus erythematosus, and cytomegalovirus infection. Such associations are, however, rare, and in the majority of cases, no clear precipitating illness, vaccination, or other event is demonstrable. Our knowledge of the pathogenesis of the disease can be briefly summarized by saying that it is unknown.

PROGNOSIS AND TREATMENT

In some cases, because of its intensity, the pain demands treatment with powerful analgesics. Some claim that corticosteroids and ACTH have a favorable effect on pain, but they do not influence the course of the disease and this author is unconvinced of their usefulness. As far as restoration of neurologic function is concerned, the prognosis is generally good. More than 80% of patients recover within the two years of onset of symptoms. This recovery is by axon regeneration and collateral sprouting of surviving axons. As such, EMG studies indicate that even in clinically strong muscles, the numbers of functioning motor units are markedly reduced following recovery. The degree of recovery is related to the severity of the initial denervation. In muscles with total denervation, regeneration is usually incomplete and atrophy and weakness in such instances is long-lasting. Some patients with severe brachial neuritis develop a syndrome analogous to post-polio syndrome, in which there is decompensation of strength around the shoulder girdle many years after recovery from the initial attack. Physical therapy is important in maintaining mobility of the shoulder joint and reducing the likelihood of formation of adhesive capsulitis.

REFERENCES

1. Burnard ED, Fox TG: Multiple neuritis of the shoulder girdle: report of nine occurring in Second New Zealand expeditionary force. NZ Med J 41:243–247, 1942.
2. Editorial: Neuralgic amyotrophy—still a clinical syndrome. Lancet 2:729–730, 1980.
3. England JD, Sumner AJ: Neuralgic amyotrophy: an increasingly diverse entity. Muscle Nerve 10:60–68, 1987.
4. Kiloh LG, Nevin S: Isolated neuritis of the anterior interosseous nerve. Br Med J 1:850–851, 1952.
5. Kraft GH: Multiple distal neuritis of the shoulder girdle: an electromyographic clarification of "paralytic brachial neuritis". Electroencephalogr Clin Neurophysiol 27:722, 1969.
6. Parsonage MJ, Turner JWA: The shoulder girdle syndrome. Lancet 1:973–978, 1948.
7. Rennels GD, Ochoa J: Neuralgic amyotrophy manifesting an anterior interosseous nerve palsy. Muscle Nerve 3:160–164, 1980.
8. Tsairis P, Dyck PJ, Mulder DW: Natural history of brachial plexus neuropathy. Arch Neurol 27:109–117, 1972.
9. Turner JWA, Parsonage MJ: Neuralgic amyotrophy (paralytic brachial neuritis). Lancet 2:209–212, 1957.

ASA J. WILBOURN, MD
JOHN M. PORTER, MD

THORACIC OUTLET SYNDROMES

Asa J. Wilbourn, MD, Director, EMG
Laboratory, Department of Neurology, The Cleveland Clinic Foundation, Cleveland, Ohio

John M. Porter, MD, Professor of
Surgery, Head, Division of Vascular
Surgery, Department of Surgery,
Oregon Health Sciences University,
Portland, Oregon

Reprint requests to:
Asa J. Wilbourn, MD
Department of Neurology
Cleveland Clinic Foundation
9500 Euclid Ave.
Cleveland, OH 44106

HISTORICAL PERSPECTIVE

The term thoracic outlet syndrome (TOS) was coined by Peet and coworkers in 1956[78] as a collective title to describe a number of disorders, of varying clinical significance, attributed to mechanical compromise of neural and/or vascular structures between the base of the neck and the axilla. The elements thus at risk include the distal cervical root and the brachial plexus fibers (neural), as well as the subclavian and proximal axillary arteries and veins (vascular) (Fig. 1).

TOS is a very confusing topic and one of the subgroups of TOS (disputed neurogenic type, discussed below) is extremely controversial as well.[27,79,135] The fact that TOS generates "much disagreement and dialogue"[54] is acknowledged in only a minority of the articles concerned with it. As a result, many physicians are unaware of the intense debate that the disputed neurogenic subgroup has spawned over the past 25 years, and assume that it has achieved the same general acceptance as have the other subgroups of TOS. Even while acquiring its name "thoracic outlet syndrome," this entity was responsible for an inordinate amount of confusion in the literature in the form of misquotes, incorrect statements, and inappropriate terminology. Many of these inaccuracies persist to the present, and merit some discussion.

By 1945, a half-dozen different syndromes had been described—beginning with the cervical rib syndrome in the early 1900s and ending with the hyperabduction syndrome in 1945—in which various components of the "neurovascular bundle" reputedly were compromised, usually by compression, at one point or another within the cervicoaxillary canal.[135] In 1956,

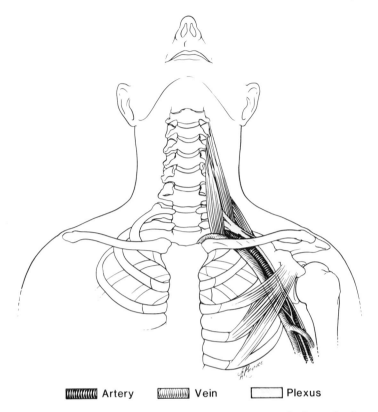

██████ Artery   ██████ Vein   □ Plexus

FIGURE 1. The thoracic outlet. Note that this area extends from the interscalene triangle proximally to behind the pectoralis minor tendon distally. Also note that the subclavian artery and brachial plexus are behind the scalenus anticus muscle, while the subclavian vein is in front of it; for this reason, the subclavian vein is seldom affected with cervical rib syndrome.

Peet, Hendriksen, Anderson and Martin, in an article published in the *Mayo Clinic Proceedings,* recommended that all these entities be "grouped together and referred to as the 'thoracic outlet syndrome,'" because they had "a similar symptom pattern."[78]

Although these authors coined the term thoracic outlet syndrome as an umbrella title for these various syndromes, they were not the first (contrary to statements made in many subsequent papers) to consider them as subdivisions of a single entity, nor were they the first to refer to them as abnormalities occurring within the "thoracic outlet." Beginning at least 15 years earlier, most of these entities (the hyperabduction syndrome often being omitted) had been discussed as a group in several articles, particularly in the British literature,[4,30,33,53,85,128] and one or another of them had been described as an abnormality occurring within the "thoracic outlet."[53,85,128,132]

In 1958, Robb and Standeven used the term thoracic outlet compression syndrome (TOCS) in a paper which, as its title suggests ("Arterial occlusion complicating thoracic outlet compression syndrome"), dealt solely with the serious consequences of arterial compromise within the cervicoaxillary canal, caused by either a cervical rib or an abnormal first rib.[84] They did not recommend using the term TOCS as a group designation for various lesions in the thoracic outlet area. In fact, they did not even mention any other subgroups of TOS in their paper. Nonetheless, in an article published in 1962—an article that is generally credited with having "reawakened" interest in this topic—Clagett made no reference to the paper by Peet et al. while implying, erroneously, that Robb and Standeven had suggested grouping all these syndromes together under the single title of TOCS.[10] Why Clagett apparently was unaware of Peet and coworkers' paper on TOS is puzzling, considering that he and they were at the same institution, and their paper had appeared in that institution's journal. Irrespective of cause, the result has been that a great number of sources dealing with TOS since 1962 have reported, incorrectly, that it was Robb and Standeven who suggested using TOCS (or TOS) as a collective title. Moreover, regardless of which term, TOS or TOCS, is used, both contain a serious flaw from a nomenclature point of view: they are anatomically inaccurate. As defined by anatomists, the thoracic outlet is the inferior opening of the thorax, bounded by the diaphragm. In contrast, the superior opening—the subject of this report— is the thoracic inlet.[130] It is ironic (but quite in keeping with the saga of TOS in general) that, among a number of equally descriptive terms available (e.g., thoracic inlet syndrome, superior aperture syndrome, and cervicoaxillary canal syndrome), the name that ultimately gained general acceptance, TOS, was (and is) the only anatomically incorrect one of the lot.

Some aspects of the term TOS are of far more than historical or academic interest. One of these is that the term was coined as a group title and has been employed in that capacity since then. This has been hailed by some physicians as a major advancement. Thus, Roos and Owens stated that "grouping the separate syndromes under the single heading of thoracic outlet syndrome has allowed more accurate diagnostic and therapeutic measures to be established."[93] Yet, other physicians hold a far different view, because under this one designation are collected a number of different entities, which have relatively little in common beyond their actual or presumed anatomical lesion site. Hence, depending upon the specific structures affected, they have different clinical presentations, are diagnosed by different diagnostic procedures, are treated by different therapeutic means, and fall into the realm of different clinical subspecialties. For this reason, using the all-encompassing term TOS may retard our understanding of these subdivisions rather than advance it. Also, since the definition of "syndrome" is a group of "symptoms occurring together and characterizing a specific . . . condition,"[29] it is obvious that TOS as presently constituted is a misnomer; when one considers the variety of disorders clustered beneath this title, the criterion of commonality is patently lacking. Because of this, Gilliatt prefers to use the term in a plural sense, i.e., thoracic outlet syndromes, as others have done,[48,59] finding "it slightly less objectionable as it implies that discrete and recognizable clinical subgroups do exist."[27]

Another confusing feature of the name TOS is that during the three decades it has been in use, the entities included under it have changed, much as a sporting team retains the same uniforms but has different players wearing them over the years. In some respects, the TOS of the late 1980s bears relatively little resemblance to the TOS of the mid-1950s. Initially, as defined by Peet and coworkers, TOS included the following subgroups: "cervical rib syndrome, scalenus-anticus syndrome, subcoracoid-pectoralis minor syndrome, costoclavicular syndrome, and first-thoracic-rib syndrome."[78] It is of interest to consider how each of these has fared over the past 30 years.

Cervical Rib Syndrome

This is by far the oldest of all the subdivisions of TOS, and it is the only one that has been universally accepted. The term cervical rib syndrome was used at least as early as 1922 by Todd.[116] According to Darling, Galen first noted these bony anomalies (circa 220 AD) and Gruber provided the first detailed description and classification of them in 1849.[17] These "supernumerary" ribs characteristically form from the transverse processes of the C7 vertebrae; they vary markedly in development, but more often are incomplete and joined to the first thoracic rib by a fibrous band. Their estimated incidence varies from one report to another, ranging from 0.17% to 1%.[53,95] They are often bilateral (50%–80%), and are found more frequently in females than males.[95] Less than 10% of them produce symptoms.[38,95] Nonetheless, it was appreciated in the early 1800s that these bony anomalies occasionally can cause upper extremity neurovascular abnormalities. In 1861, Coote performed the first reported TOS surgery by successfully removing a portion of a cervical rib which was causing progressive limb ischemia in a young woman.[12] Although isolated reports of similar surgery (primarily for arterial symptoms) sporadically appeared over the next several decades, cervical ribs achieved surgical importance only when the use of x-rays became widespread. As Murphy noted, cervical rib surgery could "be divided into the pre-röentgen and post-röentgen period,"[67] with the dividing line being approximately the year 1905.

An advance in the understanding of "cervical rib syndrome" was the recognition that symptoms and signs of both neural and vascular compromise seldom occur simultaneously.[21,56,129] As Gilliatt has noted: "although vascular and neurologic features may sometimes coexist, they are more likely to occur independently, and in different patients."[27] Which component is involved often can be predicted by the appearance of the cervical rib, as Kinnier Wilson noted as early as 1940.[49a] The findings with large, fully formed ribs usually are arterial in nature, whereas with rudimentary ribs they typically are neurogenic in nature.[27,31,62] Customarily, the "vascular" in these cases refers only to the subclavian artery; the vein is spared because it is situated anterior to the scalenus anterior muscle and consequently able to move anterior with pressure from the rear.[47,67]

Because cervical rib syndrome falls into the realm of both vascular trained and neurologically trained subspecialties, depending upon the particular structures affected, it is subdivided in this paper into the "arterial vascular type of TOS" and the "true neurogenic type of TOS."

Scalenus Anticus Syndrome (Naffziger Syndrome; Scalenus Syndrome)

This syndrome was first described and named by Ochner, Gage and DeBakey in 1935, who credited Naffziger with having first suggested that the scalenus anticus muscle could cause a "typical cervical rib syndrome" in the absence of a cervical rib.[71] In 1905, Murphy stated that the symptoms/signs of cervical rib syndrome were due to the tip of the cervical rib compressing the brachial plexus or subclavian artery against the lower border of the scalenus anticus muscle.[67] Twenty years later, Adson came to essentially the same conclusion and, in 1927, he and Coffey recommended treating cervical rib syndrome by dividing the insertion of the scalenus anticus muscle, rather than by removing the cervical rib.[3] They also described a physical examination maneuver for determining whether the subclavian artery was being compressed between the cervical rib and scalenus anticus muscle, which become known as Adson's maneuver: while sitting upright, with arms resting on knees, the patient takes a deep breath, extends the neck, and turns the head toward the affected side. An alteration of the radial pulse or blood pressure in the affected arm was considered "a pathognomonic sign of the presence of a cervical rib or scalenus anticus syndrome."[2] Eight years later, Ochner and coworkers reported that the scalenus anticus muscle could cause neurovascular compromise in certain predisposed individuals by establishing a "vicious cycle" of compression, in the absence of a cervical rib or any other type of bony anomaly. Predisposing factors included abnormally low position of the shoulder, high fixation of the sternum and ribs, and low origin of the brachial plexus (post-fixed plexus). The vicious cycle consisted of spasm of the scalene muscles which, once initiated, caused compression of the brachial plexus both directly and indirectly through abnormal elevation of the first thoracic rib. The resulting "irritation" of the brachial plexus fibers reputedly caused additional spasm of the anterior scalene muscle, which receives innervation from the brachial plexus.[71] The scalenus anticus syndrome reportedly affected women more often than men. It caused both neurologic and vascular symptoms and signs but the neurologic ones markedly predominated and primarily were manifested as pain. Marked tenderness to palpation of the lower portion of the scalenus anticus muscle and a positive Adson's maneuver were considered almost "constant features" helpful for diagnosis.[69–71] Scalenus anticus syndrome rapidly became a popular diagnosis, and soon "scalenotomies were carried out with abandon."[117] "Nearly every person who complained of pain in the shoulder extending into the arm was subjected to . . . a scalenotomy."[73] However, by the 1940s increasing skepticism was being voiced about this entity, particularly in England, where it had never been accepted with the same degree of enthusiasm as it had been in the United States. Several British authorities, as well as Nachlas in the United States, challenged the conceptual basis for scalenus anticus syndrome, particularly the "vicious cycle" theory.[68,112,128] They pointed out that the scalenus anticus muscle is a much less powerful muscle than the scalenus medius, and probably incapable of elevating the first rib if in isolated spasm. Even if it could do so, the scalene angle would increase rather than decrease, thus providing more room for the brachial plexus fibers rather than less. They also noted that the C4 through C7 cervical roots supply the scalenus anticus muscle, whereas the symptoms are experienced in C8 and T1 root distributions. Even if the fibers that derive from C4 through C7 roots were compressed by the scalenus anticus muscle, the motor nerve fibers supplying the latter would escape injury, since such compression would be occurring distal to their origin; and if somehow compression did occur proximal enough to affect them (and this is extremely unlikely, since the scalene muscles attachments at their origin are separated by rigid transverse processes), then the resultant muscle spasm would have to be much more widespread because the nerve supply to many other muscles would also be compromised. As Walshe et al. commented: "The notion of a generally atonic subject in whom one single muscle is mysteriously hypertrophied and hypertonic is not one that easily commands credence."[128] From a practical point of view, physicians became disenchanted with scalenus anticus syndrome for two interrelated reasons. First, many surgeons were experiencing unacceptably high failure rates,[10,52,81] which Adson attributed to "too liberal selection of patients for surgical treatment."[2] This was undoubtedly due, in part, to the second reason: the syndrome was being erroneously diagnosed in patients with other disorders.[30,68] As the latter were recognized, particularly cervical radiculopathy in 1943[101] and carpal tunnel syndrome in 1953,[51] the diagnosis of scalenus anticus syndrome was made less and less often. Eventually, in 1962, it was essentially rejected as a viable diagnosis, at least by name, when Clagett reported his own 60% surgical failure rate.[10] Nonetheless, as will be noted in the discussion below, many concepts regarding scalenus anticus syndrome were simply transferred, *in toto,* to disputed neurogenic TOS, and even the surgical procedure used to treat the former—scalenotomy—has been resurrected recently by some surgeons to treat the latter,[88] while others never abandoned it.[96]

First Thoracic Rib Syndrome

Of the various initial subgroups of TOS, this one is the most indefinite. At the onset, a clear distinction must be made between normal and abnormal first thoracic (or dorsal) ribs.

Abnormalities of the first thoracic rib apparently were initially reported by Hunauld in 1740. In one series, they were as common as cervical ribs.[35] They may take several different forms, similar to cervical ribs, sometimes being rudimentary. Although symptoms had been attributed to them earlier,[47] Hvoslef apparently was the first to perform surgery for one of these abnormalities, on a patient who was experiencing primarily arterial symptoms.[42] Compromise of both vascular and neural structures by abnormal first ribs has been reported many times in the literature since then, and it is generally accepted that abnormal first ribs can produce changes clinically indistinguishable from cervical ribs,[128,132] although they are more likely to produce arterial rather than neural findings.[128]

A second facet of this subgroup consists of attributing neurovascular complaints to a "normal" first thoracic rib ("normal first thoracic rib syndrome"). This subgroup also has a long history, extending back to the turn of the century. Probably the earliest proponent of this concept was Bramwell.[5] In 1903 he described a patient with the classical clinical changes of a neurogenic cervical rib syndrome (true neurogenic TOS, see below), and speculated that the findings were due to the first thoracic root being compressed by the "sharp internal border of the first rib." However, he did not obtain x-rays to substantiate this supposition, and he did not include neurogenic cervical rib syndrome in the differential diagnosis because it was just beginning to be recognized as an entity. Subsequently, he and several other authors described patients whose symptoms they attributed to compression of the neurovascular structures by normal first thoracic ribs.[6,7,65,108,131] Many of the examples cited, however, are unconvincing: in some the symptoms were quite atypical for a plexopathy, in others rudimentary cervical ribs were not excluded, while in still others cervical ribs were present but discounted, without justification, because of their small size. Nonetheless, normal first thoracic ribs were resected to treat reputed brachial plexus compression as early as 1910/1911, by T. Murphey[66] and by Stiles (reported in Bramwell and Dykes[6]).

The "normal first thoracic rib syndrome" was rarely mentioned or diagnosed in the United States after the mid-1930s, being eclipsed by the ascendency of the scalenus anticus syndrome. In England, however, where the latter was accepted with neither the same fervor nor for as long a period, the normal first dorsal rib syndrome remained a viable entity for a few decades. Often symptoms that would have been attributed to the scalenus anticus syndrome in the United States were attributed to the normal first dorsal rib syndrome in England. Both of these entities were considered by Walshe and coworkers to be due to the same underlying cause: "an altered topographical relationship . . . between the shoulder girdle and a normal thoracic outlet." Regarding the normal thoracic rib syndrome, they considered a drooping shoulder to be the precipitating factor.[128] The normal first thoracic rib syndrome is rarely mentioned in current TOS literature. Nonetheless, attributing symptom production to a normal first thoracic rib is, for most of its proponents, the quintessential component of disputed neurogenic TOS, as will be discussed subsequently.

Costoclavicular Syndrome (Costoclavicular Compression Syndrome)

This syndrome was described by Falconer and various coworkers between 1943 and 1962. Its main thesis was that the neurovascular structures could be compressed between the first rib and clavicle when the shoulder was placed in certain positions (downward and backward bracing), without there being any anatomical predisposing factors (it shared the latter point with the hyperabduction syndrome).[23] Initially it was thought that only the subclavian vessels (artery and vein), and not the brachial plexus, could be affected by this mechanism, but soon reports appeared of brachial plexus compression as well, either associated with subclavian vessel compromise or alone.[22,55]

The syndrome reportedly occurred primarily in young to middle-age females. The predominant symptom was pain, most often in a lower trunk distribution, typically continuous but fluctuating in intensity, and accentuated by both hyperabduction and by downward/backward bracing of the shoulder. Two provocative tests were described, which increased the pain: (1) digital pressure over the brachial plexus, immediately above the middle third of the clavicle, and (2) passive bracing of the shoulders downward and backward (the latter postural maneuver is often referred to as the military brace position). In some patients symptoms were severe enough to require partial or complete first rib removal.

While some surgeons considered costoclavicular compression to be a common mechanism for symptom production,[55] others, notably Telford and Mottershead, believed that compression of the brachial plexus between the clavicle and first rib was "pure supposition, unsupported by any anatomical evidence."[113]

Although the costoclavicular compression syndrome is seldom mentioned in modern-day TOS literature, one of its central concepts, that the normal first thoracic rib can act as one arm of a vice to compress neurovascular structures, has been transferred to the disputed neurogenic type of TOS by the latter's proponents.

Subcoracoid-Pectoralis Minor Syndrome (Hyperabduction Syndrome)

This syndrome was described by Wright in 1945.[138] Of the various subgroups of TOS, it was the last to be reported and probably has had the least clinical impact. Wright determined that over 80% of normal individuals experienced obliteration of the radial pulse when the arm was hyperabducted (the hyperabduction maneuver). If that position were maintained for prolonged periods of time, most often because of sleeping habits or work requirements, symptoms and signs could develop. These consisted of pain, numbness, and paresthesias, usually limited to the hands and fingers, Raynaud's syndrome, and occasionally redness and swelling of the hands and fingers. In severe cases, ulceration and gangrene of the fingertips occurred. Most of the symptoms experienced were due to arterial compromise occurring, Wright postulated, at two separate points: between the clavicle and the first rib and also posterior to the tendon of pectoralis minor muscle, beneath the coracoid process.[138] Unlike the cervical rib and scalenus anticus syndromes, the hyperabduction syndrome (similar to the costoclavicular syndrome), required no anatomical predisposing factor(s) to produce symptoms, and it involved compromise of the vein as well as the artery and brachial plexus. Also, in marked contrast to the scalenus anticus syndrome, arm elevation initiated or increased the symptoms rather than relieving them. The majority of the patients with the hyperabduction syndrome reportedly responded to conservative measures, e.g., restraining the arms at night so that they could not be hyperabducted, but occasionally extensive surgery was considered necessary.[52,58] This syndrome is seldom mentioned in the current medical literature by name. Nonetheless, we consider a mechanism such as this most likely explains the symptoms some patients experience, which are discussed below under the arterial vascular–minor type of TOS. Also, having symptoms occur or be accentuated during arm elevation is considered a characteristic presentation of disputed neurogenic TOS by many of its advocates, even by many who view the latter as a continuation of scalenus anticus syndrome; this seems contradictory, since with scalenus anticus syndrome arm elevation reputedly alleviated symptoms, rather than the reverse.[70,71]

In the 1950s and early 1960s, as the surgical failure rates from anterior scalenotomies mounted, it became fashionable to consider that neurovascular compression was occurring at more than one site simultaneously (i.e., two or more of the syndromes just described were present at the same time) and, therefore, that more than one surgical procedure was necessary.[52,58] Lang, for example, reported that by performing arteriography while putting the patient's limb and shoulder through various maneuvers, multiple compression sites frequently could be observed.[52] Nonetheless, by the time the term TOS came into general use in the late 1950s, the thoracic outlet area was losing its surgical appeal. Unequivocal cervical rib syndromes were seen too rarely to maintain interest, and yet operations performed in their absence were likely to be failures. In addition, attention was being directed toward other areas, such as the cervical roots and the median nerve at the wrist. This was the status of TOS prior to the reawakening of interest in this area, which was initiated by Clagett in 1962.[10] That renaissance will be discussed below, under Disputed Neurogenic TOS.

Unlike those who have hailed the use of TOS as a collective term, we believe it is necessary to subdivide this entity into its component parts, and examine each one of them separately, if any real appreciation of this complex topic is to be achieved.[135] Only by doing so can much of the confusion surrounding it be resolved, and the controversies regarding the disputed neurogenic TOS subdivision be understood. Nonetheless, we do not believe the "classic" subdivisions of TOS, just discussed, help in achieving this purpose, since they are based on the presumed offending structure (e.g., scalenus anticus muscle) or the reputed mechanism of insult (e.g., hyperabduction). Instead, we believe TOS is more logically approached by considering the particular neurovascular structure(s) compromised. Hence, in this review TOS will be discussed under the subdivisions listed in Table 1. Although this monograph is devoted primarily to neurologic problems, TOS, unlike the other topics discussed, has both neurologic and vascular components. Because any review of TOS would be incomplete without a discussion of the latter, the findings seen with both arterial and venous compromise in the thoracic outlet will be described.

TABLE 1.   Thoracic Outlet Syndromes

1. Vascular
    Arterial
        Major
        Minor
    Venous
2. Neurologic
    True (classical)
    Disputed
        Droopy shoulder syndrome
3. Combined Vascular and Neurologic
    True and Arterial
    True and Arterial and Venous
    Disputed

VASCULAR THORACIC OUTLET SYNDROMES

Both the arteries and veins may be compressed by muscular and/or bony structures of the thoracic outlet. For discussion, we divide vascular thoracic outlet syndrome into a major and minor arterial type as well as venous type. Each will be considered separately.

Arterial Vascular TOS–Major

The history of the major arterial type of thoracic outlet syndrome is inextricably linked to the history of the surgical treatment of cervical rib. The first reports describing an association between bony abnormalities of the thoracic outlet and neurovascular compression were those of Hilton[39] in 1853 and Wilshire[137] in 1860. As noted above, Coote in 1861 performed the first cervical rib resection for relief of progressive limb ischemia in a young woman.[12] The association between cervical rib arterial compression and the development of subclavian artery aneurysms became apparent during the last quarter of the nineteenth century. By 1916 Dr. William S. Halsted[32] had collected 716 cases of cervical rib, one third of which were associated with subclavian aneurysms. Many patients undergoing cervical rib resection with associated subclavian artery aneurysm were noted to have severe preoperative arm, hand, and finger ischemia. Interestingly, these symptoms were not initially ascribed to the subclavian aneurysm. Symonds in 1927,[110] after observing hemiplegia in two patients with subclavian aneurysm, suggested that thromboembolic debris may originate from a subclavian artery damaged by a cervical rib. Lewis and Pickering[56] seven years later accurately noted that peripheral arm embolization could originate from a similar source, and thus provided the initial explanation for the hand and finger ischemia that had been observed years earlier in certain patients with cervical rib and subclavian aneurysm.

The etiology of arterial damage in patients with cervical rib is compression of the artery between the anomalous rib posteriorly, the first rib inferolaterally, the clavicle and subclavius muscle anteriorly, and the scalenus anticus muscle medially. In severe cases, the artery is permanently compressed at this site. The arterial dilatation or aneurysm develops just distal to the site of compression as a result of fluid turbulence generated in the area of arterial stenosis. Laminated thrombus frequently is deposited in enlarging aneurysms as a result of turbulence. Portions of this thrombus may dislodge at random times and embolize distally.

By far the most frequent presenting symptom of arterial TOS is distal extremity ischemia resulting from arterial embolization.[56,103] Such patients may present with pain, ischemic finger ulceration, or, occasionally, major tissue loss to the point of requiring below- or above-elbow amputation. This type of TOS affects males and females in approximately equal numbers.[31]

Review of a number of clinical series of arterial TOS indicates that a fully developed cervical rib was present and recognized as the likely cause of the arterial damage in approximately 50% of cases.[20,46,76,99] The remaining patients generally had another bony abnormality such as a hypoplastic cervical rib, elongated C7 transverse process, or anomalous first thoracic rib. Subclavian artery damage in the absence of a bony abnormality is exceedingly rare in patients under the age of 60 years.[14] A small number of patients greater than 60 years of age develop atherosclerotic subclavian aneurysms apparently unrelated to bony abnormalities.

The usual arteriographic finding in arterial TOS is bony compression of the subclavian artery, poststenotic dilatation, and distal arterial embolization. Both rupture and total thrombotic occlusion of a subclavian aneurysm have been described, but are rare.[76]

The diagnosis of major arterial TOS requires arteriographic demonstration of the findings described above. The aneurysm itself is rarely palpable as a discrete abnormal structure. Rather, suspicions are aroused when a young patient presents with unilateral arm, hand, and/or finger ischemia of recent onset. In such patients a detailed arteriogram is mandatory to rule out a proximal cause of distal embolization. An arteriogram of a patient with a subclavian aneurysm caused by cervical rib is illustrated (Fig. 2). The usual surgical approach to this condition is through a supraclavicular or combined supra- and infraclavicular incision with resection of the abnormal bony structure and the aneurysm. The transaxillary approach, used so frequently to treat disputed neurogenic TOS, is not satisfactory for vascular repair.[31] Arterial continuity is reestablished using an autogenous vascular conduit, usually saphenous vein. If embolic material is present in the brachial or forearm arteries, a balloon catheter embolectomy is performed. Some have advocated the routine addition of cervicodorsal sympathectomy. We feel there is little evidence to support this position.

Characteristically, with this type of TOS only the artery is compromised. The brachial plexus is unaffected, although many of the findings (e.g., muscle fatigue, ischemic pain) may mistakenly be attributed to primary neurogenic involvement. As Lewis and Pickering noted, confusion exists in the literature on this point.[56] Many case reports, particularly in the older literature, describing simultaneous involvement of the artery and brachial plexus probably are examples of this type of TOS. We have performed extensive electrodiagnostic studies on a few patients with these lesions and found no evidence of a coexisting brachial plexopathy.

Unfortunately, the diagnosis of major arterial TOS is usually made only after a severe arm embolic event and resultant significant tissue loss have occurred.[46] Obviously, bony resection with arterial repair before the occurrence of distal embolization remains the therapeutic goal in treating patients with this serious condition. As it is both impractical and unnecessary to perform subclavian arteriography in all patients with a cervical rib, guidelines are needed to select appropriate patients for this invasive study. We recommend the following in

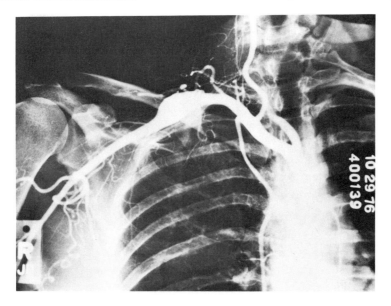

FIGURE 2. Arteriogram showing right subclavian artery aneurysm caused by a previously resected cervical rib.

patients with a cervical rib. Obtain a detailed history of any sudden arm or hand event compatible with embolization, such as the abrupt occurrence of numbness, pain, or cyanosis, even of brief duration. Persistently unilateral Raynaud's phenomenon is significant in this regard.[46] Palpate and auscultate the supraclavicular fossa for the presence of a vascular prominence or a bruit suggesting arterial ectasia or early aneurysm formation. Note presence and symmetry of arm pulses. Use noninvasive vascular laboratory Duplex examination (a combination of B-mode ultrasound vascular imaging and Doppler blood flow velocity spectral analysis) to detect arterial dilatation, stenosis, or intraluminal clot. Finally, obtain a finger photoplethysmographic tracing in all 10 fingers. This test quickly, accurately, and noninvasively detects digital arterial obstruction (40); an example is shown (Fig. 3). If digital arterial obstruction is demonstrable on the side of the cervical rib and absent on the contralateral other side, this is highly significant, suggesting unilateral embolization. If any of these tests is abnormal, a subclavian arteriogram should be obtained. If abnormal, prophylactic rib and aneurysm resection should be considered.

Arterial Vascular TOS–Minor

A condition that we consider a minor type of arterial TOS is encountered frequently. As already discussed under subcoracoid-pectoralis minor syndrome, a large number of young adults will develop diminution or obliteration of the arm pulses when the limb is placed in a position of elevation, abduction, and external rotation. In this case the subclavian-axillary artery is compressed between the clavicle and pectoralis minor anteriorly and the first rib posteriorly. As this occurs to some degree in 80% of young adults, it must be regarded as a variant of normal. Nonetheless, a small number of people clearly manifest a markedly exaggerated form of this condition. In these individuals, minor arm

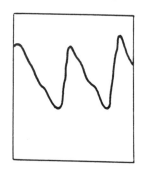

FIGURE 3. Finger plethysmographic tracing obtained with photoplethysmograph. Top tracing is normal with rapid upstroke, sharp peak, and dicrotic notch. Bottom tracing is markedly obstructive, indicating occlusion of both digital arteries in the fingers.

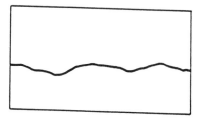

elevation to the level of the shoulder or occasionally even the breast may be associated with complete arterial compression and absence of distal pulses. Within a minute or less they experience tingling, numbness, and weakness of the arm(s), presumably as a result of nerve ischemia. Most of these individuals deal with the condition by simply avoiding the arms-elevated position. However, a small percentage of them have occupations that require work with the arms elevated. In carefully selected patients first rib removal will eliminate the posterior component of the compression pincers, and permit full arm elevation without arterial compression. Surgery is being performed in these instances for occupational convenience, not for the prevention or treatment of arterial damage. We have never seen the latter, with resultant distal embolization, occur with this condition.

Venous Vascular TOS

Spontaneous thrombosis of the subclavian and axillary vein was described initially by Paget in 1875[75] and von Schroetter in 1884.[126] The potential relationship of this condition to TOS was hypothesized by Falconer and Weddell in 1943.[23] Axillary-subclavian venous thrombosis usually occurs in young patients engaged in vigorous physical activity that emphasizes upper extremity and shoulder motion, hence, one of its synonyms: effort thrombosis. Examples include weight lifters, amateur wrestlers, competitive swimmers, baggage handlers, etc. The symptomatic onset of axillary-subclavian venous thrombosis is heralded by the occurrence of arm pain, cyanosis, and swelling, along with exercise-induced fatigue. The onset is usually sudden and dramatic, although occasional patients may have an insidious onset with only intermittent symptoms. On examination, the entire limb is typically swollen and cyanotic (bluish); dilated veins serving as collateral channels usually are prominent on the superior chest and shoulder, and the thrombosed vein may be palpable in the axilla as a thickened cord.[41]

Upper extremity phlebography is diagnostic. Unlike the situation with major arterial TOS, cervical ribs and other bony abnormalities are rarely found with venous TOS.[41]

Intermittent obstruction of the subclavian-axillary vein in its course between the scalenus anticus, clavicle, and first rib with subsequent damage to the venous endothelium is widely regarded as an important predisposing factor in a high percentage of patients with spontaneous axillary-subclavian venous thrombosis.[1,23,64]

Treatment of this condition traditionally has consisted of arm elevation and heparin, followed by warfarin anticoagulation for three to six months. The long-term outcome generally is favorable with this regimen, although arm swelling and a sensation of heaviness following prolonged use continue to be a problem in certain patients.

Axillary-subclavian venous thrombectomy using a balloon catheter has been attempted on occasion,[19,43] but long-term patency has been difficult to achieve and presently we do not recommend this procedure. Thrombolytic therapy appears to have real potential in the treatment of this condition. Most patients are healthy, young adults who present early in the course of their thrombotic process, all of which increase the likelihood of the successful use of thrombolytic therapy. We and others[72,111] have treated a small number of patients recently. Following lysis, first rib resections have been performed electively to relieve venous compression. It appears this mode of therapy will have an increasingly important role in treating this disorder in the future.

All patients with venous TOS do not present with venous thrombosis. A variable number of patients present with episodic arm swelling, cyanosis, and venous engorgement, usually related to certain positions. Positional contrast phlebography is helpful if it shows venous compression but is not diagnostic, as the spectrum of normality has never been completely defined. We have described a method of obtaining a venous pull-back catheter pressure gradient across the site of stenosis in these cases.[100] First rib resection in symptomatic patients with elevated-arm venous pressure has been associated with abolition of the pressure gradient and long term relief of symptoms. Representative phlebograms with intravenous pressures are shown (Fig. 4).

NEUROLOGIC THORACIC OUTLET SYNDROMES

True Neurogenic TOS (Classical Neurogenic TOS; Neurogenic Cervical Rib Syndrome; Cervical Rib and Band Syndrome)

Although surgery was first performed to treat the major arterial type of TOS in 1861,[12] over 40 years elapsed before it was appreciated that cervical ribs could be associated solely or very predominantly with neurologic abnormalities. Thomas and Cushing probably should be credited with the first clinical and operative description of it, which was published in 1903. Certainly, a clear description of the typical operative findings with this syndrome was provided by Cushing, who wrote "the lower cord of the plexus was compressed by a dense fibrous band which passed from the tip of the rudimentary rib under the plexus to the first thoracic rib. This band, therefore, representing continuation of the rudimentary rib and over which the lower cord of the plexus arched at rather an acute angle, was the offending agent rather than the bony projection itself."[114]

By 1921, the clinical and radiographic features of neurogenic cervical rib

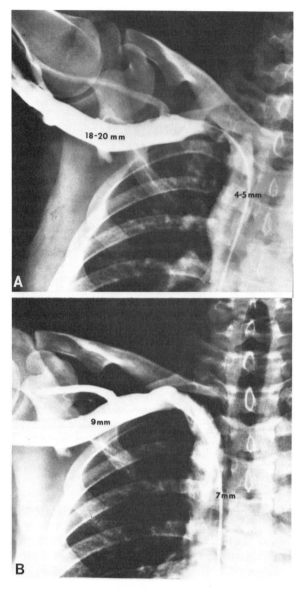

FIGURE 4 *A,* Phlebogram of young man with intermittent arm swelling, cyanosis, and venous prominence. There is a high-grade positional stenosis in the proximal subclavian vein with a 15 mm gradient brought on by arm abduction and external rotation. *B,* Following first rib resection both the position vein stenosis and gradient noted on the previous study have been eliminated.

syndrome, described below, were well known.[49,98,115] Unfortunately, however, many of those early reports included patients with weakness and wasting limited to the lateral thenar muscles, accompanied by sensory abnormalities in a median nerve distribution in the hand, rather than along the medial forearm. Thus, soon after its recognition, true neurogenic TOS had its clinical/radiographic presentation contaminated by cases of severe CTS, a then unknown entity, associated with a coincidental and asymptomatic cervical rib.[27] This confusion was to plague neurogenic cervical rib syndrome for the next 30 years. Hence, in 1945, one of the symptoms now known to be almost pathognomonic of CTS, nocturnal parasthesias (acroparaesthesia), was being attributed to a lesion at the thoracic outlet by an eminent neurologist.[127] These two entities were not clearly separated from each other until three events occurred: (1) Kraemer and coworkers described the characteristic clinical presentation of CTS in 1953;[51] (2) nerve conduction studies were introduced by Simpson[104] to diagnose CTS in 1956; and, finally, (3) Gilliatt and coworkers described the characteristic clinical and electrodiagnostic presentation of true neurogenic TOS in 1970.[28]

True neurogenic TOS is a rare lesion, having an estimated incidence of approximately one per million. The majority of patients are young to middle-aged females (female/male ratio of 9/1);[27] this contrasts sharply with the nearly equal male/female ratio seen with the arterial cervical rib syndrome previously described. The most constant feature is hand weakness and wasting. In approximately 75% of patients, all of the intrinsic hand muscles are wasted and weak, although typically the lateral thenar (abductor pollicis brevis [APB]; opponens pollicis) are the most severely affected. In the remaining 25% of cases, the wasting is essentially limited to the lateral thenar muscles, but most or all of the other intrinsic hand muscles are clinically weak. A long history of sensory complaints in the affected limb is common, typically consisting of an intermittent aching pain or paresthesia, most often limited to, or more severe along, the medial aspect of the arm, forearm, and sometimes the hand. Some patients experience intermittent "cramping" in the hand. On clinical examination, a sensory deficit frequently is found in a patchy lower trunk distribution, typically along the medial forearm and hand. When it extends into the medial fingers, it does not divide the fourth finger as an ulnar neuropathy does. Although some patients complain of the hand being cold, or the pain being exaggerated by cold, nothing suggestive of associated vascular compromise usually is seen, excluding an occasional radial pulse being diminished by arm elevation.[27,28,34]

Medical attention is directed toward the affected limb in a variety of ways. In many patients the sensory disturbances are severe enough to cause them to seek medical consultation. In others, the hand wasting triggers medical interest. Some patients notice it themselves, or have it called to their attention by relatives or acquaintances. Others have it discovered by physicians who are examining them for totally unrelated problems.

The two most helpful diagnostic procedures are x-rays of the neck and an EMG examination. Evidence of a bony abnormality is almost invariably seen on x-ray, consisting of a rudimentary cervical rib or just an elongated C7 transverse process (Fig. 5). Although the symptoms are typically unilateral, the bony abnormalities are usually bilateral, and often asymmetrical; frequently the larger anomaly is on the contralateral, asymptomatic side (which is not surprising, since it is not the bony projection compromising the brachial plexus but, rather, a taut, radiolucent band extending from the tip of the bony anomaly to the first rib).[27,49a]

Parenthetically, if bony abnormalities are not seen on x-ray, the possibility that true neurogenic TOS is present is low.[27] However, many of these are so insignificant in appearance as to be easily overlooked, so in suspected cases

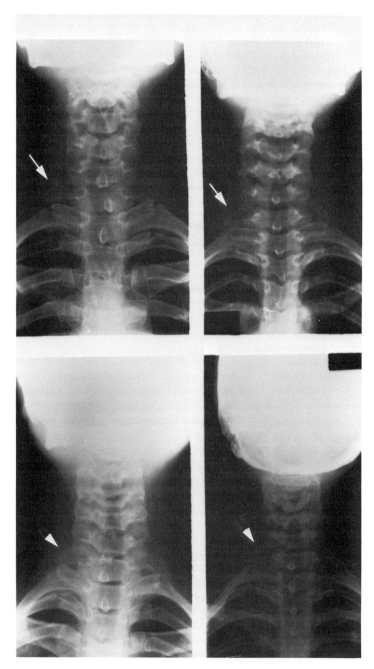

FIGURE 5. X-ray appearance of bilateral cervical ribs in four women with true neurogenic thoracic outlet syndrome. Arrows indicate those on the right. Note that most of these bony anomalies are rudimentary and hence rather inconspicuous.

clinicians should personally review the x-rays. Also, occasionally rudimentary cervical ribs are not visible on routine neck x-rays and special views (lordotic views) are necessary to demonstrate them.

The EMG examination reveals evidence of a very chronic axon-loss lower trunk brachial plexopathy, and the particular combination of nerve conduction studies is nearly pathognomonic (Table 2). Almost no other lower trunk brachial plexus lesion affects the median-innervated hand muscles more than the ulnar-innervated hand muscles. On needle electrode examination (NEE), the very chronic nature of the lesion becomes apparent. Typically, fibrillation potentials are scanty, and often are limited to the APB and sometimes one or two of the other intrinsic hand muscles. In contrast, chronic neurogenic motor unit potential (MUP) changes (i.e., MUPs of increased duration and often increased amplitude) are very prominent, as is a neurogenic MUP firing pattern (MUPs firing in decreased numbers at a rapid rate); these invariably are most prominent in the lateral thenar muscles, with the first dorsal interosseus, adductor pollicis, and often the hypothenar muscles next most affected. Other lower trunk-innervated muscles, such as flexor pollicis longus, extensor indicis proprius, and extensor pollicis brevis, show variable involvement. Although the triceps is customarily considered to be innervated by the C8 root, and should therefore be receiving innervation via the lower trunk of the brachial plexus, it characteristically appears completely normal in this entity.[136]

The appropriate treatment for this lesion is sectioning of the cervical band via a supraclavicular approach. Some surgeons also remove at least a portion of the cervical rib as well.[28,34] The transaxillary approach, used so widely in the United States for first rib resection when treating disputed neurogenic TOS, is not recommended. We are aware of one patient who suffered a severe lower trunk brachial plexus injury when her surgeons attempted to treat true neurogenic TOS by this surgical approach.

Because of the very chronic nature of this lesion, and the fact that the denervated muscles are very distal in the limb, relatively little improvement occurs in hand muscle bulk or strength after surgery. However, progression of the hand weakness and wasting is arrested, forearm muscle bulk may increase and the sensory complaints are usually alleviated.[27,27a,34]

True neurogenic TOS can be mistaken for several other lesions along the peripheral neuraxis. As already noted, for several decades this entity has been confused with CTS because the latter also can produce lateral thenar wasting. However, these disorders are readily separated from one another. First, lateral thenar wasting is a constant feature of true neurogenic TOS, but it is seen with CTS only uncommonly, in very severe, advanced cases. In contrast to patients with true neurogenic TOS, typical patients with CTS-induced lateral thenar wasting are elderly, have sensory symptoms in a median nerve distribution, and usually have at least some evidence of a similar lesion in the contralateral hand. On clinical examination, their weakness, just as their wasting, is limited to the lateral thenar muscles. Moreover, when CTS is severe enough to produce lateral thenar wasting, sensory loss in the median-innervated fingers is invariably prominent. (In contrast, sensory loss may be undetectable with true neurogenic TOS and, when present, it is found along the medial aspect of the forearm or hand and accompanied by normal sensation in the thumb, index and middle fingers.) Finally, the EMG examination, particularly the NCS component, readily differentiates CTS from true neurogenic TOS. With the former, the abnormalities will be restricted to the median nerve fibers. When severe CTS has caused lateral

TABLE 2. Basic Nerve Conduction Study Results Seen with True Neurogenic TOS Using Surface Stimulating and Recording Electrodes and Antidromic Sensory Conduction Study Techniques[27a,136]

1. Median motor (thenar) amplitude ... low/very low (often less than 2 mv; on average, less than 20% of contralateral median motor amplitude).
2. Ulnar sensory (5th finger) amplitude ... relatively low/low (usually less than 20 uv; on average, about 33% of contralateral ulnar sensory amplitude).
3. Ulnar motor (hypothenar) amplitude ... normal/mildly low (usually not lower than 5 mv; on average, about 75% of contralateral ulnar motor response).
4. Median sensory (2nd finger) amplitude ... normal (usually more than 20 uv; on average, about 90%–100% of contralateral median sensory response).
5. The distal/peak latencies and the conduction velocities usually are normal.

thenar wasting, the median sensory nerve action potentials (SNAPs) are almost always unelicitable, while the median motor response is not only quite low in amplitude (if elicitable at all) but also (in contrast to true neurogenic TOS) quite prolonged in distal latency. The ulnar SNAP is normal, while NEE reveals severe, chronic denervation limited to the median-innervated lateral thenar muscles; the other lower trunk-innervated muscles appear normal.

Occasionally, other axon-loss lower trunk brachial plexopathies are confused with true neurogenic TOS, such as the patient we studied who had carcinomatous brachial plexopathy and a coincidental cervical rib. Although lower trunk fibers are affected with both lesions, the EMG changes they produce are significantly different. With carcinoma the ulnar-innervated hand muscles are usually more severely involved than the median, or at least as severely affected; this is evident on both the NCS amplitudes and the NEE. In addition, because the lesion with carcinomatous brachial plexopathy has been present for a shorter period of time and is progressing at a more rapid pace, on NEE fibrillation potentials are much more in evidence while, conversely, chronic neurogenic MUP changes are much less prominent. Once the EMG findings are appreciated, neuroimaging of the brachial plexus usually reveals the lesion.

True neurogenic TOS also may be confused with an unusually severe, chronic C8-T1 radiculopathy. Clinical points against the latter include the absence of intrascapular pain or the history of such pain, the absence of neck pain, and the striking degree of wasting of the lateral thenar muscles. On EMG examination, the NCS findings, particularly the low or relatively low amplitude ulnar SNAP, are much more helpful in diagnosing true neurogenic TOS than are the lack of fibrillation potentials in the lower cervical paraspinal muscles on NEE, since the latter finding is not infrequently encountered with proven cervical radiculopathies.

True neurogenic TOS also may be mistaken for other cervical intraspinal canal lesions, such as an intramedullary lesion (e.g., syrinx; focal abnormality of the anterior horn cells). However, the low amplitude ulnar SNAP excludes the diagnosis of a cord lesion as well as a root lesion.

Finally, true neurogenic TOS can be misdiagnosed as a "focal myopathy." Such lesions must be extremely rare, particularly when unilateral, and they are excluded by the sensory loss on clinical examination plus the electrodiagnostic findings.

It is important to appreciate that true neurogenic TOS is not an "advanced example" of disputed neurogenic TOS. This will be discussed below.

Disputed Neurogenic TOS

The vast majority of diagnosed TOS are in this subgroup, a fact readily apparent, considering that TOS is a very popular diagnosis in some countries, particularly the United States, and yet all the other subgroups of TOS are quite rare. Hence, on review of papers reporting large series of TOS, typically one or two instances of true neurogenic TOS, arterial vascular TOS, and venous vascular TOS can be identified. All the remaining cases, which usually encompass well over 95% of those being presented, are in the disputed neurogenic TOS category (see, for example, reference 121).

In spite of the marked frequency with which this particular TOS subgroup is diagnosed, until very recently it had no formal name. We have designated it disputed neurogenic TOS to clearly separate it from the other types of TOS for discussion.[135] The term disputed was chosen because so many of its basic tenets are in dispute, either between its critics and advocates, or among its various advocates. In fact, no other reputed neurologic disorder has so many of its fundamental aspects in dispute, with so many of those disputes being between its proponents.[135]

Disputed neurogenic TOS is the only controversial subgroup of TOS. Even the structures reputedly compromised are disputed by its advocates: brachial plexus alone vs. brachial plexus plus subclavian artery. For this reason, we have had to classify it under two different headings (Table 1). This entity generally is acknowledged to have first appeared in 1962, when Clagett, in a presidential address to the American Association for Thoracic Surgery, reawakened surgical interest in the thoracic outlet region.[10] He did so by reporting that all the various types of TOS then known had a "common denominator" in their symptom production, the first thoracic rib, which was serving as one arm of a vise, compressing the neurovascular structures (the other arm varied, depending on where within the costoclavicular canal the compression was occurring). Hence, Clagett concluded, first rib removal should alleviate the symptoms, regardless of the exact site of compression. The latter point was received with considerable enthusiasm by those surgeons already performing operations in this region to treat the various syndromes ascribed to it because high failure rates were common, in spite of the alleged specificity of the various outlet maneuvers to pinpoint the exact site of compression. Equally important, Clagett's address initiated, or at least strongly stimulated, the interest of thoracic surgeons in the thoracic outlet region. He noted that this was a legitimate area for the members of that specialty to operate in, even though they might be considered "claim jumpers" by their neurosurgical colleagues, because they had the requisite surgical expertise (acquired by performing thoracotomies to treat tuberculosis).[10]

Although Clagett's address stimulated considerable surgical interest in the thoracic outlet region, that interest was not immediately translated into an increase in the number of TOS surgeries performed. The primary reason for this delay was that the surgical procedure Clagett was recommending, the posterior thoracotomy approach, was so technically demanding that most surgeons were uncomfortable performing it compared with scalenotomies (the procedure it essentially was replacing), particularly in those patients who lacked objective findings. The situation changed dramatically, however, in 1966, when Roos described a new surgical technique for first rib resection: the transaxillary approach.[92] This procedure rapidly achieved great popularity. Not only was it considered safe and simple enough to be offered to patients "with only subjective complaints,"[97] since complications were "few and temporary,"[14] but the resultant scar was inconspicuous in the axilla, an important point considering that the majority of patients (80% in one series) undergoing such surgery were young women.[119] Within a few years, thoracic outlet surgery to treat various arm, shoulder, neck, chest, and head symptoms had not only regained, but even exceeded, the popularity it once had in the 1930s and 1940s, although now the first thoracic rib, rather than the scalenus anticus muscle, was considered the offending structure. Expansion of the etiologic boundaries of TOS aided this popularity increase, as acute trauma began to be named more and more frequently as the instigating factor in its production. Because the trauma itself could have been quite mild, in fact, so trivial as to have been forgotten by the patient completely except under "close,"[14] "repeated"[96] questioning, and since it could have occurred "several days, weeks or even months" prior to the onset of symptoms,[93] TOS became a common diagnosis in legal and paralegal proceedings. Following relatively minor automobile accidents, plaintiffs with essentially normal neurologic examinations were claiming substantial neurologic disability; TOS was also implicated in workman's compensation cases.[118,139]

Similar to so many other aspects of disputed neurologic TOS, its incidence is highly controversial. Because all other subgroups of TOS are acknowledged to be rare, the perceived incidence of TOS in the general population depends almost solely on whether this type of TOS is accepted or rejected as an entity. Since its incidence is thus defined by the opinion of the individual physician, it varies enormously from one institution, city, and even country to another. It has achieved its greatest popularity in the United States. Urschel and Razzuk, for example, claim it "is recognized in about 8% of the population," or approximately 20 million persons in the United States alone.[119] In contrast, it is essentially "unknown" in Australia[63] and also relatively seldom diagnosed in England. This marked variability in incidence is unique to this subgroup of TOS, not only among the subgroups of TOS, but also among all the neural and vascular syndromes of the upper extremity, each of which typically has a generally accepted incidence that varies little from one institution, area, or country to another.[135]

Although this subgroup is diagnosed far more frequently than all the other subgroups of TOS, it is, paradoxically, far more difficult to define, primarily because its advocates agree on few of its characteristics, beyond considering it more common in women than in men, particularly young to middle-aged women. A major problem in this regard is that, of all the various types of TOS, this subgroup alone has no generally accepted pathologic substrate. The bony abnormalities typically seen on x-ray in true neurogenic TOS and arterial vascular TOS are considered to be present in disputed neurogenic TOS somewhat more commonly than in the general population—10%[88] to 30%[119]—but never in the majority of patients. What, then, is the reputed source of symptom production with this entity? Roos attributes disputed neurogenic TOS primarily to the plexus being compressed by one or more of several different types (nine being the latest count) of anomalous fibromuscular bands,[87,91] but these have been observed by few other surgeons. Many proponents believe that the developmental, dynamic and/or morphologic factors that were thought to be responsible for scalenus anticus syndrome, including a "vicious cycle" in which the scalenus anticus muscle precipitates, are responsible,[15,80,87,96,97] although all such theories were convincingly refuted in the 1940s by Nachlas, Walshe, Telford and others.[68,112,128] Ultimately, most advocates consider the symptoms are due to intermittent compression of the brachial plexus fibers at some undetermined point within the thoracic outlet, often but not always by the first thoracic rib, and the compression, being mild as well as intermittent, produces primarily symptoms rather than objective findings.

The list of symptoms attributed to disputed neurogenic TOS is long, and has continued to expand over the years. These symptoms are all-inclusive, and defy categorization.[79] The symptom complex most often quoted is essentially that attributed decades earlier to scalenus anticus syndrome which, in turn, was appropriated from the neurogenic cervical rib syndrome. It consists of pain and paresthesia in primarily a lower trunk distribution (which is often referred to as an ulnar nerve distribution), some weakness (usually described as "subtle") in the hand muscles (most proponents apparently are unaware that the median-innervated thenar muscles are supplied by the lower trunk, since they typically restrict the wasting to the ulnar-innervated interossei and hypothenar muscles) and possibly the triceps, along with supraclavicular tenderness. However, many proponents also include acroparesthesia (nocturnal paresthesias occurring in middle-aged women) as a component of this entity, presumably because this characteristic symptom of CTS was considered a symptom of a lesion in the thoracic outlet area until the 1950s.[27,127] Moreover, many of the described symptoms lack any known anatomical basis. How can pressure on the brachial plexus in the thoracic outlet, for example, produce migraine headaches, memory loss, vertigo, syncope, conjuctival swelling, or facial pain?[25,45,82,96,102]

In practice, most advocates of disputed neurogenic TOS diagnose it whenever (1) the symptoms, at least to them, are suggestive of such a diagnosis and (2) one or more "confirmatory" tests are positive for it. However, just as there is no unanimity of opinion among the advocates for the characteristic symptoms of disputed neurogenic TOS, there is no agreement regarding the nature of the useful confirmatory tests. For some proponents the diagnosis is confirmed by a particular physical examination finding, such as supraclavicular tenderness or loss of pulse on various outlet maneuvers. For others, confirmation depends upon the results of some laboratory study, such as arteriography or an electrodiagnostic procedure. In all, well over 20 of these confirmatory tests have been considered by one advocate or another as the preferred method for diagnosing disputed neurogenic TOS. Often the specific procedure championed most vigorously by one proponent is rejected as worthless by another.[135] A striking example of this is the use of the ulnar motor conduction velocity across the thoracic outlet (UMCV-TO). Urschel, a thoracic surgeon who by 1976 had performed "over 900" TOS operations,[123] considers this an almost indispensable component in the evaluation of patients with suspected TOS.[119] In contrast, Roos, another thoracic surgeon, who had performed over 1400 TOS operations by 1982, presumably for the same condition, completely rejects this particular confirmatory test.[88,90]

However, the confirmatory procedure Roos advocates, the elevated-arm stress test (EAST), also lacks credibility regarding both its conceptual basis and its specificity. The test consists of putting the hands in the "stick-up" position—elevated 90% in the AER (abduction/external rotation) position—and then repeatedly opening and closing them for 3 minutes.[87,90] When Roos and Owens first described this procedure in 1966, they considered disputed TOS to be due to both arterial and brachial plexus compromise, and they referred to the EAST procedure as a "claudication test," which it obviously is.[93] By 1974, however, Roos' view had changed; he was convinced that TOS was neurologic rather than vascular in nature.[94] He has maintained this conviction to the present, while simultaneously proclaiming that the EAST procedure is the most reliable of all confirmatory tests. He has never explained how a lesion causing brachial plexus irritation without affecting the artery produces a positive EAST procedure, except that "fortunately" it does so.[90] He has also claimed this test has great specificity, being positive with TOS but generally negative with CTS or cervical radiculopathy.[87,89,90] However, he apparently never performed any control studies to prove this assumption. Recently Costigan did so, and found the EAST procedure was an excellent test for CTS, being positive in 92% (while positive in 74% of normal controls).[13]

Many of the confirmatory tests advocated have been electrodiagnostic studies, primarily nerve stimulation techniques. These have included the UMCV-TO, positional UMCV-TO, F waves, F loops, C8 root stimulation with needle electrode and, more recently, somatosensory evoked potentials.[60,135] However, none of these techniques has gained general acceptance and most have been abandoned except for a few die-hard defenders. Literature review reveals a recurring cycle of acceptance and rejection in this regard. First, enthusiastic claims are made about the sensitivity and specificity of the particular technique for diagnosing disputed neurogenic TOS. Often these endorsements are made by surgeons who have no neurophysiological background, a fact made obvious by the naiveté displayed in regard to the detection of artifacts, distinguishing significant from insignificant changes, the range of normal variability, technical limitations of the procedure, etc. Subsequently, the technique is used in several respected EMG laboratories throughout the country where it proves unhelpful. Criticisms of the procedure then appear.[135] Finally it quietly drops from view, and proponents shift their interest to another (newer) technique. Soon the latter is being hailed as the diagnostic procedure of choice. An example of this is the UMCV-TO technique. Although Urschel had used the test since 1972—and reported that, in one year alone (1978), he had diagnosed over 720 patients using it, while evaluating over 8400 (approximately 34 per working day)[124]— in 1984 he admitted that he knew nothing about the technical aspects of performing the test. This was the explanation he provided to the editor of the *New England Journal of Medicine,* when it was shown that an article on TOS published in 1972 in that journal, and authored by Urschel and Razzuk, contained a fabricated photograph.[120] Although, according to its legend, that photograph demonstrated nerve conduction slowing across the thoracic outlet on supraclavicular stimulation in a patient with TOS, in fact it was obtained on a normal person by increasing the sweep speed during mid-arm stimulation.[83,134] At present, great claims are being made for somatosensory evoked potentials in the diagnosis of TOS.[60] However, historical perspective and recent reports suggest that these assertions, also, will prove to be unjustified as their utility is assessed in other, less biased EMG laboratories.[125]

Once the diagnosis of disputed neurogenic TOS has been suspected and then corroborated by some confirmatory test, appropriate therapy is initiated. However, similar to so many other aspects of this subgroup, there is no consensus among its proponents as to what this treatment should be. Some proponents believe the majority of patients can be treated by conservative means alone. Conversely, many others, such as Roos, believe that all but the mildest patients require operative intervention.

The contention of some proponents that this type of TOS will, if untreated, result in true neurogenic TOS with marked hand wasting lacks foundation.[15,44,77]

Bony abnormalities are a prerequisite of the true neurologic type, whereas they occur relatively seldom in the disputed type. Moreover, if this theory were true, then great numbers of true neurogenic cases should be encountered in England and Australia, where this entity is neither diagnosed nor treated in its "early" stages. Yet, the incidence of true neurogenic TOS is no greater in those countries than in the United States.[135]

If surgery is elected, then another decision immediately is required: which procedure or procedures should be performed? With few exceptions, most proponents of disputed neurogenic TOS during the first two decades of its existence considered the appropriate surgical treatment to be first rib resection. Although at least five approaches to accomplish this have been used by one proponent or another,[74] the transaxillary approach, described by Roos in 1966, has been by far the most popular.[92] However, over the last few years this concept has been increasingly questioned, and several other surgical techniques have been advocated. Interestingly enough, these include scalenotomy, which was essentially resurrected by Roos in 1982, when he described a new type of disputed neurogenic TOS, the "upper plexus" type, which he contends requires this procedure.[88] However, he states he removes the entire scalenus muscle ("scalenectomy"), and considers this technical modification to represent a marked advance over the formerly performed "scalenotomy". Although unstated, presumably first rib resection had proved ineffective in these patients; otherwise, what was the necessity for reviving this surgical technique? Some patients now are undergoing multiple operative procedures at one sitting, most often first rib resection plus scalenectomies, based on the belief that more than one type of TOS is present.[80,88] This situation is highly reminiscent of the waning days of scalenus anticus syndrome, when patients were thought to have multiple compression sites, each of which required separate surgical procedures.[52,58]

Droopy Shoulder Syndrome

This subset of disputed neurogenic TOS has recently been identified; it merits discussion because it reportedly has a symptom complex distinctive enough to allow it to be considered a syndrome.[109] Beginning with Todd in 1912, abnormal descent of the shoulder girdle, resulting in low position of shoulders and high fixation of the sternum and ribs, has been considered a predisposing factor for the development of TOS.[116a] Patients, usually women, with sloping shoulders and long necks have been referred to as the "anatomical type," or "bottle-necks."[26,105] This physiognomy was considered a predisposing factor in both the cervical rib syndrome by Adson,[2] and the scalenus anticus syndrome by Ochner, Gage, and DeBakey.[71] In 1983, Swift and Nichols delineated the droopy shoulder syndrome, using a name supplied earlier by Clein,[11] which they attributed to brachial plexus stretch. The patients are primarily women with low-set shoulders and long "swan-like" necks, who complain of pain and paresthesias in the head, neck, chest, shoulder, and arm, usually bilaterally but asymmetrically. These symptoms are exaggerated by brachial plexus palpation and downward arm traction, and relieved by passive shoulder elevation. There is no evidence of vascular compromise, objective neurologic findings, or electrodiagnostic abnormalities. However, on neck x-ray at least the second thoracic vertebra is visible above the shoulders (Fig. 6).[109] Swift and Nichols reported that first rib removal was likely to exaggerate rather than alleviate the symptoms, because surgery simply produces additional brachial plexus stretch.

Although this type of TOS is concise enough to be considered a syndrome, the fact that it is not associated with a detectable abnormality in the thoracic outlet and it produces neither clinical nor electrophysiologic abnormalities causes us to classify it as a subgroup of disputed neurogenic TOS.

We have considerable reservations about disputed neurogenic TOS for a number of reasons. First, many of the patients so diagnosed, and often treated with TOS surgery, have functional complaints. Even many proponents admit that their patients are anxious and depressed.[74,118,139] While they often prefer to consider these secondary phenomena produced by the disputed neurogenic TOS, it seems just as logical to consider them the primary event, and the TOS symptoms the manifestations of a disturbed psyche. The fact that TOS has played an ever increasing role in personal injury litigation and in workman's compensation cases is disturbing.[61,96,139] The possibility of secondary gain factors being operative in these situations is quite high.[8,61] How else can one explain the observation of Youmans and Smiley that the success of TOS surgery in patients who develop their symptoms following automobile accidents varies significantly, depending on whether or not they have retained a lawyer?[139] Even surgeons who have performed great numbers of these operations, some of whom have reported initial high success rates, are now conceding that having patients involved in compensation lawsuits "diminishes clinical success."[61,118,122,139]

Second, we are concerned that patients diagnosed as having disputed neurogenic TOS may actually have a structural neurologic lesion that is being overlooked. This was obviously the case a few decades ago when almost every patient with shoulder and arm pain was considered to have scalenus anticus syndrome. However, the surgeons of that era could offer, in retrospect, the justification that other entities, such as cervical radiculopathy and particularly CTS, were then unknown. This excuse obviously is no longer valid. Nonetheless, while all proponents of disputed neurogenic TOS discuss these entities in their differential diagnosis, some refuse to use modern methods to exclude them. Particularly distressing in this regard is Roos' rejection of the EMG examination, specifically the median NCS, to diagnose CTS. Although a host of investigators whose training and experience are primarily in neurologic disorders have shown that this is an extremely sensitive technique for confirming or refuting the clinical impression of CTS (especially if palmar NCS is performed),[18,50,106,107] Roos refuses to acknowledge its benefit, reporting it is "too expensive," "too painful," and "yields confusing results."[87,90] Instead, he advocates diagnosing CTS by history, employing some criteria that reflect a lack of appreciation of its typical presentation (e.g., insisting that paresthesias be limited to the median-innervated fingers and that symptoms not be increased by arm elevation), and a few "simple" physical examination procedures,[89] many of which (e.g., Tinel's sign; Phalen's sign) have been shown to have far less than optimal sensitivity, and some of which (e.g., thenar wasting) will be positive only with far advanced disease.[18,36,107] Using such imprecise and insensitive methods, a great number of patients with CTS will have that diagnosis unjustifiably excluded and will have their symptoms, instead, erroneously attributed to a lesion of the thoracic outlet. This is particularly likely to happen if the EAST procedure, with its alleged sensitivity and specificity for TOS, is also used. The result often will be unwarranted and unhelpful TOS surgery. This parallels the state of confusion that existed with regard to CTS and true neurogenic TOS until electrodiagnostic studies were developed which allowed the two to be distinguished from each other.[27]

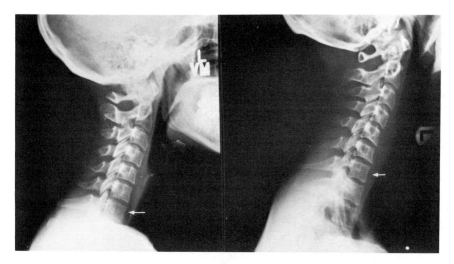

FIGURE 6. Lateral cervical x-ray of normal young woman (left) contrasted with that of young woman with droopy shoulder syndrome (right). Arrow indicates C7 vertebral body in each photograph.

Third, and finally, in recent years it has become apparent that TOS surgery is not as innocuous as once thought. Dale was the first to call attention to this, when he surveyed the members of one surgical organization (The International Cardiovascular Society) and found that slightly over half of those who reported performing this surgery had encountered, as a group, almost 300 brachial plexus injuries severe enough to produce clinical weakness, nearly one-fifth of which were permanent.[16] Subsequently, reports describing the characteristic type of iatrogenic brachial plexus lesions seen, as well as other significant complications such as infections and life-threatening hemorrhage, have been published.[9,16,133] The fact that only a small percentage of patients experience these complications must be weighed against the fact that many of them would not have been subjected to surgery at all if more stringent operative selection criteria had been used. This is a course recommended initially by Lord[57] and subsequently by Dale,[16] and one that seems particularly prudent as: (1) reports are appearing that describe large numbers of failed TOS surgery,[86,89,102,118] and (2) TOS surgery is playing an increasing role in medicolegal litigation.[16,24] In this regard, Urschel recently noted that "this operation is one of the prime causes" for law suits filed against thoracic surgeons in the state of Texas.[122]

The evidence presented above strongly indicates to us that the existence of the disputed neurogenic type TOS is doubtful. It is interesting to note that in all the large surgical series published to date, the assessment of clinical benefit has invariably been determined by the operating surgeon, who is hardly a disinterested observer. Considering the large volume of patients reported, it would appear easy to design an appropriate study to permit the objective assessment of the efficacy of rib resection or the other types of TOS surgery performed. A group of patients deemed surgical candidates should be randomly allocated to either "surgery" or "no surgery" and both groups carefully followed longitudinally by a disinterested neurologist. Until this is done we will continue to regard the disputed neurogenic TOS with great skepticism.

If we are not seeing TOS, then what are we seeing? We are unsure on this point, although patients with sore shoulders and arms have been haunting physicians' offices for at least 75 years. As noted above, many surgical procedures have been proposed over the decades as treatment for this condition, all based on the assumption that the discomfort being described is a manifestation of chronic nerve fiber compression in the thoracic outlet. However, this remains an unproven assumption, in spite of multiple attempts over the years to discover an objective neurologic or electrophysiologic diagnostic procedure.

COMBINED VASCULAR AND NEUROLOGICAL TOS

As already discussed, simultaneous compromise of both vascular and neurologic structures is uncommon.[21,56,129] Although it occasionally occurs,[55] many of the older reports most probably were describing compromise of the artery alone, with ischemic symptoms mistakenly considered "neurologic."[56] Also, until the mid-1970s, most proponents of disputed neurogenic TOS considered it was caused by compression of both the artery and brachial plexus. While a few advocates still cling to this concept,[77] the vast majority have accepted Roos' contention that all the symptoms are due to brachial plexus "irritation."[87,91]

SUMMARY

TOS is complex topic, since the term actually encompasses a number of different entities. Both the vascular subgroups and the neural subgroup associated with a cervical band have characteristic clinical and laboratory findings, but both types are quite rare. One subgroup of TOS, considered by some proponents to be solely neurogenic in nature and by others to have both a neurogenic and arterial component, is highly controversial; it is considered very common by some physicians and nonexistent by others, depending upon their orientation. This disputed type is controversial because it is not usually associated with a bony abnormality in the thoracic outlet, and has no generally accepted characteristic symptomatology or objective confirmatory diagnostic tests. Nonetheless, the vast majority of TOS surgery performed in the United States is for this type.

REFERENCES

1. Adams JT, DeWeese VA, Mahoney EB et al: Intermittent subclavian vein obstruction without thrombosis. Surgery 63:147–165, 1968.
2. Adson AW: Cervical ribs: symptoms, differential diagnosis and indications for section of the insertion of the scalenus anticus muscle. J Int Coll Surg 16:546–559, 1951.
3. Adson AW, Coffey JR: Cervical rib: a method of anterior approach for relief of symptoms by division of the scalenus anticus. Ann Surg 85:839–853, 1927.
4. Beyer JA, Wright IS: The hyperabduction syndrome. Circulation 4:161–172, 1951.
5. Bramwell E. Lesion of the first dorsal nerve root. Rev Neurol Psychiatry 1:236–239, 1903.
6. Bramwell E, Dykes JHB: Rib pressure and the brachial plexus. Edinburgh Med J 27:65–88, 1921.
7. Brickner WM: Brachial plexus pressure by the normal first rib. Ann Surg 85:858–872, 1927.
8. Busuttil RW: In discussion of Qvarfordt et al, reference 80.
9. Cherington M, Happer I, Machanic B, et al: Surgery for thoracic outlet syndrome may be hazardous to your health. Muscle Nerve 9:632–634, 1986.
10. Clagett OT: Presidential address: research and prosearch. J Thoracic Cardiovasc Surg 44:153–166, 1962.
11. Clein LJ: The droopy shoulder syndrome. Can Med Assoc J 114:343–344, 1976.
12. Coote H: Exostosis of the left transverse process of the seventh cervical vertebrae, surrounded by blood vessels and nerves, successful removal. Lancet 1:360–361, 1861.
13. Costigan DA, Wilbourn AJ: The elevated arm stress test: Specificity in the diagnosis of the thoracic outlet syndrome. Neurology 35(Suppl 1):74–75, 1985.
14. Dale WA, Lewis MR: Management of thoracic outlet syndrome. Ann Surg 181:575–585, 1975.

15. Dale A: Thoracic outlet compression syndrome. In Management of Vascular Surgical Problems. New York, McGraw-Hill, 1985, pp 562–587.
16. Dale WA: Thoracic outlet compression syndrome: critique in 1982. Arch Surg 117:1437–1445, 1982.
17. Darling HCR: The surgery of cervical rib. Med J Austral 2:389–395, 1915.
18. Dawson DM, Hallett M, Millender LH: Carpal tunnel syndrome. In: Entrapment Neuropathies. Boston, Little, Brown and Co., 1983, pp 5–59.
19. DeWeese JA, Adams JT, Gaiser DL: Subclavian venous thrombectomy. Circulation 16(Suppl 2):158, 1970.
20. Etheredge S, Wilbur B, Stoney RJ: Thoracic outlet syndrome. J Surg 138:175–182, 1979.
21. Eden KC. The vascular complications of cervical ribs and first thoracic rib abnormalities. Br J Surg 27:111–139, 1939.
22. Falconer M, Li FW. Resection of first rib in costoclavicular compression of the brachial plexus. Lancet 1:59–63, 1962.
23. Falconer MA, Weddell G. Costoclavicular compression of the subclavian artery and vein. Lancet 2:539–544, 1943.
24. Ferguson TB: Presidential address: Crisis of excellence. J Thorac Cardiovasc Surg 84:161–171, 1982.
25. Fernandez Noda EL, Lopez S: Thoracic outlet syndrome: diagnosis and management with a new surgical technique. Herz 9:52–56, 1984.
26. Freiberg JA: The scalenus anterior muscle in relation to shoulder and arm pain. J Bone Joint Surg 20:860–869, 1938.
27. Gilliatt RW. Thoracic outlet syndromes. In Dyck PJ, Thomas PK, Lambert EH, et al (eds): Peripheral Neurology, 2nd ed. Philadelphia, W.B. Saunders Co. 1984, pp 1409–1424.
27a. Gilliatt RW, Willison RG, Dietz V, et al: Peripheral nerve conduction in patients with a cervical rib and band. Ann Neurol 4:124–128, 1978.
28. Gilliatt RW, LeQuesne PM, Logue V, Sumner AJ: Wasting of the hand associated with a cervical rib or band. J Neurol Neurosurg Psychiatry 33:615–624, 1970.
29. Guralnik DB (ed): Webster's New World Dictionary, 2nd college ed. New York, Simon and Schuster, 1980, p 1444.
30. Haggert GE. Value of conservative management in cervicobrachial pain. JAMA 137:508–513, 1948.
31. Haimovici, H: Arterial thromboembolism secondary to thoracic outlet compression. In Haimovici H (ed): Vascular Surgery: Principles and Techniques, 2nd Ed, Norwalk, CT, Appleton-Century-Crofts, 1984, pp 903–910.
32. Halsted WS. An experimental study of circumscribed dilation of an artery immediately distal to a partially occluding band, and its bearing on the dilation of the subclavian artery observed in certain cases of cervical rib. J Exp Med 24:271, 1916.
33. Hansson KG. The cervico-brachial syndrome. Arch Phys Med 22:662–666, 1941.
34. Hardy RW, Wilbourn A, Hanson M. Surgical treatment of compressive cervical band. Neurosurgery 7:10–13, 1980.
35. Haven H. Neurocirculatory scalenus anticus syndrome in the presence of developmental defects of the first rib. Yale J Biol Med 11:443–445, 1939.
36. Heller L, Ring H, Costeff H, Solzi P: Evaluation of Tinel's and Phalen's signs in diagnosis of carpal tunnel syndrome. Eur Neurol 25:40–52, 1986.
37. Hempel GK, Rusher AH, Wheeler CG, et al: Supraclavicular resection of the first rib for thoracic outlet syndrome. Am J Surg 14:213–215.
38. Hill RM. Vascular anomalies of upper limbs associated with cervical ribs; report of case and review of literature. Br J Surg 27:100–110, 1939.
39. Hilton J. On Rest and Pain, 2nd ed. New York, William Wood and Co., 1879, p 113.
40. Holmgren K, Baur GM, Porter JM. The role of digital photoplethysmography in the evaluation of Raynaud's syndrome. Bruit 5:19, 1981.
41. Hughes ESR. Venous obstruction in the upper extremity (Paget-Schrotter's syndrome): A review of 320 cases. Surg Gynecol Obstet 88 (International Abstr. Surg):89–127, 1949.
42. Hvoslef J. Abnormal first thoracic rib simulating cervical rib. J Minn. State Med. Assoc. and NW Lancet. 31:251–253, 1911.
43. Inahara T. Surgical treatment of "effort" thrombosis of the axillary and subclavian veins. Am Surg 34:479, 1968.
44. Jerrett SA, Cuzzone LJ, Pasternak BM: Thoracic outlet syndrome: Electrophysiological reappraisal. Arch Neurol 41:960–963, 1984.
45. Johnson CR: Treatment of thoracic outlet syndrome by removal of first rib and related entrapments through posterolateral approach: a 22 year experience. J Thorac Cardiovasc Surg 68:536–545, 1974.

46. Judy KL, Heymann RL: Vascular complications of thoracic outlet syndrome. Am J Surg 123:521, 1972.
47. Keen WW: The symptomatology, diagnosis, and surgical treatment of cervical ribs. Am J Med Sci 133:173–218, 1907.
48. Kinmouth JB, Rob CG, Simeone FA: Vascular Surgery. Baltimore, Williams and Wilkins Co., 1963.
49. Kinnier Wilson SA: Some points in the symptomatology of cervical rib, with especial reference to muscular wasting. Proc Roy Soc Med (Clin Sect) 6:133–141, 1912.
49a. Kinnier Wilson SA, Bruce AN (eds): Neurology, vol. 2. Baltimore, Williams and Wilkins, 1940, p 1414.
50. Kimura J, Machida M, Kimura A: Median neuropathies. In Brown WF, Bolton CF (eds): Clinical Electromyography. Boston, Butterworths 1987, pp 75–96.
51. Kremer M, Gilliatt RW, Golding JS, et al. Acroparesthesia in the carpal tunnel syndrome. Lancet 2:590–595, 1953.
52. Lang EK: Neurovascular compression syndromes. Dis Chest 50:572–580, 1966.
53. Learmouth JR: Some sequels of abnormality at the thoracic outlet. Thorax 2:1–20, 1947.
54. Lederman R: Thoracic outlet syndromes: review of the controversies and a report of 17 instrumental musicians. Med Prob Perform Art 2:87–91, 1987.
55. LeVay AD. Costoclavicular compression of brachia plexus and subclavian vessels. Lancet 2:164–166, 1945.
56. Lewis T, Pickering GW: Observations upon maladies in which the blood supply to digits ceases intermittently or permanently, and upon bilateral gangrene of digits; observations relevant to so-called "Raynaud's disease." Clin Sci 1:327–366, 1934.
57. Lord JW: Thoracic outlet syndromes: Real or imaginary? NY State J Med 81:1488–1489, 1981.
58. Lord JW: Surgical management of shoulder girdle syndromes. Arch Surg 66:69–83, 1953.
59. Lord JW, Rosati LM: Thoracic-outlet syndromes. Ciba Symposia 23:1–32, 1971.
60. Machleder HI, Moll F, Nuiver M, Jordon S: Somatosensory evoked potentials in the assessment of thoracic outlet syndrome. J Vasc Surg 6:177–184, 1987.
61. Mark JBD: In discussion of Qvarfordt et al, reference 80.
62. Martinez NS, Uhrich J, Bryar G, et al: Reassessment of the significance of cervical rib in the thoracic outlet syndrome overlooking the ribs, failure to demonstrate them and their role in arterial compression. Vasc Surg 14:57–72, 1980.
63. Mellick SA: In discussion of Dale, reference 16.
64. Mercier CP, Branchereau A, Dimarino V, et al: Venous thrombosis of the upper limb: Effort or compression. J Cardiovasc Surg 14(Suppl 1):519, 1973.
65. Morley J: Brachial pressure neuritis due to a normal first thoracic rib: its diagnosis and treatment by excision of rib. Clin J 42:461–464, 1913.
66. Murphey T: Brachial neuritis caused by pressure of first rib. Aust Med J 15:582–585, 1910.
67. Murphy, JB: The clinical significance of cervical ribs. Surg Gynecol Obstet 3:514–520, 1906.
68. Nachlas IW. Scalenus anticus syndrome or cervical foraminal compression? South Med J 35:663–667, 1942.
69. Naffziger HC: The scalenus syndrome (editorial). Surg Gynecol Obstet 64:119–120, 1937.
70. Naffziger HC, Grant WT: Neuritis of the brachial plexus, mechanical in origin: the scalenus syndrome. Surg Gynecol Obstet 67:722–730, 1938.
71. Ochner A, Gage M, DeBakey M: Scalenus anticus (Naffziger) syndrome. Am J Surg 28:669–695, 1935.
72. O'Donnell TF Jr: In discussion of Donayre CE, White GGH, Mehringer SM, et al: Pathogenesis determines late morbidity of axillosubclavian vein thrombosis. Am J Surg 152:179, 1986.
73. Overton LM: The causes of pain in the upper extremities: a differential diagnosis study. Clin Orthop 51:27–44, 1967.
74. Owens JC: Thoracic outlet compression syndromes. In Haimovici H (ed): Vascular Surgery: Principles and Techniques, 2nd ed. Norwalk, CT, Appleton-Century-Crofts, 1984, pp 877–902.
75. Paget J: Clinical Lecture and Essays. London, Longmans, Green and Co., 1875.
76. Pailero PC, Walls JT, Payne WS, et al: Subclavian-axillary artery aneurysms. Surgery 90:757–763, 1981.
77. Pang D, Wessel HB: Thoracic outlet syndrome. Neurosurgery 22:105–121, 1988.
78. Peet PM, Henriksen JD, Anderson TP, Martin GM. Thoracic outlet syndrome: evaluation of a therapeutic exercise program. Mayo Clin Proc 31:281–287, 1956.
79. Porter JM, Rivers SP, Coull BM, et al. Thoracic outlet syndrome: a conservative approach. Vasc Diagn Ther 3:35–42, 1982.

80. Qvarfordt PG, Ehlenfeld WK, Stoney RJ: Supraclavicular radical scalenectomy and transaxillary first rib resection for the thoracic outlet syndrome: A combined approach. Am J Surg 148:111–116, 1984.
81. Raaf J: Surgery for cervical rib and scalenus anticus syndrome. JAMA 157:219–223, 1955.
82. Raskin NH, Howard MN, Ehrenfeld WK: Headache as the leading symptom of the thoracic outlet syndrome. Headache 25:208–210, 1985.
83. Relman A: Responsibilities of authorship: where does the buck stop? (editorial). N Engl J Med 310:1048–1049, 1984.
84. Robb CG, Standeven A: Arterial occlusion complicating thoracic outlet compression syndrome. Br Med J 2:709–712, 1958.
85. Rogers L: Upper limb pain due to lesions of the thoracic outlet. Br Med J 2:956–958, 1949.
86. Roos DB: Reoperations for thoracic outlet syndrome. In Bergan JJ, Yas JST (eds): Reoperative Arterial Surgery. Orlando, FL, Grune & Stratton, Inc. 1986, pp 475–491.
87. Roos DB: Thoracic outlet and carpal tunnel syndromes. In Rutherford RB (ed): Vascular Surgery. Philadelphia, W.B. Saunders Co., 1984, pp 708–724.
88. Roos DB: The place for scalenectomy and first rib resection in thoracic outlet syndrome. Surgery 92:1077–1085, 1982.
89. Roos DB: Recurrent thoracic outlet syndrome after first rib resection. Acta Chir Belg 79:363–372, 1980.
90. Roos DB: New concepts in the etiology, diagnosis and surgical treatment of thoracic outlet syndrome. In Greep JM, Lemmen HAJ, Roos DB, Urschel HC (eds): Pain in the Arm and Shoulder: An Integrated View. The Hague, Martinus Nijhoff, 1979, pp 201–210.
91. Roos DB: Congenital anomalies associated with thoracic outlet syndrome. Am J Surg 132:771–777, 1976.
92. Roos DB: Transaxillary approach for first rib resection to relieve thoracic outlet syndrome. Ann Surg 163:354–358, 1966.
93. Roos DB, Owens JC. Thoracic outlet syndrome. Arch Surg 93:71–74, 1966.
94. Roos DB: In discussion of Johnson CR, reference 45.
95. Rosati LM, Lord JW. Neurovascular Compression Syndromes of the Shoulder Girdle. New York, Grune and Stratton, 1961.
96. Sanders RJ, Monsour JW, Gerber WF, et al: Scalenectomy versus first rib resection for treatment of thoracic outlet syndrome. Surgery 85:109–121, 1979.
97. Sanders RJ, Monsour JW, Baer SB: Transaxillary first rib resection for the thoracic outlet syndrome. Arch Surg 97:1014–1023, 1968.
98. Sargent P: Lesions of the brachial plexus associated with rudimentary ribs. Brain 44:95–124, 1921.
99. Schein CJ, Harmovici H, Young H: Arterial thrombosis associated with cervical ribs and surgical considerations. Surgery 40:428–443, 1956.
100. Schubart PJ, Halberlin JR, Porter JM: Intermittent subclavian venous obstruction: Utility of venous pressure gradients. Surgery 99:365, 1986.
101. Semmes RE, Murphey F: The syndrome of unilateral rupture of the sixth intravertebral disk with compression of the seventh cervical nerve root: A report of four cases with symptoms simulating coronary disease. JAMA 121:1209–1214, 1943.
102. Sessions RT: Recurrent thoracic outlet syndrome: causes and treatment. South Med J 75:1453–1461; 1466, 1982.
103. Short DW: The subclavian artery in 16 patients with complete cervical ribs. J Cardiovasc Surg 16:135–141, 1975.
104. Simpson JA: Electrical signs in the diagnosis of carpal tunnel and related syndromes. J Neurol Neurosurg Psychiatry 19:275–280, 1956.
105. Stammers FAR: Pain in the upper limb from mechanisms in the costoclavicular space. Lancet 1:604–607, 1950.
106. Stevens JC, Sun S, Beard CM, et al: Carpal tunnel syndrome in Rochester, Minnesota, 1961–1980. Neurology 38:134–137, 1988.
107. Stewart JD, Aguayo: Compression and entrapment neuropathies. In Dyck PJ, Thomas PK, Lambert EH, Bunge R (eds): Peripheral Neuropathy, 2nd ed. Philadelphia, W.B. Saunders, 1984, Vol. 2, pp 1435–1457.
108. Stopford JSB, Telford ED: Compression of the lower trunk of the brachial plexus by a first dorsal rib. Br J Surg 7:168–177, 1919/1920.
109. Swift TR, Nichols FT: The droopy shoulder syndrome. Neurology 34:212–214, 1984.
110. Symonds CP: Two cases of thrombosis of the subclavian artery with contralateral hemplegia of sudden onset, probably embolic. Brain 50:259, 1927.
111. Taylor LM Jr, McAllister WR, Dennis DR et al: Thrombolytic therapy followed by first rib

resection for spontaneous ("effort") subclavian vein thrombosis. Am J Surg 149:644, 1985.

112. Telford ED, Mottershead S: Pressure at the cervico-brachial junction. J Bone Joint Surg 30B:249–265, 1948.

113. Telford ED, Mottershead S: The "costoclavicular syndrome." Br Med J 1:325–328, 1947.

114. Thomas HM, Cushing HG: Exhibition of two cases of radicular paralysis of the brachial plexus. One from the pressure of a cervical rib with operation. The other of uncertain origin. Johns Hopkins Hosp Bull 14:315–319, 1903.

115. Thorburn W: The symptoms due to cervical ribs. In Brockbank EM (ed): Dreschfeld Memorial Volume. Manchester, University Press, 1908, pp 85–111.

116. Todd TW: Posture and the cervical rib syndrome. Ann Surg 75:105–109, 1922.

116a.Todd TW: The descent of the shoulder after birth; its significance in the production of pressure symptoms on the brachial plexus. Anat Anz 41:385, 1912.

117. Tytus JS. Scalenus anticus syndrome, fact or fancy. Bull Mason Clin 19:149–166, 1965.

118. Urschel HC, Razzuk MA: The failed operation for thoracic outlet syndrome: the difficulty of diagnosis and management. Ann Thorac Surg 42:523–528, 1986.

119. Urschel HC, Razzuk MA: Thoracic outlet syndrome. In Sabiston DC, Spencer FC: Gibbon's Surgery of the Chest. Philadelphia, W.B. Saunders Co., 1983, pp 437–452.

120. Urschel HC, Razzuk MA: Thoracic outlet syndrome. N Engl J Med 286:1140–1143, 1972.

121. Urschel HC, Paulson DL, McNamara JJ: Thoracic outlet syndrome. Ann Thorac Surg 6:1–10, 1968.

122. Urschel HC: In discussion of Urschel HC, Razzuk MA, reference 118.

123. Urschel HC: In discussion: Stalworth JM, Quinn GH, Aiken AF: Is rib resection necessary for relief of thoracic outlet syndrome? Ann Surg 581–592, 1977.

124. Urschel HC: In discussion of McGough EC, Pearce MB, Byrne JP: Management of thoracic outlet syndrome. J Thorac Cardiovasc Surg 77:169–174, 1979.

125. Veilleux M, Stevens JC, Campbell JK: Value of somatosensory evoked potentials in the diagnosis of thoracic outlet syndrome. Muscle Nerve 9:655, 1986.

126. von Schroetter L. Erkrankungen der Gefasse. In Nathnagel Handbuch der Pathologie und Therapie. Vienna, Holder, 1884.

127. Walshe FMR: On "acroparesthesia" and so-called "neuritis" of the hands and arms in women. Br Med J 2:596–598, 1945.

128. Walshe FMR, Jackson H, Wyburn-Mason R: On some pressure effects associated with rudimentary and "normal" first ribs, and the factors entering into their causation. Brain 67:141–177, 1944.

129. Walshe FMR: Nervous and vascular pressure syndromes of the thoracic inlet and cervico-axillary canal. In Feiling A (ed): Modern Trends in Neurology. New York, Paul B. Hoeber, Inc., 1951, pp 542–566.

130. Warwick R, Williams PL: Gray's anatomy, 35th British ed. Philadelphia, W.B. Saunders Co, 1973, pp 254–255.

131. Wheeler, WI de C: Compression neuritis due to normal first dorsal rib. Practitioner c.v.; 409–414, 1920.

132. White JC, Poppel MH, Adams R: Congenital malformations of the first thoracic rib. Surg Gynecol Obstet 81:643–659, 1945.

133. Wilbourn AJ: Thoracic outlet syndrome surgery causing nerve brachial plexopathy. Muscle Nerve 11:66–74, 1988.

134. Wilbourn AJ, Lederman RJ: Evidence for conduction delay in thoracic outlet syndrome is challenged (letter to editor). N Engl J Med 310:1052–1053, 1984.

135. Wilbourn AJ. Thoracic outlet syndrome. In syllabus, Course D: Controversies in Entrapment Neuropathies. American Association of Electromyography and Electrodiagnosis. Rochester, Minnesota, 1984, pp 28–38.

136. Wilbourn AJ: Case Report No. 7: True neurogenic thoracic outlet syndrome. American Association of Electromyography and Electrodiagnosis, Rochester, Minnesota, 1982.

137. Wilshire WH. Supernumerary first rib: clinical records. Lancet 2:633, 1860.

138. Wright IS. The neurovascular syndrome produced by hyperabduction of the arms. Am Heart J 29:1–19, 1945.

139. Youmans CR, Smiley RH: Thoracic outlet syndrome with negative Adson's and hyperabduction maneuvers. Vasc Surg 14:318–329, 1980.

SAID R. BEYDOUN, MD

FOCAL ENTRAPMENT NEUROPATHIES OF THE ARM

Signs, Symptoms, Electrodiagnosis, and Etiologic Considerations

Associate Professor of Neurology, University of Southern California; Director of Electromyography Laboratory at Los Angeles County Hospital, Los Angeles, California

Reprint requests to:
Said R. Beydoun, MD
Los Angeles County-USC Medical Center
1200 North State St.
Unit I, Room 5641
Los Angeles, CA 90033

Entrapment neuropathies represent a group of neuropathies sharing in common focal dysfunction of the nerve secondary to mechanical compression at certain "vulnerable" sites, such as narrow spaces or tunnels[138] through which the nerve passes or sharp edges against which the nerve can be pushed, angulated, squeezed, or stretched. Intrinsic causes include space-occupying lesions, fibrous edges,[50] and aponeuroses of muscles.[42,43] Extrinsic causes are external pressure or certain traumatic conditions (acute or chronic). These may occur at sites where the nerve courses superficially close to a bone, or across a joint, thereby predisposing it to external compression. A few conditions in this last category would be classified as focal mononeuropathies, rather than the classical entrapment ones.

Numerous factors favor the development of entrapment neuropathies: congenital factors such as the size of the space through which a nerve is passing,[12] occupational/habit factors,[116] and medical factors. A common medical cause is the presence of certain preexisting neuropathies,[7,104,114,153] making the nerve more susceptible to compression.

Almost any nerve is subject to compressive neuropathy. The objective of this chapter is to cover the common entrapment neuropathies of the arm in terms of their pathogenesis, clinical features, electrodiagnostic localization, and treatment. Two frequently encountered entrapment syndromes, the carpal tunnel syndrome and ulnar nerve entrapment at the elbow, will be discussed in more detail. Some of the focal mononeuropathies that are secondary to external factors (e.g., after injury) will also be described.

PATHOPHYSIOLOGY

A distinction is to be made whether the pathophysiologic changes and clinical manifestations in entrapment neuropathy are due to a direct effect of pressure or to ischemia. Originally it was proposed by Denny-Brown[30,31] that compression of a nerve produces dysfunction secondary to ischemia. This was illustrated in acute experimental compressive neuropathies (tourniquet paralysis) by applying high pressure (supersystolic) conditions to a nerve for a short time. However, pathologic studies in nerves subjected to tourniquet paralysis challenged the ischemia hypothesis because changes in those nerves were consistent with direct pressure effects rather than ischemia.[125] Changes begin with a paranodal swelling of the nerve; a sharp pressure gradient then results, distorting the nerve and causing intussusception of one internodal segment of an axon with its myelin into the adjacent axonal segment. The axon and the myelin are displaced from the region of high pressure to the region of low pressure, with the paranodal myelin breaking down after having been stretched. Paranodal demyelination results, with progression to focal segmental demyelination.

Using an analogy from chronic entrapment experiments in animals,[1,4,45,46] it was found that in chronic human entrapment neuropathies ischemia plays a minor role. Pathologic changes in nerves entrapped by chronic low pressure application are consistent with a direct mechanical effect.[100,126] Segmental changes of focal demyelination and remyelination have been observed, affecting preferentially the outer fibers and the large diameter myelinated fibers.[1] This process results in conduction block and is the basis for the clinical and electrophysiologic findings in most entrapment neuropathies. Initially, distal segments remain intact; with more severe and long-standing compression, distal axonal degeneration can result. Swelling of the proximal segment has been observed in most cases.[152,157,161] In summary, direct pressure damage is thought to be the major cause for the dysfunction in human chronic entrapment neuropathies. Ischemia, however, does play a role in some of the symptoms experienced by patients with nerve entrapment. It can result in remitting numbness and tingling, which people experience after assuming a certain posture (lying on their arm or on the side of their leg). It is usually not associated with any pathologic change and is fully reversible. Long-standing ischemia can, however, result in axonal degeneration.

ELECTRODIAGNOSIS

Routine electrodiagnostic techniques for localization and diagnosis of entrapment neuropathies consist of nerve conduction studies and needle electromyography. A brief basic explanation of these tests and interpretation of results will be discussed. A more detailed explanation is found in many available EMG textbooks.[3,53,75]

Motor Nerve Conduction Studies

Commonly used techniques consist of percutaneous stimulation of a nerve at two or more accessible sites and recording the response over the muscle using surface electrodes. The elicited response is a compound muscle action potential (CMAP). Its amplitude represents the summation of activation of individual muscle fiber potentials which, in turn, reflects the summation of activation of the individual conducting axons. By stimulating at different sites, responses identical in waveform morphologies and amplitudes but different in latencies are elicited. Knowing the distance between the two stimulation points and the latencies difference, the conduction velocity can be calculated. The latter is a function of the integrity of the myelin and the number of large myelinated axons. In general, findings associated with low CMAP amplitudes are designated as axonal neuropathies, whereas those associated with prolonged distal latencies and slowed conduction velocities are demyelinative ones. For localization purposes, which is generally important in entrapment neuropathy studies, one additionally stimulates the nerve at sites proximal and distal to the presumed entrapment. Three possible sets of responses can result (Fig. 1).

Response (a): Equivalent CMAP amplitude at proximal and distal sites with normal conduction velocity across the entrapment site.

Response (b): Normal CMAP amplitude distally, low CMAP amplitude proximally with similar or different morphology. Conduction velocity across the entrapment site can be normal or slowed.

Response (c): Low CMAP amplitude proximally and distally (the contralateral site serves as control).

Response (a) is seen commonly in some entrapment neuropathies despite clinical symptoms and signs for the following reasons: (1) some of these neuropathies cause minimal block of conduction and are missed on routine electrophysiologic studies; (2) the patient's fleeting symptoms could be caused by ischemia rather than direct pressure with sparing of large myelinated fibers; (3) symptoms can also be due to intermittent nerve compression without any fixed deficit at the time of electrodiagnostic study.

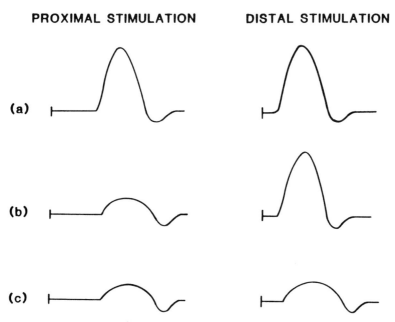

PROXIMAL STIMULATION   **DISTAL STIMULATION**

(a)

(b)

(c)

FIGURE 1. Compound muscle action potential (CMAP) amplitude obtained in response to stimulation of a nerve, proximal and distal to its entrapment site. Three responses are possible (normal, low amplitude proximally, and low amplitude distally and proximally).

TABLE 1.   Distinction Between Lesions Causing Neuropraxia Versus
Axonotmesis by Electrophysiologic Studies

Pathology	Nerve Conduction Studies	Electromyographic Findings
Neuropraxia	1. Slowed conduction velocity across the compressed segment 2. Decrease CMAP amplitude proximal to the entrapment site 3. Normal CMAP amplitude distal to the entrapment	1. No fibrillations or positive sharp waves 2. Decreased number of motor units
Axonotmesis	Decrease CMAP amplitude proximal and distal to the entrapment	Fibrillations, positive sharp waves, and decreased number of motor units

Response (b) is characteristically seen in early entrapment neuropathies. It is found in 10–30% of chronic ulnar and median entrapment neuropathies respectively.[20] Its physiologic term, "neuropraxia," reflects conduction block across the compressed nerve segment (Table 1). Fewer myelinated axons conduct the impulse and, therefore, the CMAP amplitude is smaller proximally than distally. There is no axonal loss, which is reflected by normal CMAP amplitude, distal to the entrapment site.

Response (c) is characterized by progression of the conduction block to axonal wallerian degeneration. It is called axonotmesis, the low CMAP amplitude at the distal site reflecting axonal loss (Table 1).

Response (b) can progress to (c) by showing on a later electrodiagnostic setting a lower CMAP amplitude distally.

Sensory Nerve Conduction Studies

Techniques consist of either stimulating the nerve and recording from the skin (antidromic techniques) or nerve recording with stimulation of the cutaneous innervated area (orthodromic techniques). Since sensory fibers are very sensitive to axonal loss,[93] the amplitude of the sensory nerve action potential (SNAP) can be used as an indicator of the severity of the process when compared to the asymptomatic contralateral site. The drop in SNAP amplitude from a distal to a proximal site cannot be used to assess conduction block because SNAPs normally show a drop in amplitude proximally compared to distally, secondary to physiologic dispersion.

Late Responses

One of these, known as an "F" response (Fig. 2), is used to assess conduction along the whole nerve, including its proximal segment. The technique consists of antidromic stimulation of the nerve with recording made from the muscle. Although it can assist in the diagnosis of proximal entrapment neuropathies, it is not very useful because the "F" wave latency can be normal if the area of conduction block is small or incomplete, thus being diluted by the normal conduction of the whole nerve segment.

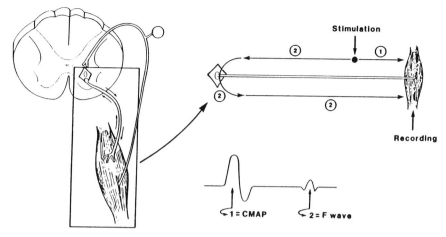

FIGURE 2. "F" wave response. Its longer latency and small amplitude response represents the antidromic excitation of few anterior horn cells. The shorter latency, large amplitude response is the CMAP.

Electromyography

This is a useful complementary test to document axonal loss. It consists of inserting a needle in muscles supplied by the nerve distal to the entrapment site, assessing insertional and spontaneous activity, motor unit action potential morphology, and their numbers on full contraction as well as discharge rate. Abnormal spontaneous activity is seen in conditions associated with response (c), showing denervation potentials (fibrillations and positive sharp waves) secondary to wallerian axonal degeneration. Depending on the distance between the muscles and the sites of entrapment, these denervation potentials occur between 5–35 days after the onset of wallerian degeneration. In conditions associated with responses (b) and (c) and in which weakness is present, needle EMG reveals only decreased number of activated motor units, due to the loss of "functional" conducting axons secondary to the conduction block. The absence of denervation potentials documents the integrity of the axons innervating the muscle.

Having briefly discussed the basis of routine electrodiagnostic testing, it is essential to mention that adequate history and physical examination with detailed attention to occupational habits and associated medical conditions constitute the key for diagnosis. Thorough knowledge of the anatomy of nerves and muscles, including anomalous innervation, usage of proper electrophysiologic techniques, and awareness of factors that can affect electrodiagnostic parameters, is essential for precise localization and diagnosis.

The next section focuses on specific nerve entrapment syndromes of the upper extremity.

THE MEDIAN NERVE

Anatomy

The median nerve (Fig. 3) is formed by the union of the lateral (C5–C7) and medial (CB–T1) cords of the brachial plexus.[57] After exiting the axilla, it

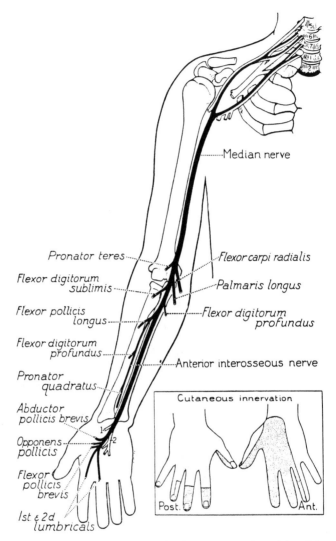

Median nerve

Pronator teres

Flexor digitorum sublimis

Flexor pollicis longus

Flexor digitorum profundus

Pronator quadratus

Abductor pollicis brevis

Opponens pollicis

Flexor pollicis brevis

1st & 2d lumbricals

Flexor carpi radialis

Palmaris longus

Flexor digitorum profundus

Anterior interosseous nerve

Cutaneous innervation

Post.   Ant.

FIGURE 3. The median nerve, its course in the arm, and the origin of the motor and sensory branches. The cutaneous branches and cutaneous distribution are shown respectively in stipple and in the inset. (1) designates the palmar cutaneous branch of the median nerve; (2) represents the palmar digital branches. (Reproduced with permission from Haymaker W, Woodhall B: Peripheral Nerve Injuries. Philadelphia, W. B. Saunders, 1945, p 155.)

lies on the medial aspect of the upper arm, close to the brachial artery and to the radial and ulnar nerves. It crosses the anticubital fossa, medial to the brachial artery, and the biceps tendon. After exiting the elbow, the median nerve passes beneath the lacertus fibrosus, a fascial band extending from the biceps tendon to the forearm fascia. In the forearm, it usually courses between the superficial and deep heads of the pronator teres. It then dips under a tendinous arch connecting the two heads of the flexor digitorum superficialis (Fig. 4). Distal to the innervation of the latter muscle, the anterior interosseous nerve originates from the median nerve. This nerve has only motor functions, supplying the flexor digitorum profundus (I and II), the flexor pollicis longus, and the pronator quadratus. At the wrist, the median nerve enters the hand through the carpal tunnel. Its boundaries include the carpal bones dorsally and laterally, and the tranverse carpal ligament volarly. In addition to the median nerve, the contents of the carpal tunnel include the tendon of flexor pollicis longus, the four tendons of the flexor digitorum superficialis, and the four tendons of the flexor digitorum profundus.

Distal to the carpal ligament, the nerve divides into branches. The motor branch supplies the abductor pollicis brevis, the opponens pollicis, the superficial head of the flexor pollicis brevis, and the lateral two lumbricals. The sensory branch supplies the palmar surfaces of the thumb, index and middle fingers, and the radial half of the ring finger. The sensory branch to the thenar region originates 3 cm proximal to the transverse carpal ligament.

In discussion of median nerve anatomy, one should mention the Martin-Gruber anastomosis[60,172] an anomalous median to ulnar nerve connection in the forearm, present in 15–30% of normal persons. The presence of this anomaly can cause variations in the clinical presentation and electrophysiological findings.

The median nerve is subject to entrapment at various sites along its course. These entrapment syndromes are described in the next section.

Carpal Tunnel Syndrome

CLINICAL FEATURES
Etiology.   It is caused by entrapment of the median nerve at the wrist within a closed space,[136-138] mostly due to nonspecific tenosynovitis.[176] It is more common in women, ascribed partly to a congenitally smaller carpal tunnel.[29] It is usually bilateral in 55% of patients. People with certain occupational activities such as knitting, typing, or painting tend to develop this syndrome with increased frequency, probably due to a repeated rise in intracarpal tunnel pressure during such maneuvers.[49] Other conditions associated with increased incidence of carpal tunnel include increased susceptibility to pressure palsies seen in certain familial neuropathies[7,49,104] and other neuropathies including the diabetic ones.[114] Disorders that lead to an increase in the content of carpal canal, either secondary to swelling or to tissue infiltration and enlargement, are frequent causes of carpal tunnel syndrome. These include myxedema,[117] acromegaly,[127] amyloidosis, the mucopolysaccharidoses,[95] and pregnancy,[56,122] Rheumatoid arthritis resulting in flexor tenosynovitis and thickening of the synovium and joint capsule is another common cause of carpal tunnel syndrome.[119] Other disorders include osteoarthritis with secondary osteophyte formation, exostoses, ganglia, lipomas, and anomalous tendons and muscles. Acute carpal tunnel syndrome has been associated with Colles' fracture[32] and forearm crushing injuries with secondary Volkmann's ischemic contracture.

Symptoms.   Presenting symptoms consist of paresthesias in the hand and digits.[91,137] Sensory complaints are rarely restricted to the palmar aspect of the thumb, index, middle digit, and radial aspect of the ring finger. They may involve the tips of the fingers, only one digit, or the entire hand. A common complaint includes hand pain. Forearm, elbow, and shoulder pain are not uncommon presentations.[23] Neck pain is not present, which helps to differentiate

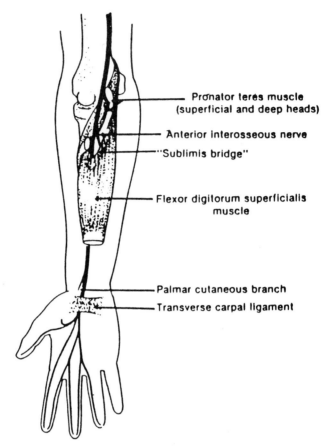

Pronator teres muscle
(superficial and deep heads)

Anterior Interosseous nerve

"Sublimis bridge"

Flexor digitorum superficialis
muscle

Palmar cutaneous branch

Transverse carpal ligament

FIGURE 4.   The course of the median nerve in the forearm, showing its passage between the two heads of the pronator teres. The origin of the anterior interosseous nerve and the sublimis bridge are also shown. (Reproduced with permission from Stewart JD: Focal Peripheral Neuropathies. New York, Elsevier, 1987, p 135.)

it from cervical radiculopathy. Pain and paresthesias are felt during maneuvers that produce repeated wrist flexion and are more common during sleep hours at night. Probable stasis and venous engorgment are precipitating factors. Shaking the hand can sometimes relieve the tingling and the pain. Motor manifestations are late ones. They consist of clumsiness of the hand, stiffness complaints probably reflecting loss of dexterity, and weakness of pinch. Autonomic manifestations, including Raynaud's phenomenon, are occasionally present.[2]

   Physical Findings.   These vary from being normal in mild cases of carpal tunnel syndromes to classical sensory findings in the distribution of the median nerve cutaneous innervation. The area over the thenar eminence is usually spared, since the sensory nerve supplying it arises 3 cm proximal to the transverse carpal ligament. Sensory findings include numbness and paresthesias, which can be discerned over the tips of index and the middle fingers (autonomous zone of median nerve innervation). Tinel's sign, which consists of tingling sensation in the median nerve–innervated digits after tapping over the volar wrist crease, is present in 45–73% of patients with carpal tunnel syndrome,[137,156] but is also present in 29% of normal individuals.[156] Phalen's sign, which consists of passive wrist flexion for 30 to 60 seconds, is reported to be present in 80% of patients.[137] Motor weakness consists of difficulty in elevating the thumb perpendicular to the plane of the palm and in opposing the thumb to the little finger secondary to weakness of the abductor pollicis brevis and opponens pollicis, respectively. Only in advanced stages does one see atrophy of the thenar eminence.

DIAGNOSTIC EVALUATION

Electrodiagnosis.   This is the most reliable way to diagnose carpal tunnel syndrome. Various electrodiagnostic parameters can be applied as summarized in Table 2.[27,73,74,90,155,163] They include the following:

Median sensory conduction study. Some of the techniques described consist of stimulating at fixed distances, proximal and distal to the carpal ligament (at the wrist and at the palm), using either antidromic or orthodromic stimulation and comparing it to the ulnar sensory conduction latencies at similar points and to the conduction velocity across the wrist. Inching technique, as described by Kimura,[74] consists of stimulating the median nerve at multiple increments of 1 cm across the wrist. In patients with carpal tunnel syndrome, a disproportionate focal slowing is found usually between 2 to 4 cm distal to the distal wrist crease. Comparing the median nerve electrodiagnostic parameters to other nerves, such as the radial and ulnar, is important in order to rule out a generalized neuropathy.

Median motor conduction study. This is a less sensitive parameter in the electrodiagnosis of carpal tunnel syndrome than the sensory conduction study. However, in few cases, distal median motor latency can be prolonged with normal median sensory parameters. Also, in rare cases where only the recurrent motor branch to the thenar muscles is compressed,[10] patients present with weakness, thenar muscles wasting, and no sensory complaints. Electrodiagnostic abnormalities are then only restricted to the median motor nerve. It is important to differentiate this entity from certain disorders such as C8–T1 radiculopathy or motor neuron disease.

It is worth mentioning that the degree of electrodiagnostic abnormalities does not correlate with the severity of symptoms. This is due to the fact that some of the symptoms (e.g., pain and paresthesias) reflect ischemic nerve dysfunction rather than direct pressure effects, and the former is not well appreciated on routine conduction studies. The electrodiagnostic abnormalities do, however, correlate with the duration and severity of compression. They are very helpful in these settings: (1) confirming the diagnosis; (2) ruling out certain entities that may mimic carpal tunnel syndrome; (3) prior to surgery to assess the degree of compression; and (4) for follow-up after surgery.

Thermography.   In recent years, this noninvasive test has been reported to be of some use in the diagnosis of peripheral nerve injuries,[17,167] including carpal tunnel syndrome. The abnormality obtained reflects involvement of the small sympathetic fibers that mediate skin temperature changes in the median nerve–innervation distribution.[2]

TABLE 2. Some of the Various Electrodiagnostic Parameters Used in the Diagnosis of Carpal Tunnel Syndrome

1. Absent or prolonged median SNAP latency at the wrist (N < 3.4 msec at 13 cm)[163]
*2. Ratio of the median to the ulnar SNAP amplitudes (N > 1.0)[90]
3. Comparing the palmar median SNAP latency to the palmar ulnar SNAP latency (N < 0.2 msec difference)[27]
4. Comparing the median CMAP latency to the ulnar CMAP latency at the wrist (N < 1.8)[163]
†5. Comparing the median CMAP and SNAP latencies at the wrist to the contralateral site (N < 1.0 msec for motor and <0.5 msec for sensory)[163]
6. Distal median CMAP latency prolongation at the wrist (N < 4.2 msec)
7. Slowing of the median sensory conduction velocity across the wrist[73]
8. Segmental, serial 1 cm stimulation across the carpal tunnel (inching technique)[74]

* Rarely useful by itself; usually associated with distal latency prolongation.
† Not too useful, given the bilaterality of carpal tunnel syndrome.
N = Normal, SNAP = sensory nerve action potential, CMAP = compound muscle action potential.

DIFFERENTIAL DIAGNOSIS

(1) Cervical radiculopathy C6 or C7, is the most common entity in the differential diagnosis of carpal tunnel syndrome. It is, however, associated with neck pain, reflex changes, and weakness in the biceps and/or triceps muscle without thenar atrophy or weakness. (2) Transient ischemic attacks or simple partial seizures with secondary sensory complaints can be confused if the paresthesias involve the whole hand. Reflex changes, lack of pain, presence of other neurologic findings, and a careful history and physical examination are useful in clarifying the diagnosis. (3)Thenar muscle weakness and atrophy can be a presenting feature of the rare entity of neurogenic thoracic outlet syndrome.[50] It is secondary to compression of the C8–T1 roots by an accessory rib, a fibrous band, or a hypertrophied muscle; however, it causes sensory complaints in the ulnar aspect of the hand and forearm (C8–T1 distribution). (4) Motor neuron disease, which can present with thenar wasting, causes painless weakness not restricted to a peripheral nerve or root distribution with other neurologic findings and absent sensory complaints. (5) Reflex sympathetic dystrophy[80] can be associated with carpal tunnel syndrome or may follow carpal tunnel surgery. It is characterized by diffuse paresthesias, lack of specific motor and sensory dysfunction in the distribution of the median nerve, temperature changes, and trophic alterations in the skin and nail. (6) Occasionally, carpal tunnel syndrome may be a presenting feature of a symmetric generalized neuropathy or part of a mononeuritis multiplex. The latter occurs in disorders associated with ischemic nerve pathology and in certain collagen-vascular diseases. History, physical examination and electrodiagnosis would distinguish it from carpal tunnel syndrome.

TREATMENT

The indication for a given treatment modality is a function of the severity of symptoms and signs. It is primarily a clinical decision guided by the electrodiagnostic findings. For example, a patient who has severe pain and paresthesias, thenar wasting, and denervation on EMG would be considered a candidate for surgery.[137] On the other hand, a patient with minimal paresthesias, without weakness, and without electromyographic evidence of denervation would be tried on conservative treatment, even if the nerve conduction parameters were abnormal. Clinical and electrodiagnostic follow-up are indicated to assess the response to treatment and the degree of progression.

Initially, a simple volar wrist splint held in the neutral position is indicated. It can be worn at night and during the day if it does not interfere with daily activities. The patient is instructed to avoid certain hand activities that usually precipitate the symptoms. If relief is incomplete, local corticosteroid injection in the carpal tunnel is then carried out,[138] with no more than two injections usually advised.[28] Pregnant patients who develop carpal tunnel syndrome are managed by either of these two treatment modes. Patients with severe complaints that are refractory to splinting and corticosteroid injection, and who have progressive weakness are referred for surgery. This consists of surgical decompression, excising the transverse carpal ligament using a curved interthenar incision in order to avoid the palmar cutaneous branch of the median nerve.[160] The recurrent thenar branch should be avoided and the whole ligament should be excised.

Surgical Complications. Surgical complications include incomplete or blind resection of the ligament, fibrosis in the carpal tunnel, palmar cutaneous branch damage with painful neuroma formation, causalgic pain, and reflex sympathetic dystrophy.[94] The latter can be avoided by advising the patient to perform passive hand exercises within 24 hours after surgery. This will facilitate regaining of finger motion. Results of surgery are usually very good, with 90% of patients achieving satisfactory relief provided that they are referred with the right diagnosis and operated on with good surgical techniques.[155] In most patients normalization of the electrodiagnostic parameters takes up to many months after surgery.[54,105]

Proximal Median Nerve Entrapment Syndromes

These are much less common than the median entrapment neuropathy at the wrist. Compression may occur at various sites: (1) in the axilla and upper arm; (2) above and at the elbow; and (3) in the forearm. In the axilla and the arm, compression can occur in isolation but usually occurs in association with other neuropathies (e.g., radial and ulnar). Etiologies vary and include anterior dislocation of the shoulder,[13] direct compression from poorly fitted crutches, honeymoon or sleeping palsies,[98,143] humeral fractures,[158] and anomalous vessels.[149] Above the elbow, compression can occur within the ligament of Struthers.[101] The latter is an anomalous structure that is present in 0.7–2.7% of the population.[162] It extends between the medial epicondyle and a humeral anteromedial supracondylar spur, 5 cm above the spur (Fig. 5). The median nerve and brachial artery may pass through it, with neural and vascular symptoms consequent to the compression. Other causes of median nerve palsies at this level include supracondylar fractures and elbow dislocation.[151,154]

Two main proximal entrapment neuropathies will be discussed in more detail: the pronator teres syndrome and the anterior interosseous nerve syndrome.

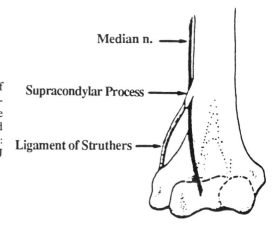

FIGURE 5. The ligament of Struthers, extending from a humeral supracondylar spur to the medial epicondyle. (Reproduced with permission from Wiggins CE: Pronator syndrome. South Med J 75:241, 1982.)

Median n.

Supracondylar Process

Ligament of Struthers

Pronator Teres Syndrome

CLINICAL FEATURES

Etiology.   This syndrome is due to compression of the median nerve at any of the following sites:[61,69,82,144,148] (1) under the lacertus fibrosus (a fascial band connecting the biceps tendon to the forearm fascia); (2) between the superfical and deep heads of the pronator teres by a hypertrophied muscle or anomalous band; and (3) under the arch of the flexor digitorum sublimis (see Fig. 4). Excessive forearm muscular activity and hypertrophic muscles have also been reported to cause this syndrome.[113] A rise in intracompartmental pressure associated with an anatomic predisposition is a possible cause in some of the latter patients.

Symptoms.   Vague discomfort and aching in the volar forearm are intensified by repeated elbow flexion, extension, and pronation. The patient reports weakness with poorly defined sensory problems in the median nerve territory.

Physical Findings.   There is sparing of the pronator teres muscle with various degrees of weakness of the remaining median-innervated muscles. Because the flexor carpi ulnaris is supplied by the ulnar nerve, ulnar deviation of the wrist occurs on flexion. Tenderness over the pronator teres bulk is a common sign. Increased firmness of the muscle and Tinel's sign have been described in some.

DIAGNOSTIC EVALUATION

Radiographic examination of the elbow is indicated in cases of trauma and to rule out space-occupying lesions. The main aid to diagnosis is electromyography. It reveals denervation changes in the median-innervated muscles, sparing the pronator teres. Nerve conduction study is useful in ruling out carpal tunnel syndrome.

Differential Diagnosis.   Proximal and distal median segment neuropathies (Table 3) as well as radiculopathies must be ruled out. They are characterized by the following: (1) in proximal median neuropathies at the axilla or the arm, there is weakness of the pronator teres muscle; (2) in the anterior interosseous nerve syndrome, there is selective weakness of the flexor digitorum

TABLE 3. Median Mononeuropathies: Localization of the Lesion Site by Motor and Sensory Examination

Compression Site	Motor Deficit	Sensory Deficit
1. Axilla/upper arm/above elbow	All median innervated muscles	Similar to CTS in addition to palmar cutaneous branch
2. Pronator teres syndrome	As above, except that the pronator teres is spared	As above
3. Anterior interosseous nerve syndrome	Flexor pollicis longus Flexor digitorum profundus I and II Pronator quadratus	None
4. Carpal tunnel syndrome (CTS)	Intrinsic median-innervated hand muscles	Volar aspect of the thumb, index, middle finger and radial half of the ring finger

profundus I and II, the flexor pollicis longus and the pronator quadratus without any sensory deficit; (3) carpal tunnel syndrome is differentiated by normal strength of the median-innervated forearm flexor muscles, normal sensation over the thenar eminence due to sparing of the palmar cutaneous branch of the wrist, sensory complaints worsened by wrist flexion, and characteristic electrophysiologic findings; (4) in C6 or C7 radiculopathy, weakness and reflex changes are present in non-median innervated C6 or C7 muscles, as is pain that is worsened by neck movements. Electromyographic abnormalities are sought in the paraspinal muscles and in non-median innervated C6 or C7 limb muscles; (5) thoracic outlet syndrome, which causes vague arm pain and thenar wasting, can resemble the pronator teres syndrome. However, the pain is referred to the medial aspect of the forearm. Electrodiagnostic findings of ulnar nerve involvement are also characteristic.

TREATMENT
For patients with slight, intermittent, and nonprogressive symptoms, conservative treatment is recommended. The patient is advised to wear an elbow splint and to avoid maneuvers that precipitate the symptoms. Patients who fail conservative treatment, as well as patients with progressive weakness and muscle atrophy, are referred for surgical exploration and decompression of the nerve at any of the above-mentioned potential compressive sites.[61]

Anterior Interosseous Nerve Syndrome

CLINICAL FEATURES
Etiology. Conditions associated with this syndrome[72] include: (1) the presence of an anomalous structure associated with a fibrous band originating from the deep head of pronator teres, the flexor pollicis longus, or the flexor digitorum superficialis;[41] (2) an accessory head to the flexor pollicis longus (Gantzer muscle);[96] (3) certain forearm or supracondylar fractures;[151,171] (4) complication of certain operative procedures;[59] (5) external pressure of a cast or a supportive beam;[170] and (6) certain vascular pathologies.[150] Spontaneous

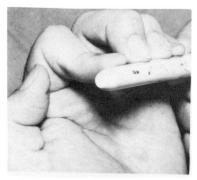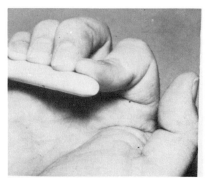

FIGURE 6. Partial bilateral anterior interosseous nerve palsies. Patient presented with inability to flex the distal interphalangeal joints of both index fingers.

cases have been reported,[170] as well as palsies occurring after intense exercise. Anterior interosseous nerve palsy is also a relatively common finding in patients with the brachial plexus neuritis syndrome (Parsonage-Turner).[132]

Symptoms.   Patients present with pain in the forearm and weakness limited to the flexor pollicis longus, flexor digitorum profundus (I and II), and pronator quadratus. Various degrees of involvement of those muscles, isolated muscle involvement,[144] and bilateral involvement have been described (Fig. 6).[118]

Physical Findings.   The weakness consists of difficulty flexing the distal interphalangeal joints of the thumb, index, and middle fingers, with a characteristic triangular-appearing pinch. Weakness of pronation is difficult to discern, secondary to the preserved pronator teres, but can be tested with the elbow in flexion to decrease the contribution of the latter. Sensory function is normal. Tinel's sign may be positive in some patients.

DIAGNOSTIC EVALUATION

Forearm and elbow radiographic studies are indicated in cases of trauma or when intrinsic etiology is suspected. Electromyography is useful in documenting selective abnormalities of the involved muscles.

Differential Diagnosis.   Given the selective involvement of few muscles, few disorders are confused with this entity. It is easily distinguished from proximal median neuropathies and carpal tunnel syndromes as shown in Table 3. Patients with rheumatoid arthritis can have spontaneous rupture of the flexor pollicis longus and flexor digitorum profundus tendons.[97] Radiographic and electromyographic studies can differentiate those mechanical causes from the true anterior interosseous nerve palsy.

TREATMENT

Conservative treatment is recommended in the initial stages (8–12 weeks) of spontaneous palsies and in certain extrinsic and traumatic conditions.[48] The patient is instructed to rest his arm and to avoid any exercise that worsens the symptoms. Surgical intervention, including exploration and/or decompression, is recommended after a period of 8–12 weeks in patients who are progressing or showing lack of improvement.[62] Spontaneous, nonsurgical improvement has been reported, however, up to 18 months after onset in one patient.[118]

THE ULNAR NERVE

Anatomy

The ulnar nerve (Fig. 7) is derived from the medial cord (C8–T1) of the brachial plexus.[57] It courses in the axilla and then in the upper arm where it lies medial to the brachial artery. At the middle of the arm it angles posteriorly, piercing the intermuscular septum, which separates the flexor and extensor muscle groups. It then lies close to the humerus adjacent to the medial head of the triceps. In some instances, it crosses the arcade of Struthers. The latter is formed by fibers of the medial head of the triceps muscle and the deep fascia including the internal brachial ligament attachment. At the elbow, the ulnar nerve passes in a superficial location in the ulnar condylar groove between the medial epicondyle of the humerus and the olecranon of the ulna. After emerging from this groove and immediately distal to the elbow, it passes through the cubital tunnel (Fig. 8). This important structure is a fibrosseous canal whose roof is formed by the humero-ulnar aponeurotic arcade, site of attachment of the flexor carpi ulnaris to the medial epicondyle and olecranon. Other boundaries of the cubital tunnel include the medial epicondyle anteriorly, the humero-ulnar ligament laterally, and the flexor digitorum profundus forming part of the floor. The ulnar nerve then courses through the forearm between the flexor carpi ulnaris and the flexor digitorum profundus, continuing medial to the ulnar artery, to the wrist. At the wrist, the nerve enters a space between the pisiform bone and hook of the hamate. This tunnel is known as Guyon's canal; its roof is formed by the volar carpal ligament and its floor is the transverse carpal ligament. Unlike the carpal tunnel, there are no flexor tendons traversing the canal.

The branches of the ulnar nerve begin at the elbow without any proximal branch. Motor branches arise at the elbow with two to three branches to the heads of the flexor carpi ulnaris and another branch originating in the distal cubital tunnel to the medial head of the flexor digitorum profundus. The origin of the branches to the flexor carpi ulnaris is variable. In a recent autopsy study of 30 cadavers, the branches were found to originate distal to the medial epicondyle in 27 cases and proximal to it in only 3 cases.[21] The range of origin of the first branch was found between 5 mm proximal to 37 mm distal to the medial epicondyle. For clinical localization purpose, it is important to known that the ulnar nerve does not have any sensory innervation above the wrist. At about 5 to 8 cm proximal to the wrist, a dorsal cutaneous sensory branch arises between the flexor carpi ulnaris and the ulna. The ulnar nerve then winds around and courses distally to supply sensation to the dorsum of the hand, the dorsal ulnar half of the fourth digit, and the dorsal aspect of the fifth finger.

Within Guyon's canal, the ulnar nerve divides into a superficial terminal branch and a deep motor branch (see Fig 7). The former is sensory, supplying sensation to the medial border of the palm, the medial half of the fourth digit, and the entire fifth digit. The deep motor branch exits the canal and gives its first branch to the hypothenar muscles, then bends and continues its course in the palm to supply the interossei, the third and fourth lumbricals, the adductor pollicis, and the deep head of the flexor pollicis brevis.

The ulnar nerve can be compressed at various sites: (1) in the axilla and upper arm; (2) in the middle and distal arm while passing through the inter-

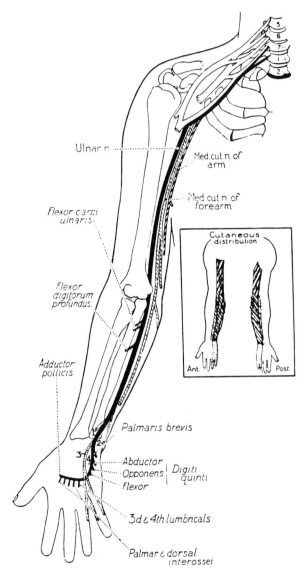

FIGURE 7. The ulnar nerve, its course, and origin of motor and sensory branches. The medial cutaneous nerves of the arm and forearm, originating from the C8–T1 medial cord are also shown. The sensory branches and cutaneous distribution are shown respectively in stipple and in the inset: (1) designates the palmar branch; (2) is the dorsal sensory branch; (3) is the superficial terminal branch; and (4) is the deep motor branch. (Reproduced with permission from Haymaker W, Woodhall B: Peripheral Nerve Injuries. Philadelphia, W. B. Saunders, 1945, p 163.)

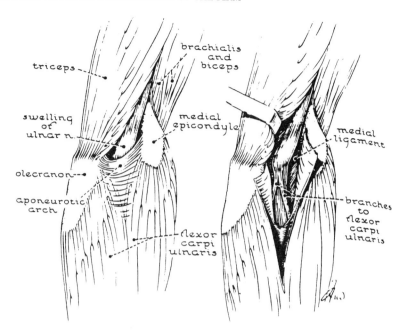

FIGURE 8. Posterior view of the elbow, showing the cubital tunnel closed (left) and opened (right) by splitting of the aponeurosis. The ulnar nerve passes between the olecranon and the medial epicondyle, under the aponeurotic arch of the flexor carpi ulnaris muscle. Left, swelling of the nerve proximal to the tunnel; right, constriction under the arch. (Reproduced with permission from Feindel W, Stratford J: The role of the cubital tunnel in tardy ulnar palsy. Can J Surg 1:292, 1958.)

muscular septum beneath the arcade of Struthers; (3) at the elbow; and (4) at the wrist. The former two are very rare. Only the latter entrapment sites will be discussed: the more common one at the elbow and the relatively less common one at the wrist.

Knowing the anatomy and origin of the ulnar nerve branches, one can extrapolate the following clinical findings (Table 4): (1) all ulnar neuropathies do not cause sensory signs in the forearm; (2) ulnar neuropathies at the elbow affect sensation over the dorsum of the wrist. The latter is spared by ulnar compression at the wrist; (3) ulnar neuropathies above the elbow affect the flexor carpi ulnaris and the flexor digitorum profundus (III and IV), which can be spared in certain compressions at the elbow; and (4) depending on the level of entrapment, ulnar neuropathies at the wrist can cause mixed sensory-motor involvement, isolated motor, or pure sensory involvement.

Ulnar Neuropathies at the Elbow

CLINICAL FEATURES

Etiology.   Ulnar neuropathies at the elbow represent a syndrome caused by different etiologies. The first is the entity of tardy ulnar palsy, usually associated with a remote history of trauma to the elbow with or without elbow joint deformity.[131] Later, patients manifest ulnar nerve dysfunction. The second

TABLE 4. Ulnar Compressive Neuropathies: Localization of Entrapment Site
by Clinical Examination

Compression Site	Forearm Sensation	Flexor Carpi Ulnaris & Flexor Digitorum Profundus (III & IV)	Intrinsic Hand Muscles	Sensation over Dorsum of Hand	Volar Hand Sensation
Axilla/upper arm/above elbow	Normal	Weak	Weak	Abnormal	Abnormal
Elbow 1. Condylar groove 2. Cubital tunnel	Normal	Variable	Weak	Abnormal	Abnormal
Wrist (Guyon's canal)	Normal	Normal	Weak	Normal	Abnormal
Mid/distal palm	Normal	Normal	Weak	Normal	Normal

entity is usually due to recurrent ulnar nerve injury, secondary to frequent external compression (for example, excessive elbow leaning). This occurs more commonly in individuals with a shallow ulnar groove; in these patients prolapse of the ulnar nerve from the condylar groove into a position close to, and anterior to the medial epicondyle can occur.[26] The third entity, which is the most common, is the cubital tunnel syndrome.[42,43] It has been erroneously used to indicate any type of ulnar nerve compressive neuropathy at the elbow. It is due to compression of the nerve under the humero-ulnar aponeurotic arch and is usually bilateral. Repeated elbow flexion in these individuals can compress the nerve, since the aponeurotic arch tightens secondary to widening of the space between the olecranon and medial epicondyle (sites of attachment of the aponeurosis).[42] Bulging of the floor of the cubital tunnel also occurs.

All these three entities do, however, share a similar clinical presentation. Routine electrodiagnostic testing to separate them in general is difficult and controversial.[19] Resorting to special techniques, including intraoperative recording, is sometimes indicated.

Symptoms. Unlike carpal tunnel syndrome, where severe sensory complaints are predominant, in ulnar neuropathies at the elbow, motor disability is a major complaint in many patients. Initial presentation consists of pain that is poorly localized to the ulnar nerve distribution. It can be referred to the elbow, forearm, or hand. Sensory complaints consisting of paresthesias and numbness are usually well localized to the ulnar aspect of the hand (palm, medial half of the ring finger, and the fifth digit). Pain and sensory complaints are worse with repeated elbow flexion and extension, and occasionally worse at night. In longstanding ulnar neuropathies, intrinsic hand muscle wasting results. In few patients, it is not uncommon to find muscle atrophy as the sole and presenting complaint.

Since the ulnar nerve innervates all intrinsic hand muscles, excluding the four median-innervated muscles (abductor pollicis brevis, opponens pollicis, first two lumbricals, and superficial head of the flexor pollicis brevis), motor manifestations of ulnar neuropathy are usually severe.[28] The combination of weakness of the intrinsic hand muscles and the medial head of the flexor digitorum profundus can result in significant disability. By understanding the functions of these muscles and their coordination in various finger maneuvers, one can derive the specific resulting motor signs and symptoms. Patients usually present with loss of dexterity and hand clumsiness. Weakness of the flexor carpi ulnaris is usually not significant because wrist flexion can be compensated by other wrist flexors including the palmaris longus and the flexor carpi radialis. Flexor digitorum profundus weakness usually results in selective inability to flex the distal phalanges of the last two digits. Intrinsic muscle weakness results in a weak pinch. Long-standing ulnar nerve paralysis results in a claw-hand deformity, which consists of flexion of metacarpophalangeal joints and extension of the interphalangeal joints of the last two digits. Sparing of the index and middle finger lumbrical muscles is due to their median nerve innervation.

Physical Findings.   Physical findings consist of sensory signs below the wrist crease, with normal sensation above it, since sensory innervation of the medial forearm is from the medial cutaneous nerve of the forearm, a branch of the medial cord of the brachial plexus. Sensory findings in the last two digits are variable. They are usually evident over their distal ends, the autonomous zones of ulnar nerve innervation. Motor signs due to muscle weakness include Froment's sign, which is due to weakness of the first dorsal interosseous and adductor pollicis. It is tested by asking the patient to hold a piece of paper tightly between his thumb and index finger, with the examiner attempting to pull it. To compensate for the weakness, the patient attempts to use the long thumb flexor, resulting in its flexion (Fig. 9). Wartenburg's sign, which is due to weakness of the third palmar interosseous, results in an abducted posture of the fifth digit.

Diagnostic Evaluation

Radiography.   X-ray of the elbow is indicated to rule out bony, soft tissue masses or elbow joint deformity, which usually occurs in the setting of a history of trauma.

Electrodiagnosis.   In order to document focal slowing and/or conduction block across the elbow segment, ulnar motor and sensory conduction studies are performed, using four point stimulation (wrist, below elbow, above elbow and axilla).[38,39,133] Electrodiagnostic documentation of a focal lesion is difficult for the following reasons: (1) it is present in not more than 25% of patients with ulnar neuropathies;[66] (2) many ulnar neuropathies result in axonal loss lesions and may be associated with diffuse slowing, a nonlocalizing finding; (3) electrodiagnostic abnormalities may be absent in early stages; and (4) routine conduction studies do not usually separate the various entities of ulnar neuropathies at the elbow.

Various nerve conduction abnormality criteria have been set for the diagnosis of focal ulnar lesions at the elbow. Some of these include the following: (1) an absolute prolongation of the elbow ulnar motor latency to more than 9.0 msec;[39] (2) slowing of the across elbow ulnar conduction velocity to less than 38 m/sec;[39] and (3) slowing of the across elbow velocity relative to the forearm velocity. However, slowing can be present in asymptomatic individuals, which is also influenced by the position of the limb during the nerve conduction test.[22] Various laboratories adopt different techniques regarding arm position. The arm can either be fully extended at the elbow or flexed to 90 or 135 degrees. When the arm is in an extended position, the velocity across the elbow can be slower

FIGURE 9. Positive Froment's sign on the right. Due to weakness of the ulnar innervated adductor pollicis and the first dorsal interosseous, the patient uses the long flexor of the thumb when asked to hold tightly to a piece of paper. (Reproduced with permission from Haymaker W, Woodhall B: Peripheral Nerve Injuries. Philadelphia, W. B. Saunders, 1945, p 169.)

than the forearm velocity by as much as 15 m/sec even in normal individuals. The reason for this is that the nerve is more redundant in the extended limb position, and an underestimation of its length occurs when surface skin measurements are being done.

A very important criterion useful in diagnosing a focal ulnar neuropathy is the presence of focal conduction block. It is evidenced by the presence of a dispersed and a lower compound muscle action potential amplitude when stimulating above the elbow compared to below the elbow. In this condition, the electromyographer should be sure to rule out the presence of a Martin-Gruber anastomosis in the forearm, which can simulate a focal ulnar nerve conduction block at the elbow.[172]

Other electrodiagnostic techniques include a four-point ulnar sensory conduction study, found by some investigators to increase the sensitivity of diagnosis.[88,133] Inching techniques and near-nerve needle recording would also increase the yield.[107,128] In inching techniques, it was found by Miller[107] that the site of slowing in cubital tunnel syndrome extends between 1.5—4.0 cm below the medial epicondyle. Thus, when one performs a routine four-point stimulation study, the below-elbow stimulating electrode should be placed at least 4.0 cm distal to the medial epicondyle. The above-elbow stimulation site should be at least 10 cm distant from it, in order to avoid an overestimation of conduction error due to short distances.[76] A dorsal ulnar sensory nerve action potential study[65] should be performed to differentiate an ulnar neuropathy at the elbow from an ulnar neuropathy at the wrist. Ulnar neuropathies at the elbow resulting in axonal loss abolish the dorsal ulnar sensory nerve action potential which is, however, preserved in ulnar neuropathies at the wrist.

Electromyographic examination should consist of assessing four muscles (flexor carpi ulnaris, flexor digitorum profundus, abductor digiti minimi and first dorsal interosseous). The examination may be normal, may show an increase in the number of polyphasic motor units, or may reveal fibrillations and positive sharp waves. The flexor digitorum profundus and especially the flexor carpi ulnaris can be spared in more than 50% of cases.[9,38,39] This is because the location of the branches within the nerve to those muscles are deep, making them less sensitive to ischemia and compression.[168] Electrodiagnostic abnormalities are summarized in Table 5. As shown in the table, certain ulnar neuropathies result in severe axonal loss with low ulnar distal CMAP amplitude, absent ulnar SNAP, and diffuse motor conduction slowing.[173] Should this situation exist, localization of the entrapment site at the elbow cannot then be established.

DIFFERENTIAL DIAGNOSIS

Diseases that result in ulnar-innervated muscle weakness should be ruled out. However, these result in additional signs and symptoms that can be easily distinguished from ulnar neuropathies, and include (1) C8–T1 radiculopathies; (2) C8–T1 inferior trunk and medial cord brachial plexopathies. Differentiating points are the presence of sensory signs in a C8–T1 distribution (medial forearm) and C8–T1 motor signs, with weakness in non-ulnar innervated muscles. The lower trunk/medial cord brachial plexopathies may be due to infiltrative neoplasms, radiation damage, or, rarely, are part of the entity of neurogenic thoracic outlet syndrome;[50] and (3) early motor neuron disease in patients with isolated intrinsic hand muscle weakness. In these patients, the sensory examination is normal, pain is absent, deep tendon reflexes are brisk, and weakness is present in non-ulnar innervated muscles.

TREATMENT

The choice of treatment is dictated by the severity of signs and symptoms, and by the type of lesion, i.e., whether it is a retrocondylar compression, due to recurrent nerve prolapse, or secondary to compression at the cubital tunnel. Conservative measures are indicated in patients with minimal sensory complaints who have no motor weakness and no electromyographic evidence of denervation. Avoiding repeated elbow flexion and wearing a splint to keep the elbow in an extended position are usually very successful measures.

On the other hand, patients who have intractable pain not relieved by conservative measures and who have progressive sensory and motor complaints as well as EMG evidence of denervation should be considered for surgery. Surgical techniques are variable, depending on the etiology. Anterior transposition of the nerve is indicated in patients with tardy ulnar palsy who have elbow joint deformity or shallow ulnar grooves, which predispose the nerve to external pressure.[35,103] This can be combined with medial epicondylectomy.[55,70] Correction of an elbow joint deformity, which predisposes to nerve stretching, is sometimes indicated.[139] Soft tissue masses should be resected if present.[5] For patients with the cubital tunnel syndrome, a successful approach that should be considered in all patients is decompression of the ulnar nerve between the two heads of the flexor carpi ulnaris.[42,175]

In general results of surgery are a function of the severity of the clinical signs: patients with minimal evidence of neuropathy do better than patients who already have wasting. Pain is alleviated in most.[103]

TABLE 5. Electrodiagnostic Findings in Ulnar Neuropathy at the Elbow

---

A. Establishing the presence of a focal conduction abnormality:
  1. Slow conduction velocity across the elbow segment.
  2. Drop in CMAP amplitude with or without dispersion proximal to the elbow, on supramaximal stimulation and in the absence of an anomalous innervation.
B. Axonal loss lesions:
  a. Mild: Denervation in the abductor digiti minimi, first dorsal interosseous, with or without flexor carpi ulnaris and flexor digitorum profundus involvement.
  b. Moderate: Decrease or absent ulnar sensory nerve action potential at the wrist and absent ulnar dorsal cutaneous SNAP in addition to (a).
  c. Severe: Decrease distal ulnar CMAP amplitude with generalized diffuse slowing in addition to (a) and (b).

Surgical Complications.   Complications depend on the type of the surgical procedure used,[18,175] and include painful neuroma formation at the site of transposition, recurrent subluxation of the nerve, fibrosis of the nerve, and incomplete decompression in certain cases of cubital tunnel syndrome.

Acute Ulnar Neuropathies at the Elbow

Unlike the previously described syndromes, which represent chronic ulnar entrapment at the elbow, an acute ulnar neuropathy entity has been described.[106,111] It occurs in patients undergoing cardiac surgery with medial sternotomy under general anesthesia. In addition to motor deficits, patients with this syndrome present with greater pain and sensory complaints than in chronic entrapment. This is important to mention because almost all patients recover within 8 to 12 weeks and without the need for surgical exploration. The syndrome is thought to be due to vascular compromise of the nerve at a proximal site. The mechanism of damage is believed to be ischemia rather than direct pressure.

Ulnar Neuropathies at the Wrist

Ulnar neuropathies at the wrist are much less common than ulnar neuropathies at the elbow. Compression can occur within the canal of Guyon or distal to it.

CLINICAL FEATURES
Etiology.   The causes can be exogenous or intrinsic. Exogenous causes include acute trauma, such as metacarpal bone fracture, or recurrent external trauma from occupational habits.[37,64] The latter have been described in cyclists and mechanics who commonly use their palms to exert pressure on objects with resulting deep motor palmar branch compression. Extrinsic causes include bony masses, pisiform arthritis, soft tissue masses such as ganglia, cysts, or lipomas.[68,142]
Symptoms and Physical Findings.   Depending on the level of entrapment (Fig. 10), various clinical findings result: (1) compression within the canal of Guyon causes weakness of all the ulnar intrinsic hand muscles and decreased sensation over the volar medial aspect of the palm, the medial part of the ring finger, and the fifth digit;[146] (2) mid-palm compression results in painless muscle weakness and wasting.[129] It can involve all the intrinsic ulnar-innervated muscles, with or without hypothenar muscle sparing, depending on whether the compres-

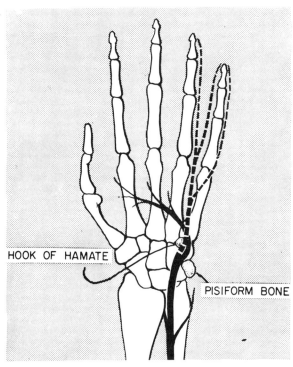

HOOK OF HAMATE

PISIFORM BONE

FIGURE 10. The course of the ulnar nerve distally, through the canal of Guyon, between the pisiform bone and the hook of the hamate. Broken lines designate terminal sensory branches. Compression can occur within or distal to the canal of Guyon (see text). (Reproduced with permission from Shea JD, McClain EJ: Ulnar nerve compression syndromes. J Bone Joint Surg 51A:1099, 1969.)

sion is proximal or distal to the origin of the hypothenar branch. Long-standing compression can result in atrophy of these muscles and the appearance of claw-hand deformity; and (3) isolated sensory manifestations due to compression of the superficial digital branch with motor sparing may occur rarely.

DIAGNOSTIC EVALUATION

Radiography.   X-rays of the wrist, including oblique and carpal tunnel views, are indicated to rule out soft tissue masses or bony joint abnormalities.[28]

Electrodiagnosis.   This is the main tool to confirm the diagnosis.[36] Depending on the site of compression, one of four electrodiagnostic findings is possible: (1) Absent or decreased ulnar sensory nerve action potential (SNAP) amplitude from the fifth digit, decreased ulnar compound muscle action potential (CMAP) amplitudes, and/or prolonged distal latencies from the abductor digiti minimi (ADM) and first dorsal interosseous (FDI) with electromyographic (EMG) evidence of denervation. (2) Normal ulnar SNAP, abnormal ulnar CMAP parameters, and EMG abnormalities of FDI and ADM. (3) Normal ulnar SNAP, ulnar CMAP and EMG abnormalities restricted to the FDI. (4) Abnormal ulnar SNAP parameters, normal ulnar CMAP parameters and normal EMG of the FDI and ADM.

Number 1 is due to mixed motor-sensory ulnar nerve involvement within the canal of Guyon; number 2 is due to deep motor palmar involvement; number

3 is due to deep motor palmar involvement distal to its hypothenar branch; and number 4, the least common, is due to isolated superficial ulnar sensory involvement. In all these conditions, the dorsal ulnar SNAP is normal, which helps in differentiating them from ulnar nerve compression at the elbow.[65] EMG of the flexor carpi ulnaris and flexor digitorum profundus is also normal.

DIFFERENTIAL DIAGNOSIS

Proximal ulnar neuropathies (see Table 4), C8–T1 root and C8–T1 brachial plexus lesion should be ruled out. A history of wrist or hand trauma, occupational habits, radiographic examination, and electrodiagnostic testing help in establishing the diagnosis of distal ulnar nerve entrapment. In cases of isolated deep palmar motor branch compression, the differential diagnosis would include an early form of motor neuron disease.

TREATMENT

The patient should be advised to avoid activities that result in palmar compression of the nerve. Surgical exploration is indicated in cases of failed conservative measures, progressive motor and sensory complaints, wrist joint deformities, or space-occupying lesion.[28] Depending on the etiology, surgery should consist either of decompression or excision of the mass.

THE RADIAL NERVE

Anatomy

The radial nerve (Fig. 11) is the major continuation of the posterior cord (C5–T1) of the brachial plexus.[57] It courses down the lateral wall of the axilla and enters the arm anteromedially, along the long head of the triceps on the medial aspect of the humerus. It then winds around the posterior aspect of the humerus, entering the spiral groove and passing deep to the lateral head of the triceps. At the junction of the middle and lower thirds of the humerus, it turns forward and pierces the lateral intermuscular septum, where it lies in a relatively superficial position close to the bone with no overlying muscle. The nerve then lies between the brachioradialis and the brachialis muscles, and continues its course in the anterior compartment of the arm. After passing anterior to the lateral epicondyle, and about 3–4 cm distal to it, the radial nerve divides into a superficial branch (sensory) and a deep (motor) branch, the posterior interosseous nerve (Fig. 12). The superficial branch descends along the anterior aspect of forearm, becoming cutaneous at the level of the lower one-third of the forearm, where it emerges from under the tendon of the brachioradialis. It then divides, supplying sensation to the posterior radial half of the hand and dorsum of the first three digits to the proximal phalanges. The posterior interosseous branch descends anterior to the radial neck and winds around the lateral aspect of the radius to reach the supinator, where it pierces the superficial head of the supinator. The point at which it pierces the muscle is the arcade of Frohse[44] (Fig. 12), which represents a curved fibrous arch in the origin of the muscle between the lateral and medial aspects of the lateral epicondyle. In its course within the supinator, the nerve is close to the bursae of the elbow. Distally, it is in close contact with the radius. After emerging from the supinator, the posterior interosseous nerve descends in the forearm and gives off its terminal muscular branches.

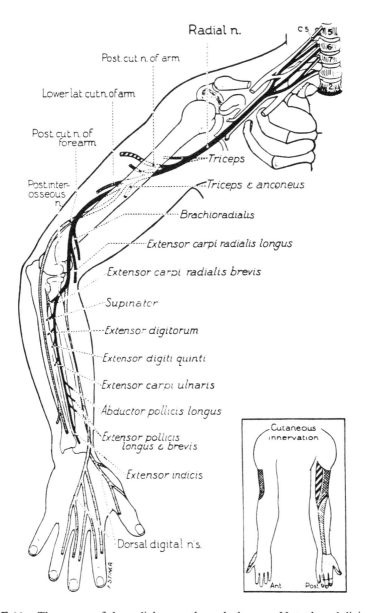

FIGURE 11. The course of the radial nerve through the arm. Note the subdivisions of the nerve and the origin of the posterior interosseous nerve at the level of the supinator muscle. The cutaneous branches are shown in stipple. The cutaneous sensory distribution is shown in the inset. (Reproduced with permission from Haymaker, Woodhall B: Peripheral Nerve Injuries. Philadelphia, W. B. Saunders, 1945, p 174.)

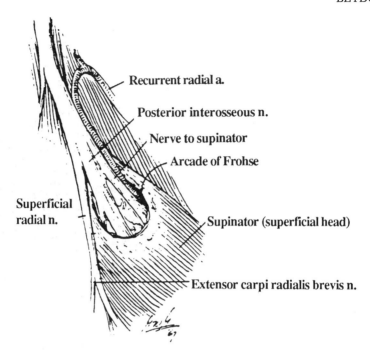

Recurrent radial a.

Posterior interosseous n.

Nerve to supinator

Arcade of Frohse

Superficial
radial n.

Supinator (superficial head)

Extensor carpi radialis brevis n.

FIGURE 12. The bifurcation of the radial nerve into the superficial radial nerve and the posterior interosseous nerve. Note the relationship of the latter to the supinator muscle and the arcade of Frohse. (Reproduced with permission from Spinner M: The arcade of Frohse and its relationship to posterior interosseous nerve paralysis. J Bone Joint Surg 50B:810, 1968.)

The branches of the radial nerve begin at the level of the axilla (see Fig. 11). First is a sensory branch, the posterior cutaneous nerve of the arm, which supplies a small area of skin over the posterior aspect of the arm, and then a motor branch, which innervates the long head of the triceps. In the arm and during its course in the spiral groove, it gives the posterior cutaneous nerve of the forearm and two motor branches to the lateral and medial head of the triceps. After it pierces the intermuscular septum, the radial nerve supplies branches to the brachioradialis and the extensor carpi radialis longus. After its division, the posterior interosseous nerve supplies the extensor carpi radialis brevis and the supinator before entering the arcade of Frohse. After its exit from the supinator, it supplies the following muscles: extensor digitorum communis, extensor digiti minimi, extensor carpi ulnaris, abductor pollicis longus, extensor pollicis longus, extensor pollicis brevis, and extensor indicis (proprius).

Potential entrapment sites of the radial nerve include: (1) the level of the axilla; (2) the level of intermuscular septum; and (3) its course in the spiral groove. The deep posterior interosseous branch is usually entrapped within the arcade of Frohse. Common entrapment sites of the superficial sensory radial branch are at the level at the posterolateral distal forearm and at the wrist.

Given the relatively "fixed" sets of the radial nerve branches to its muscles, one can easily localize the level of the lesion based on the following clinical points (Table 6): (1) a high axillary lesion will affect all the muscles innervated

TABLE 6. Radial Mononeuropathies: Localization of Lesion Site by Clinical Examination

Compression Site	Muscles Spared	Sensory Findings
Axilla	None	Posterior arm, forearm, and dorsum of the hand
Spiral groove/intermuscular septum	Triceps	Dorsum of the hand and part of the first three digits ± forearm
Arcade of Frohse	Triceps Brachioradialis Extensor carpi radialis (longus and brevis) Supinator	None
Distal forearm	All	Dorsum of the hand and of the first three digits

by the nerve; (2) a lesion distal to the spiral groove and at the intermuscular septum will spare the triceps; (3) a lesion at the arcade of Frohse will spare the brachioradialis, the extensor carpi radialis longus, the extensor carpi radialis brevis, and the supinator. Numbers 1 and 2 result in additional sensory deficits, whereas number 3 results in motor involvement only. Entrapment of the superficial branch of the radial nerve at the forearm results in sensory deficit alone.

Radial Entrapment Neuropathies

Etiology. With the exception of posterior interosseous nerve palsy, intrinsic entrapment neuropathies of the radial nerve are rare. They are usually caused by extrinsic compression and trauma.

In the axilla and upper arm, the radial nerve can be affected by poorly fitted axillary crutches, so-called crutch palsy. It can be compressed by tightly applied pneumatic tourniquets around the upper arm,[14] rifle slings,[115] shoulder straps of a back pack, and wheelchairs.[63] It is seen in association with fractures of the humerus, either due to displaced bone fragments or as a delayed manifestation of a healed fracture.[145] Some cases of radial neuropathies have been reported after attempted closed reduction of the fracture. The most common cause of radial neuropathy encountered in routine clinical practice is the so-called "Saturday night palsy."[159] This occurs in patients who are in deep sleep or coma from alcohol or drugs and lie in a certain posture, with the arm externally rotated, predisposing it to radial nerve compression. Honeymoon palsy results from the pressure of a sleeping partner's head resting on the upper arm. In these two conditions, the site of the compression is at the level of the intermuscular septum, where the nerve is superficial and close to the humerus not covered by muscles. Rare instances of intrinsic radial nerve palsies have been described in patients following intense muscular exercise, secondary to compression of the nerve under a fibrous arch of the lateral head of the triceps.[92]

Superficial branch radial nerve palsies, known as cheiralgia paresthetica, have been reported in association with wearing tight wristwatch bands, handcuffs, or casts.[102] Laceration of the nerve at the distal forearm and wrist are, however, much more common.[87]

Posterior interosseous nerve palsies have been described in association with fractures of the ulna,[112] fractures and dislocations of the radial head, deformed elbow joint secondary to osteomyelitis,[86] and rheumatoid synovitis.[99] Soft tissue masses such as cysts, ganglia, and lipomas should be ruled out in every case of nontraumatic posterior interosseous nerve palsy.[15,110] Idiopathic posterior interosseous nerve palsy is secondary to compression of the nerve under the arcade of Frohse.[123] Occasional cases have been reported after strenuous exercise consisting of pronation and supination movements.

The clinical features of two compression syndromes will be discussed: radial nerve entrapment at the arm and posterior interosseous nerve palsy.

Radial Neuropathies at the Arm

CLINICAL FEATURES

Symptoms and Physical Findings.   Patients present mainly with motor deficit consisting of wrist drop. When the compression occurs distal to the spiral groove, the triceps muscle is spared and elbow extension is normal. Despite weakness of the brachioradialis and supinator, elbow flexion and supination will be mediated by the biceps. Extension of the wrist is absent, as is extension at the metacarpophalangeal joints. Extension at the interphalangeal joints is spared because this is mediated by the median and ulnar-innervated intrinsic hand muscles. Sensory complaint is minor, and objective sensory findings may be restricted only to the dorsum of the hand.

DIAGNOSTIC EVALUATION

The history will provide a clue to the etiology in most cases. X-ray of the humerus is indicated in cases of preceding trauma. Electrodiagnosis localizes the level of involvement.[34,67,166] In axonal loss lesions, denervation changes by EMG are found in all radial-innervated muscles excluding the triceps. Four-point motor conduction study has been described, stimulating at the forearm, above the lateral epicondyle between the biceps and the brachioradialis, at the posterolateral aspect of the humerus below the deltoid insertion (level of the intermuscular septum), and at Erb's point. Recording is done from an extensor muscle such as the extensor indicis. Because of the deep location of the nerve within large muscles, inadvertent stimulation of neighboring nerves occurs with spread of volume conducted potentials, necessitating needle recording in most cases. Slowing across the compressed segment can be documented in some cases.

Differential Diagnosis.   The differential diagnosis of radial neuropathy includes: (1) C7 root pathology; (2) C7 middle trunk brachial plexus lesion; and (3) posterior cord plexopathy. C7 involvement can be documented by the clinical and electrophysiologic involvement of non-radial innervated C7 muscles, e.g., flexor carpi radialis, pronator teres, and latissimus dorsi. In a C7 lesion, the supinator and brachioradialis are spared because they are C5–6 muscles. In addition to clinical and radiographic clues, these electrophysiologic findings are helpful: (1) C7 radiculopathies are confirmed by the presence of denervation in the C7 paraspinals muscles; (2) in C7 middle trunk plexopathies, the median sensory nerve action potential from the middle finger is abnormal; and (3) posterior cord lesions are confirmed by additional axillary nerve involvement with denervation changes in the deltoid.

Treatment

Most cases of Saturday night palsies are neuropraxic, recovering within 8–12 weeks.[165] If axonal degeneration results, recovery is slower,[145] although it will eventually occur in the majority.[121] A cock-up splint for wrist drop is advised. For other causes of radial neuropathy, surgical exploration is controversial. In general, it is indicated in a few conditions associated with displaced distal spiral humeral fractures,[130] in palsies occurring after closed reduction of the fracture, and in non-recovering palsies after closed humeral fractures.

Posterior Interosseous Nerve Compression

Clinical Features

Symptoms. Patients present with partial wrist drop with or without elbow or forearm pain.[152] The onset may be acute or gradual depending on the etiology, and the extent can be partial or complete.

Physical Findings. Wrist drop is due to involvement of the extensor carpi ulnaris. It is partial since it is compensated by the extensor carpi radialis longus and brevis. This usually results in a radially deviated wrist on wrist extension testing. Extension of the digits at the metacarpophalangeal joints is impaired. There are reported cases of partial interosseous nerve palsies with selective involvement of few digits.[51] Sensory examination is normal in all cases.

Diagnostic Evaluation

X-rays of the elbow and forearm are indicated in cases of trauma and in all nontraumatic conditions to rule out space-occupying lesions. Electrodiagnostic studies can confirm the diagnosis and localize it by documenting a normal radial sensory nerve action potential and by sparing of muscles innervated by the radial nerve proximal to the posterior interosseous nerve origin.

Differential Diagnosis. One must rule out proximal radial nerve lesions (see Table 6), C7 root lesion, and C7 brachial plexus lesions (middle trunk, and posterior cord), as discussed in the preceding section. One entity that belongs in the differential diagnosis of posterior interosseous nerve palsy is resistant tennis elbow syndrome.[120] This is secondary to lateral epicondylitis or tendinitis at the origin of the forearm extensor muscles. The true frequency and etiology of the syndrome, i.e., whether it is due to posterior interosseous nerve palsy, are still controversial.[169] Unlike patients with true posterior interosseous nerve palsy, patients with the tennis elbow syndrome present with: (1) predominant pain over the lateral epicondyle; (2) greater tenderness over the lateral epicondyle than over the forearm extensors; (3) increasing pain on wrist and finger flexion with the elbow extended, rather than on forearm supination; and (4) no muscle weakness.[89]

Treatment

Surgical exploration is indicated for all patients with soft tissue masses and in some post-traumatic and idiopathic conditions, where lack of improvement (later than 12 weeks after onset) or progressive deficit occurs.

THE SUPRASCAPULAR NERVE

Anatomy

The suprascapular nerve is the first branch of the upper trunk (C5–C6) of the brachial plexus.[57] It courses beneath the trapezius in the posterior triangle of the neck and then reaches the upper border of the scapula through the scapular notch (Fig. 13).[141] The latter is a fibrosseous tunnel formed at the junction of the roof of the coracoid process and the superior border of the scapula. The transverse scapular ligament forms its roof. The nerve reaches the supraspinous fossa, innervates the supraspinatus, and gives two branches to the glenohumeral and acromioclavicular joints. It then supplies the infraspinatus muscle after entering the infraspinatus fossa by passing around the lateral margin of the scapular spine. The suprascapular nerve has no sensory cutaneous distribution.

Suprascapular Neuropathy

CLINICAL FEATURES
Etiology. Causes of suprascapular neuropathy include: (1) compression of the nerve as it passes through a shallow scapular notch. It is usually precipitated by forward motion and depression of the shoulder, causing stretching of the nerve;[79] (2) traction injury from falls which results in an increase in the acromiomastoid angle; (3) shoulder trauma with occasional selective scapular notch fractures;[147,164] and (4) rare cases of space-occupying lesions, e.g., ganglia.[47]

Symptoms and Physical Findings. Patients present with nonradiating shoulder pain that is aggravated by movements causing forced scapular protraction and external rotation of the shoulder.[81] The deficit is exclusively motor, consisting of weakness of the infraspinatus and supraspinatus muscles with resultant shoulder abduction and external rotation weakness. Local tenderness on scapular notch palpation is noted in some patients.

DIAGNOSTIC EVALUATION
X-ray of the shoulder should be performed when a history of trauma is elicited. Electrodiagnostic studies consist of comparing the supraspinatus or the infraspinatus compound muscle action potential latency to the contralateral site.[71] Needle electrodes are used for recording with percutaneous stimulation of the nerve performed at Erb's point. Electromyography will show denervation changes if axonal loss results.

Differential Diagnosis. The differential diagnosis includes ruling out: (1) C5–C6 radiculopathies, which are characterized by involvement of other C5–C6 motor and sensory functions, the presence of radiating pain in the arm originating from the neck, and the absence of pain by maneuvers that stretch the suprascapular nerve; (2) brachial plexus neuritis, which presents with shoulder pain and is usually associated with additional muscle involvement;[132] and (3) non-neurogenic causes of shoulder pain, such as bicipital tendinitis, subacromial bursitis, acromioclavicular synovitis, and rotator cuff injury.[33] Radiographic abnormalities and absence of denervation on EMG are typical findings in the latter group.

TREATMENT
After a period of observation is allowed, surgical exploration is indicated in patients who had spontaneous palsies and are worsening. Surgery would

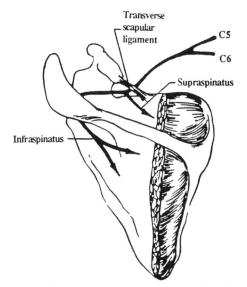

FIGURE 13. The course of the suprascapular nerve under the transverse scapular ligament, where it is subject to entrapment. (Reproduced with permission from Johnson EW (ed): Practical Electromyography. Baltimore, Williams and Wilkins, 1980, p 223.)

consist of resection of soft tissue masses, if present, or decompression with resection of the scapular ligament.[140]

THE AXILLARY NERVE

Anatomy

The axillary nerve (Fig. 14), primarily of C5–C6 derivation, is the smaller branch of the posterior cord of the brachial plexus.[57] It innervates the deltoid and teres minor muscles after descending in the quadrilateral space. This space is bound by the surgical neck of the humerus laterally, the long head of the triceps medially, the teres minor superiorly, and the teres major posteriorly. The nerve provides cutaneous innervation to a small area over the lower portion of the deltoid.

Axillary Neuropathy

CLINICAL FEATURES

Etiology.   Although the axillary nerve can rarely be compressed by hypertrophied muscles,[78] the most common etiology of an axillary neuropathy is trauma. Blunt trauma,[11] fractures of the humerus,[13] and shoulder dislocation[11] are more common causes.

Symptoms.   Patients present with a shoulder abduction weakness that can be partially compensated by other muscles.

DIAGNOSTIC EVALUATION

X-ray of the shoulder and the humerus is indicated in cases of trauma. Nerve conduction study will reveal a prolonged latency and/or a decreased

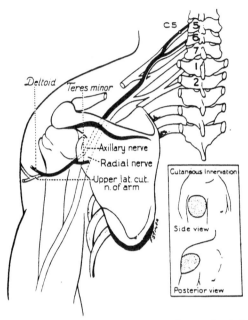

FIGURE 14. The axillary nerve. The nerve is a small branch of the posterior cord of the brachial plexus. The cutaneous branch and its innervation are shown respectively in stipple and in the inset. (Reproduced with permission from Haymaker W, Woodhall B: Peripheral Nerve Injuries. Philadelphia, W. B. Saunders, 1945, p 148.)

compound muscle action potential amplitude, stimulating at Erb's point and recording from the deltoid.[83] Denervation changes are noted in axonal loss lesions.

Differential Diagnosis. C5 radiculopathies, C5 upper trunk, and posterior cord plexopathies are ruled out by additional motor and sensory involvement.

TREATMENT

Depending on the etiology, surgical exploration consisting of decompression, neurolysis, or nerve graft is indicated in patients who are not improving.[135] Poor prognosis has been reported in some of the stretch injuries.[85]

THE MUSCULOCUTANEOUS NERVE / LATERAL CUTANEOUS NERVE OF THE FOREARM

Anatomy

The musculocutaneous nerve (Fig. 15) is a branch of the lateral cord (C5–C6) of the brachial plexus.[57] After crossing the inferior border of the pectoralis minor, it pierces the coracobrachialis and then lies in a septum between the brachialis and the biceps muscles, where it innervates them. About 3 cm above the elbow, the nerve pierces the fascia and continues subcutaneously as the lateral cutaneous nerve of the forearm, supplying the skin over the radial aspect of the forearm.

Musculocutaneous Neuropathy

CLINICAL FEATURES
Etiology. Isolated neuropathy of this nerve is very rare. It has been reported after heavy exercise, assumed to be secondary to coracobrachialis hypertrophy.[16] Trauma causing traction injury of the shoulder,[108] or stretch injury of the nerve can, rarely, result in musculocutaneous palsy.[40] Entrapment of the lateral cutaneous nerve of the forearm has been reported by Nunley,[124] occurring secondary to compression by the lateral edge of the biceps aponeurosis.

Symptoms and Physical Findings. Patients present with weak elbow flexion, weak forearm supination, and a longitudinal band of sensory loss over the radial forearm region. When only the lateral cutaneous nerve is affected, patients present with isolated sensory findings and elbow pain exacerbated by extension.

DIAGNOSTIC EVALUATION
Nerve conduction and EMG studies establish the isolated nature of the lesion and rule out other nerve involvement.[83] In cases of trauma, x-ray of the shoulder and the humerus should be performed.

Differential Diagnosis. A C5–C6 radiculopathy and an upper trunk plexopathy are ruled out by additional motor involvement and sensory deficit.

TREATMENT
Surgical intervention is indicated in cases of non-recovering palsies after conservative measures have failed.[124]

THE LONG THORACIC NERVE

Anatomy
The long thoracic nerve is an exclusively motor nerve formed by the union of the branches of C5,C6 and C7 roots. It courses behind the clavicle, entering the axilla, and descending along the thoracic wall to supply the serratus anterior (Fig. 16).

Long Thoracic Neuropathy

CLINICAL FEATURES
Etiology. Long thoracic neuropathy is mainly secondary to trauma causing traction or stretch injury of the nerve.[52,58] It may occur spontaneously or idiopathically.[6] It is frequently involved in the brachial plexus neuritis syndrome.[132]

Symptoms and Physical Findings. Patients present with scapular winging barely noted at rest. It is more pronounced during forward flexion of the extended arm, due to poor fixation of the scapula to the thorax.

DIAGNOSTIC EVALUATION
Nerve conduction of the long thoracic nerve consists of stimulating the nerve at Erb's point and recording over the serratus anterior between the anterior and mid-axillary lines over the fifth rib.[134] Compound muscle action potential parameter abnormalities and EMG evidence of denervation localize the lesion.

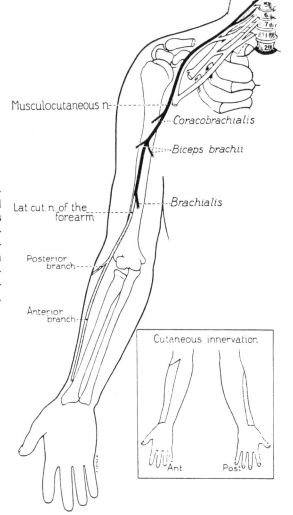

FIGURE 15. The musculocutaneous nerve course and branches. The lateral cutaneous nerve of the forearm is a continuation of the nerve. (Reproduced with permission from Haymaker W, Woodhall B: Peripheral Nerve Injuries. Philadelphia, W. B. Saunders, 1945, p 152.)

Differential Diagnosis.   Very few entities have similar presentation. Spinal accessory neuropathy causing scapular winging can be differentiated by other characteristic physical findings (see next section). In brachial plexus neuritis, the long thoracic nerve is commonly affected in addition to other parts of the brachial plexus.

TREATMENT
Conservative treatment usually results in good recovery in the traction-induced neuropathies.[58] Surgery is indicated for post-traumatic, non-improving conditions.[52]

THE SPINAL ACCESSORY NERVE

Anatomy
This nerve (cranial nerve XI) originates from spinal cord segments C1, C2,

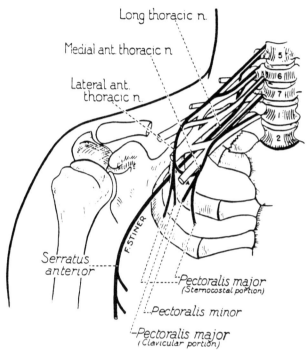

FIGURE 16. Origin and course of the long thoracic nerve. The nerve supplies the serratus anterior only. Anterior thoracic nerves are also shown in this illustration. (Reproduced with permission from Haymaker W, Woodhall B: Peripheral Nerve Injuries. Philadelphia, W. B. Saunders, 1945, p 139.)

C3, and C4.[57] After uniting, it ascends through the foramen magnum and exits through the jugular foramen to supply the sternocleidomastoid and the trapezius. Before it innervates the trapezius muscles, it lies superficially in the posterior neck triangle, covered only by subcutaneous tissue and skin (Fig. 17).

Spinal Accessory Neuropathy

CLINICAL FEATURES

Etiology.   In addition to its entrapment at the base of the skull by various pathologies such as tumor, trauma, or infection, the most common site of injury is in the posterior neck triangle, where the nerve lies superficially. Injury is primarily iatrogenic, complicating routine surgeries such as lymph node dissection.[77] This results only in trapezius weakness, since the nerve is injured distal to the sternocleidomastoid branch.

Symptoms and Physical Findings.   Patients present with weakness of shoulder elevation, scapular winging accentuated by arm abduction, and drooping of the shoulder. A late manifestation is loss of shoulder contour with prominence of the supraclavicular fossa.

DIAGNOSTIC EVALUATION

Spinal accessory nerve conduction is easily accessible to percutaneous stim-

POSTERIOR TRIANGLE OF NECK

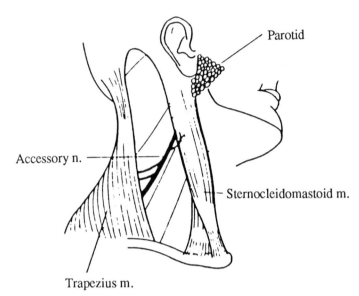

Parotid

Accessory n.

Sternocleidomastoid m.

Trapezius m.

FIGURE 17. Course of the spinal accessory nerve in the posterior neck triangle. Note its superficial location, where it is subject to iatrogenic injuries. (Reproduced with permission from Goodgold J: Anatomical Correlates of Clinical Electromyography, 2nd ed. Baltimore, William & Wilkins, 1984, p 13.)

ulation with surface recording made from the upper trapezius muscle.[25] Comparison of the compound muscle action potential amplitude to the contralateral site, as well as EMG of the muscle determine respectively the amount and presence of axonal loss.

Differential Diagnosis. The diagnosis is easily established when a prior surgical procedure at the posterior triangle of the neck has been performed. In cases of isolated monoscapular winging, one should differentiate this lesion from serratus anterior palsy, which is characterized by the nature and accentuation of scapular winging on shoulder motion testing (i.e., absent at rest and more pronounced with forward flexion of the extended arm than arm abduction).

TREATMENT

Although the nerve is sometimes sacrificed in radical neck dissection, its dysfunction causes discomfort and limitation of motion at the shoulder joint. Conservative treatment is recommended initially: the patient should be advised to wear supportive slings. Surgery, including nerve suture, has been described for some cases.[24]

THE DIGITAL NERVES

Digital Neuropathy

The digital nerves are the terminal sensory branches of the median, ulnar, and radial nerves (Fig. 18). Digital neuropathy is due to intrinsic entrapment

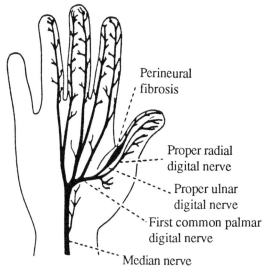

Perineural fibrosis

Proper radial digital nerve

Proper ulnar digital nerve

First common palmar digital nerve

Median nerve

FIGURE 18. Diagram of the digital nerves. Perineural fibrosis of the ulnar digital nerve is shown. (Reproduced with permission from Minkow and Bassett: Clin Orthop 83:116, 1972.)

of the digital nerves by space-occupying lesions,[28] or to extrinsic causes, such as external compression secondary to occupational habits.[8,109] Laceration injuries are, however, much more common causes than compression.[28] Patients present solely with sensory complaints, including dysesthesias and sensory loss. Electrodiagnosis helps in establishing the diagnosis by comparing the sensory nerve action potential at the involved site to the contralateral one. Treatment consists of instructing the patient to avoid external pressure in occupational conditions. However, treatment is mainly surgical for post-traumatic cases such as lacerations and for spontaneously occurring neuropathies to rule out space-occupying lesions.[174]

REFERENCES

1. Aguayo A, Nair CPV, Midgley R: Experimental progressive compression neuropathy in the rabbit. Arch Neurol 24:358, 1971.
2. Aminoff MJ: Involvement of peripheral vasomotor fibers in carpal tunnel syndrome. J Neurol Neurosurg Psychiatry 42:649, 1979.
3. Aminoff MJ: Electromyography in Clinical Practice: Electrodiagnostic Aspects of Neuromuscular Diseases, 2nd ed. New York, Churchill Livingstone, 1987.
4. Anderson MH, Fullerton PM, Gilliatt RW, Hern JEC: Changes in the forearm associated with median nerve compression at the wrist in the guinea pig. J Neurol Neurosurg Psychiatry 33:70, 1970.
5. Barber KW Jr, Blanco AJ Jr, Soule EK Jr: Benign extraneural soft-tissue tumors of the extremities causing compression of nerves. J Bone Joint Surg 34B:391, 1952.
6. Bassam BA, Meyer MD, Canado JA: Recurrent idiopathic serratus anterior palsy. Muscle Nerve 10:663, 1987.
7. Behse, F, Buchthal F, Carlsen F, Krappeis GG: Hereditary neuropathy with liability to pressure palsies: Electrophysiological and histopathological aspects. Brain 95:777, 1972.
8. Belsky MR, Millender LH: Bowler's thumb in a baseball player: A case report. Orthopedics 3:122, 1980.
9. Benecke R, Conrad B: The value of electrophysiological examination of the flexor carpi ulnaris in the diagnosis of ulnar nerve lesions at the elbow. J Neurol 223:207, 1980.
10. Bennett JB, Crouch CC: Compression syndrome of the recurrent motor branch of the median nerve. J Hand Surg 7:407, 1982.
11. Berry H, Bril V: Axillary nerve palsy following blunt trauma to the shoulder region: A clinical and electrophysiological review. J Neurol Neurosurg Psychiatry 45:1027, 1985.

12. Bleecker ML, Bohlman M, Moreland R, Tipton A: Carpal tunnel syndrome: Role of carpal tunnel size. Neurology 35:1599, 1985.
13. Blom S, Dahlback LD: Nerve injuries in dislocations of the shoulder joint and fractures of the neck of the humerus: A clinical and electromyographical study. Acta Chir Scand 136:461, 1970.
14. Bolton CF, McFarlane RM: Human pneumatic tourniquet paralysis. Neurology 28:787, 1978.
15. Bowen TL, Stone RH: Posterior interosseous nerve paralysis caused by a ganglion at the elbow. J Bone Joint Surg 48B:774, 1966.
16. Braddom R, Wolfe C: Musculocutaneous nerve injury after heavy exercise. Arch Phys Med Rehab 59:290, 1978.
17. Brelsford KL, Uematsu S: Thermographic presentation of cutaneous sensory and vasomotor activity in the injured peripheral nerve. J Neurosurg 62:711, 1985.
18. Brody AS, Leffert RD, Smith RJ: Technical problems with ulnar nerve transposition at the elbow: Findings and results of reoperation. J Hand Surg 3:85, 1978.
19. Brown WF: Ulnar neuropathies. In controversies in entrapment neuropathies (Course D). Seventh Annual Continuing Educational Course. American Association of Electromyography and Electrodiagnosis. Kansas City, 1984, p 23.
20. Brown WF, Kates SK: The quantitative assessment of conduction block in human entrapment neuropathies synopsia. Seventh International Congress of Electromyography, Munich, 1983. Electroencephalography and Clinical Neurophysiology, Vol 56, 1983.
21. Campbell WW, Pridgeon RM, Leahy M, Crostic G: Sparing of the flexor carpi ulnaris in ulnar neuropathy at the elbow. Muscle Nerve 10:652, 1987.
22. Checkles NS, Russokov AD, Piero DL: Ulnar nerve conduction velocity—effect of elbow position on measurement. Arch Phys Med Rehab 52:362, 1971.
23. Cherington M: Proximal pain in carpal tunnel syndrome. Arch Surg 108:69, 1974.
24. Cherington M, Hendec R, Roland R: Accessory nerve palsy. A painful cranial neuropathy: Surgical cure. Headache 18:274, 1978.
25. Cherington M: Accessory nerve conduction studies. Arch Neurol 18:708, 1968.
26. Childress HM: Recurrent ulnar nerve dislocation at the elbow. J Bone Joint Surg 38A:978, 1956.
27. Daube JR: Percutaneous palmar median nerve stimulation for carpal tunnel syndrome. Electroencephalogr Clin Neurophysiol 43:139, 1977.
28. Dewson DM, Hallett M, Millender LH: Entrapment Neuropathies. Boston, Little, Brown and Co., 1983.
29. Dekel S, Coates R: Primary carpal stenosis as a cause of "idiopathic" carpal tunnel syndrome. Lancet 2:1024, 1979.
30. Denny-Brown D, Brenner C: Lesion in peripheral nerve resulting from compression by spring clip. Arch Neurol Psychiatry 52:1, 1944.
31. Denny-Brown D, Brenner C: Paralysis of nerve induced by direct pressure and by tourniquet. Arch Neurol Psychiatry 51:1, 1944.
32. Dobyns J, Linschied R: Fracture and dislocation of the wrist. In Reckwood CA Jr, Green DP (eds): Fractures, Vol. 1. Philadelphia, J. B. Lippincott, 1975.
33. Donovan WH, Kraft GH: Rotator cuff tear versus suprascapular nerve injury—a problem in differential diagnosis. Arch Phys Med Rehab 55:424, 1974.
34. Downie AW, Scott TR: An improved technique for radial nerve conduction studies. J Neurol Neurosurg Psychiatry 30:332, 1967.
35. Eaton R, Crowe JF, Parkes JC: Anterior transposition of the ulnar nerve using a non-compressing fasciodermal sling. J Bone Joint Surg 62A:820, 1980.
36. Ebeling P, Gilliott RW, Thomas PK: The clinical and electrical study of ulnar nerve lesion in the hand. J Neurol Neurosurg Psychiatry 23:1, 1960.
37. Eckman PB, Perlstein G, Altrocchi PH: Ulnar neuropathy in bicycle riders. Arch Neurol 32:130, 1975.
38. Eisen A, Danon J: The mild cubital tunnel syndrome: Its natural history and indications for surgical intervention. Neurology 24:608, 1974.
39. Eisen A: Early diagnosis of ulnar nerve palsy: An electrophysiological study. Neurology 24:256, 1974.
40. Ewing MR: Postoperative paralysis in the upper extremity. Lancet 1:99, 1950.
41. Fearn CBD, Goodfellow JW: Anterior interosseous nerve palsy. J Bone Joint Surg 47B:91–93, 1965.
42. Feindel W, Stratford J: The role of the cubital tunnel in tardy ulnar palsy. Can J Surg 1:287, 1958.

43. Feindel W, Stratford J: Cubital tunnel compression in tardy ulnar palsy. Can Med Assoc J 78:351, 1958.
44. Frohse LE, Frankel M: Die Muskeln menschlichen Armes. Jena, G. Fischer, 1908.
45. Fullerton PM, Gilliatt RW: Pressure neuropathy in the hind foot of the guinea pig. J Neurol Neurosurg Psychiatry 30:18, 1967.
46. Fullerton PM, Gilliatt RW: Median and ulnar neuropathy in the guinea pig. J Neurol Neurosurg Psychiatry 30:393, 1967.
47. Ganzhorn R, et al: Suprascapular nerve entrapment: A case report. J. Bone Joint Surg 63A:492, 1981.
48. Gardner-Thrope C: Anterior interosseous nerve palsy: Spontaneous recovery in two patients. J Neurol Neurosurg Psychiatry 37:1146, 1974.
49. Gelberman RH, Hergenroeder PT, Hargens AR: The carpal tunnel syndrome: A study of carpal canal pressures. J Bone Joint Surg 63A:380, 1981.
50. Gilliatt RW, LeQuesne PM, Logue V, Sumner AJ: Wasting of the hand associated with a cervical rib or band. J Neurol Neurosurg Psychiatry 33:615, 1970.
51. Goldman S, Honet JC, Sobel R, Goldstein AS: Posterior interosseous nerve palsy in the absence of trauma. Arch Neurol 21:435, 1969.
52. Gonza ER, Harris WR: Traumatic winging of the scapula. J Bone Surg 61A:1230, 1979.
53. Goodgold J, Elberstein A: Electrodiagnosis of Neuromuscular Disease, 3rd ed. Baltimore, Williams and Wilkins, 1983.
54. Goodwill CJ: The carpal tunnel syndrome: Long term follow-up showing relation of latency measurements to response to treatment. Ann Phys Med 8:12, 1965.
55. Gore D, Larson S: Medical epicondylectomy for subluxing ulnar nerve. Am J Surg 111:851, 1966.
56. Gould JS, Wissinger HA: Carpal tunnel syndrome in pregnancy. South Med J 771:144, 1978.
57. Gray H: In William PL, Warwick R (eds): Gray's Anatomy, 36th British ed. New York, Churchill Livingstone, 1980.
58. Gregg JR, Labosky D, Harty M et al: Serratus anterior paralysis in the young athlete. J Bone Joint Surg 61A:825, 1979.
59. Griffiths JC: Nerve injuries after plating of forearm bones. Br Med J 2:277, 1966.
60. Gutmann L: Median-ulnar nerve communication and carpal tunnel syndrome. J Neurol Neurosurg Psychiatry 40:982, 1977.
61. Hartz CR, Linscheid RL, Gramse RR, et al: The pronator teres syndrome: Compression neuropathy of the median nerve. J Bone Joint Surg 63A:885, 1981.
62. Hill NA, Howard FM, Huffer BR: The incomplete anterior interosseous nerve syndrome. J Hand Surg 10A:4, 1985.
63. Hortigan JD: The dangerous wheelchair. J Am Geriatr Soc 30:572, 1981.
64. Howard FM: Ulnar nerve palsy in wrist fractures. J Bone Joint Surg 43A:1197, 1961.
65. Jabre J: Ulnar nerve lesions at the wrist: New techniques for recording from the sensory dorsal branch of the ulnar nerve. Neurology 30:873, 1980.
66. Jabre J, Wilbourn AJ: The EMG findings in 100 consecutive ulnar neuropathies. Acta Neurol Scand 60(Suppl 73):91, 1979.
67. Jebsen RH: Motor conduction velocity in proximal and distal segments of the radial nerve. Arch Phys Med Rehab 47:597, 1966.
68. Jenkins SA: Osteoarthritis of the pisiform-triquetrial joint: Report of three cases. J Bone Joint Surg 33B:532, 1951.
69. Johnson RK, Spinner M, Shrewsbury MM: Median nerve entrapment in the proximal forearm. J Hand Surg 4:48, 1979.
70. Jones RE, Gauntt C: Medial epicondylectomy for ulnar nerve compression at the elbow. Clin Orthop 139:174, 1979.
71. Khalili AA: Neuromuscular electrodiagnostic studies in entrapment neuropathy of the suprascapular nerve. Orthop Rev 3:27, 1974.
72. Kiloh L, Nevin S: Isolated neuritis of the anterior interosseous nerve. Br Med J 1:850, 1952.
73. Kimura J: A method for determining median nerve conduction velocity across the carpal tunnel. J Neurol Sci 38:1, 1978.
74. Kimura J: The carpal tunnel syndrome: Localization of conduction abnormalities within the distal segment of the median nerve. Brain 102:619, 1979.
75. Kimura J. Electrodiagnosis in Diseases of Nerve and Muscle: Principles and Practice. Philadelphia, F.A. Davis, 1983.
76. Kincaid JC, Phillips LH, Daube JR: The evaluation of suspected ulnar neuropathy at the elbow: Normal conduction study values. Arch Neurol 43:44, 1986.

77. King RJ, Molta G: Iatrogenic spinal accessory nerve palsy. Am R Coll Surg Engl 65:35, 1983.
78. Kirby JR, Kraft GH: Entrapment neuropathy of the anterior branch of axillary nerve, report of a case. Arch Phys Med Rehab 53:338, 1972.
79. Klein LJ: Suprascapular entrapment neuropathy. J Neurosurg 43:337, 1975.
80. Kleinert HE, Cole NM, Wayne L, et al: Posttraumatic sympathetic dystrophy. Orthop Clin North Am 4:917, 1973.
81. Kopell HP, Thompson WAL: Pain and frozen shoulder. Surg Gynecol Obstet 109:92, 1959.
82. Kopell HP, Thompson WAL: Peripheral entrapment neuropathies. Huntington, NY, Robert E. Krieger, 1976, 113.
83. Kraft GH: Axillary, musculocutaneous, and suprascapular nerve latency studies. Arch Phys Med Rehab 53:383, 1972.
84. Krag C: Isolated paralysis of the flexor pollicis longus muscle. Scand J Plast Reconstr Surg 8:250, 1974.
85. Leffert RD, Seddon H: Infraclavicular brachial plexus injuries. J Bone Joint Surg 47B:9, 1965.
86. Lichter RL, Jacobsen T: Tardy palsy of the posterior interosseous nerve with a Monteggia fracture. J Bone Joint Surg 57A:124, 1975.
87. Linscheid RL: Injuries to the radial nerve at the wrist. Arch Surg 91:942, 1965.
88. Lippman SM, Kimura I, Ayyar DR: Ulnar sensory conduction across the elbow in tardy ulnar palsy. Neurology 33(Suppl 2):197, 1983.
89. Lister GD, Belsole RB, Kleinert HE: The radial tunnel syndrome. J Hand Surg 4:52, 1979.
90. Long EW, Wolfgang JW: Serial stimulation of the median nerve across the carpal canal. Muscle Nerve 6:528, 1983.
91. Loong SC: The carpal tunnel syndrome: A clinical and electrophysiological study of 250 patients. Proc Aust Assoc Neurol 14:51, 1977.
92. Lotem M, Fried A, Levy M et al: Radial palsy following muscular effort. J Bone Joint Surg 53B:500, 1971.
93. Ma DM, Kraft GH, Wilbourn AJ: Unusual sensory conduction studies: Techniques. (AAEE Workshop) American Association of Electromyography and Electrodiagnosis. Rochester, Minnesota, 1984.
94. MacDonald RI, Lichtman DM, Hanlon JJ, Wilson JN: Complications of surgical release for carpal tunnel syndrome. J Hand Surg 3:70, 1978.
95. MacDougal B, Weeks PM, Wray RC Jr: Median nerve compression and trigger finger in mucopolysaccharidoses and related diseases. Plast Reconstr Surg 53:260, 1977.
96. Mangini U: Flexor pollicis longus muscle. Its morphology and clinical significance. J Bone Joint Surg 42A:467, 1960.
97. Mannerfelt L, Norman O: Attrition rupture of flexor tendons in rheumatoid arthritis caused by bony spurs in the carpal tunnel. J Bone Joint Surg 51B:270, 1969.
98. Marinacci AA: The value of electromyogram in the diagnosis of pressure neuropathy from "hanging arm". Electromyogr Clin Neurophysiol 7:5, 1967.
99. Marmor L, Lawrence JF, Dubois E: Posterior interosseous nerve paralysis due to rheumatoid arthritis. J Bone Joint Surg 49A:981, 1967.
100. Marotte LR: An electron microscope study of chronic median nerve compression in the guinea pig. Acta Neuropathol 27:69, 1974.
101. Marquis JW, Bruwer AJ, Keith HM: Supracondyloid process of the humerus. Proc Staff Meet Mayo Clin 32:691, 1957.
102. Massey EW, Pleet BA: Handcuffs and cheiralgia paresthetica. Neurology 28:1312, 1978.
103. McGowan AJ: The results of transposition of the ulnar nerve for traumatic ulnar neuritis. J Bone Joint Surg 32B:293, 1950.
104. Meier C, Moll C: Hereditary neuropathy with liability to pressure palsies. J Neurol Sci 47:385, 1980.
105. Melvin JL, Johnson EW, Duran R: Electrodiagnosis after surgery for the carpal tunnel syndrome. Arch Phys Med Rehab 49:502, 1968.
106. Miller RG, Camp PE: Postoperative ulnar neuropathy. JAMA 242:1636, 1979.
107. Miller RG: The cubital tunnel syndrome: Diagnosis and precise localization. Ann Neurol 6:56, 1979.
108. Milton GW: The mechanism of circumflex and other nerve injuries in dislocation of the shoulder, and the possible mechanism of nerve injuries during reduction of dislocation. Aust J Surg 23:25, 1953.
109. Minkow FV, Bassett FH: Bowler's thumb. Clin Orthop 83:115, 1972.
110. Moon N, Marmor L: Parosteal lipoma of the proximal part of the radius. J Bone Joint Surg 46A:608, 1964.
111. Morin JE, Long R, Elleker MG, Eisen A: Upper extremity neuropathies following median sternotomy. Ann Thorac Surg 34:181, 1982.

112. Morris AH: Irreducible Monteggia lesion with radial nerve entrapment. J Bone Joint Surg 56A:1744, 1974.
113. Morris HH, Peters BH: Pronator syndrome: Clinical and electrophysiological features in seven cases. J Neurol Neurosurg Psychiatry 39:461, 1976.
114. Mulder DW, Lambert EH, Bastron JA: The neuropathies associated with diabetes melitus. Neurology 11:275, 1961.
115. Muntz HH, Coonrad RW, Murchison RA: Rifle-sling palsy. US Armed Forces Med J 6:353, 1955.
116. Murphy EL: Observations on craft palsies. Trans Assoc Industr Med Offrs 5:113, 1955.
117. Murray IPC, Simpson IA: Acroparaesthesia in myxoedema: A clinical and electromyographic study. Lancet 1:1360, 1958.
118. Nakano KK, Lundergan C, Okihoro MM: Anterior interosseous nerve syndromes. Arch Neurol 34:477, 1977.
119. Nakano R: Entrapment neuropathies in rheumatoid arthritis. Orthop Clin North Am 6:243, 1975.
120. Narakas A: Epicondylite et syndrome compressif du nerf. Radial Med Hyg (Geneve) 1129:2067, 1974.
121. Negrin P, Fardin P: The electromyographic prognosis of traumatic paralysis of radial nerve: Study of its myelinic and axonal damage. Electromyogr Clin Neurophysiol 24:481, 1984.
122. Nicholas GG, Noone RB, Graham WP: Carpal tunnel syndrome in pregnancy. Hand 3:80, 1971.
123. Nielson HO: Posterior interosseous nerve paralysis caused by fibrous band compression at the supinator muscle: A report of four cases. Acta Orthop Scand 47:301, 1976.
124. Nunley JA, Bassett FH: Compression of the musculocutaneous nerve at the elbow. J Bone Joint Surg 64A:1050, 1982.
125. Ochoa J, Fowler TJ, Billiatt RW: Anatomical changes in peripheral nerves compressed by pneumatic tourniquet. J Anat 113:433, 1972.
126. Ochoa J, Marotte L: The nature of the lesion caused by chronic entrapment in the guinea pig. J Neurol Sci 19:491, 1973.
127. O'Duffy JD, Randall RV, MacCarty CS: Median neuropathy (carpal-tunnel syndrome) in acromegaly: A sign of endocrine overactivity. Ann Intern Med 78:379, 1973.
128. Okudote K, Elsen A: An electrophysiological quantitation of the cubital tunnel syndrome. Can J Neurol Sci 6:403, 1979.
129. Olney RK, Wilbourn AJ, Miller RG: Ulnar neuropathies at or distal to the wrist. Neurology 33(Suppl 2):815, 1983.
130. Packer JW, Foster RR, Garcia A, Granthan SA: The humeral fracture with radial nerve palsy. Is exploration warranted? Clin Orthop 88:34, 1972.
131. Panas P: Sur une cause peu conue de paralysis du nerf cubital. Arch Gen Med 2:5, 1878.
132. Parsonage MJ, Turner JW: Neuralgic amyotrophy: The shoulder girdle syndrome. Lancet 1:973, 1948.
133. Payan J: Electrophysiological localization of ulnar nerve lesions. J Neurol Neurosurg Psychiatry 32:208, 1969.
134. Petrera JE, Trojaborg W: Conduction studies of the long thoracic nerve in serratus anterior palsy of different etiology. Neurology 34:1033, 1984.
135. Petrucci FS, Morelli A, Raimondi PL: Axillary nerve injuries—21 cases treated by nerve graft and neuroloysis. J Hand Surg 7:271, 1982.
136. Phalen GS: The carpal tunnel syndrome. Clin Orthop 83:29, 1978.
137. Phalen GS: Reflections on 21 years' experience with the carpal tunnel syndrome. JAMA 212:1365, 1970.
138. Phalen GS: The carpal tunnel syndrome. Seventeen years experience in diagnosis and treatment of 654 hands. J Bone Joint Surg 48A:211, 1966.
139. Platt H: The pathogenesis and treatment of traumatic neuritis of the ulnar nerve in the postcondylar groove. Br J Surg 13:409, 1926.
140. Rask MR: Suprascapular nerve entrapment: A report of two cases treated with suprascapular notch resection. Clin Orthop 123:73, 1977.
141. Rengachary SS, Neft JP, Singer PA, Bracket EE: Suprascapular nerve entrapment neuropathy: A clinical anatomical and comparative study. Neurosurgery 5:441, 1979.
142. Richmond DA: Carpal ganglion with ulnar nerve compression. J Bone Joint Surg 45B:13, 1963.
143. Roth G, Ludy JP, Engloff-Baer S: Isolated proximal median neuropathy. Muscle Nerve 5:247, 1982.
144. Seyffarth H: Primary myoses in the M. pronator teres as cause of lesion of the N. medianus (the pronator syndrome). Acta Psychiatr Scand 74(Suppl):251, 1951.

145. Shah JJ, Bhatti NA: Radial nerve paralysis associated with fractures of the humerus. Clin Orthop 172:171, 1983.
146. Shea JD, McClain EJ: Ulnar nerve compression at and below the wrist. J Bone Joint Surg 51A:1095, 1969.
147. Solheim LF, Roaas A: Compression of the suprascapular nerve after fracture of the scapular notch. Acta Orthop Scand 443:338, 1978.
148. Solnitzky O: Pronator syndrome: Compression neuropathy of the median nerve at level of pronator teres muscle. Georgetown Med Bull 13:232, 1960.
149. Spinner M: Injuries to the Major Branches of Peripheral Nerves of the Forearm. Philadelphia, W. B. Saunders, 1972.
150. Spinner M: The anterior interosseous nerve syndrome: With special attention to its variations. J Bone Joint Surg 52A:84, 1970.
151. Spinner M, Schrieber SN: Anterior interosseous nerve paralysis as a complication of supracondylar fractures of the humerus in children. J Bone Joint Surg 51A:1584, 1969.
152. Spinner S: The arcade of Frohse and its relationship to posterior interosseous nerve paralysis. J Bone Joint Surg 50B:809, 1968.
153. Staal A, De Weerdt CJ, Went LN: Hereditary compression syndrome of peripheral nerves. Neurology 15:1008, 1965.
154. Steiger RN, Larrick RB, Meyer TL: Median nerve entrapment following elbow dislocation in children. J Bone Joint Surg 51A:381, 1969.
155. Stevens KC: The electrodiagnosis of carpal tunnel syndrome (AAEE minimonograph #26). American Association of Electromyography and Electrodiagnosis. Rochester, Minnesota, 1987.
156. Stewart JD, Eisen A: Tinel's sign and the carpal tunnel syndrome. Br Med J 2:1125, 1978.
157. Sunderland S: Nerve lesion in the carpal tunnel syndrome. J Neurol Neurosurg Psychiatry 39:615, 1976.
158. Sunderland S: Nerves and Nerve Injuries. Edinburgh, Churchill Livingstone, 1978.
159. Sunderland S: Traumatic injuries of peripheral nerves. I. Simple compression injuries of the radial nerve. Brain 68:58, 1945.
160. Taleisnik J: Palmar cutaneous brand of the median nerve. J Bone Joint Surg 55A:1213, 1973.
161. Tanzer RC: The carpal tunnel syndrome: A clinical and anatomical study. J Bone Joint Surg 41A:626, 1959.
162. Terry RJ: A study of the supracondyloid process in the living. Am J Phys Anthropol 4:129, 1921.
163. Thomas JE, Lambert EH, Cseuz KA: Electrodiagnostic aspects of the carpal tunnel syndrome. Arch Neurol 16:635, 1967.
164. Toon TN, Bravois M, Guillen M: Suprascapular nerve injury following trauma to the shoulder. J Trauma 21:652, 1981.
165. Trojaborg W: Rate of recovery in motor and sensory fibers of the radial nerve: Clinical and electrophysiological aspects. J Neurol Neurosurg Psychiatry 33:625, 1970.
166. Trojaborg W, Sindrup EH: Motor and sensory conduction in different segments of the radial nerve in normal subjects. J Neurol Neurosurg Psychiatry 32:354, 1969.
167. Uematsu S: Thermographic imaging of cutaneous sensory segments in patients with peripheral nerve injury. J Neurosurg 62:716, 1985.
168. Vanderpool DW et al: Peripheral compression lesions of the ulnar nerve. J Bone Joint Surg 50B:792, 1968.
169. Van Rossum J, Buruma OJS, Komphuisen HAC et al: Tennis elbow—a radial tunnel syndrome? J Bone Joint Surg 60B:197, 1978.
170. Vichare NA: Spontaneous paralysis of the anterior interosseous nerve. J Bone Joint Surg 50B:806, 1968.
171. Warren JD: Anterior interosseous nerve palsy as a complication of forearm fractures. J Bone Joint Surg 45B:511, 1963.
172. Wilbourn AJ, Lambert E: The forearm median to ulnar nerve communication: Electrodiagnostic aspects. Neurology 86:368, 1976.
173. Wilbourn AJ: Ulnar neuropathies. In basic electrophysiologic testing in mononeuropathy (Course A). American Association of Electromyography and Electrodiagnosis. Las Vegas, p 27, 1985.
174. Wilgis EPS, Maxwell GP: Distal nerve grafts: Clinical and anatomical studies. J Hand Surg 4:439, 1979.
175. Wilson DH, Krout R: Surgery of ulnar neuropathy at the elbow: Sixteen cases treated by decompression without transposition. J Neurosurg 38:780, 1973.
176. Yanagushi DM, Lipscomb PR, Soule EH: Carpal tunnel syndrome. Minn Med 48:22, 1965.

WILLIAM T. COULDWELL, MD
MARTIN H. WEISS, MD

LEG RADICULAR PAIN AND SENSORY DISTURBANCE
The Differential Diagnosis

From the Department of Neurosurgery, University of Southern California School of Medicine, Los Angeles, California

Reprint requests to:
Martin H. Weiss, MD
Department of Neurosurgery
1200 N. State St., Ste. 5046
Los Angeles, CA 90033

Radicular leg pain associated with low back pain is a costly and ubiquitous problem. Lumbar disc prolapse is an endemic disease associated with bipedal ambulation, and was an ailment described in antiquity. Even in the primitive era, sciatica was depicted as an "evil display of Demon Magic."[40] By fifth century Greece, leg radicular pain was widely recognized but etiologies were speculative. Caelius Aurelianus, the Roman State intellectual, had recognized numerous causes of sciatica, including falls, lifting objects, digging in ground, or "engaging in immoderate sexual intercourse." One of his more interesting conjectures was the precipitation of sciatica with the "termination of hemorrhoidal bleeding, especially in the sexually active young male."[40] As recently as the first third of the twentieth century, the etiology of many of the low back pain and sciatica syndromes remained obscure.[36] It was not until the landmark paper of Mixter and Barr[33] that the anatomical basis for the overwhelming majority of cases of leg radicular pain—the prolapsed nucleus pulposus with nerve root impingement—was recognized based on direct surgical observation. Since this milestone work, there has been a litany of different reported etiologies of radicular leg pain.

It is estimated that 80% of people will experience low back pain (LBP or lumbago) at some time in their lifetimes; Harod has speculated that 35% of these will develop associated sciatica. In consideration of such a prevalent condition, it behooves all physicians to be familiar with the more common etiologies. Often this symptom complex is wrongly attributed to a herniated disc when other more important pathologic entities are overlooked which may have been differentiated clinically. It must be remembered that segmental pain and sensory disturbances may originate from pathology anywhere along the sensory pathway from spinal cord to peripheral nerve. In this chapter we present a rational and convenient classification of the causes of segmental sensory disturbance and radicular pain in the lower extremity, and outline some of the salient clinical features.

It is intuitively easiest to consider the etiology of radicular pain and sensory disturbance from an anatomical standpoint; thus the classification devised follows this scheme (Table 1).

SPONDYLOGENIC ORIGINS

The most common source of radicular symptoms is spondylogenic (i.e., arising from the axial skeleton and supporting structures). It follows logically that it is perhaps best characterized with respect to the etiologic factors and specificity of symptoms produced. Intervertebral disc prolapse represents the single most common source of radicular symptoms with or without concomitant LBP.

DISC HERNIATION SYNDROMES

Anatomically the intervertebral disc is composed of two separate components: the central nucleus pulposus, a soft, gelatinous matrix of glycosaminoglycan surrounded by a fibrous lamellar ring, and the annulus fibrosis, which merges indiscernably with the anterior and posterior longitudinal ligaments and is firmly attached to the vertebral body endplates. This structure facilitates axial load bearing, smooth multiplanar motion, and spinal stability.[27] With aging the nucleus pulposus undergoes progressive cellular death with corresponding desiccation (87% to 70% water content) and alteration of the glycosaminoglycan profile. The annulus also degenerates, producing cracks that radiate centrifugally and result in weaknesses that predispose to nucleus prolapse.[41] As the annulus is supported posteromesially by the posterior longitudinal ligament, disc protrusion usually occurs laterally, impinging on one (occasionally two, see below) nerve roots, resulting in radicular pain and possible neurologic dysfunction. Only 30% of herniations in the lumbar region are associated with sciatica. Disc herniation itself is associated with LBP; however as an isolated source of LBP without radiation, it is difficult to diagnose clinically. Commonly intermittent backache precedes the onset of sciatica for variable periods of time, occasionally up to 6–10 years,[47] and presumably is secondary to early disc prolapse without root compromise.[4] Disc prolapse occurs most commonly between the ages of 30 and 50, the incidence decreasing in senescence as the nucleus pulposus desiccates and becomes fibrotic. Disc prolapse is rare in children; radicular symptoms in this age group should prompt a search for other causes. The clinical hallmark of discogenic disease is intermittent backache associated with radicular leg pain. This characteristic description with a long history (> 5–10 years) virtually excludes more serious pathologic causes. There is an inconsistent history of a stressful precipitating event. The L4–L5 and L5–S1 disc spaces produce 98% of all lumbar lesions requiring surgery[4] and are associated with classic sciatica ("sciatica" by strict definition refers to radicular pain radiating below the knee; elements of L4–S3 roots comprise the sciatic nerve).

TABLE 1. Etiologies of Radicular Leg Pain and Segmental Sensory Disturbance: An Anatomical Classification

MYELOGENIC
    Spinal cord tumor
        Ependymoma
        Astrocytoma
        Hemangioblastoma
    Multiple sclerosis
ROOT
    Spondylogenic
        Prolapsed disc
        Spinal stenosis
        Foraminal stenosis/lateral recess syndrome
        Ankylosing spondylitis
        Achondroplasia
        Metabolic—Paget's disease, osteoporosis, extramedullary hematopoiesis
        Bone lesion—Chordoma, chondrosarcoma, aneurysmal bone cyst, osteoma, osteogenic
            sarcoma, eosinophilic granuloma, other bone tumors, sacral cyst, infection—Pott's
            disease, discitis
    Non-bony Tumors
        Neurofibroma/schwannoma
        Meningioma
        Ependymoma
        Lipoma
        Metastasis (breast, lung, thyroid, prostate, renal cell, multiple myeloma)
    Infection/inflammation
        Herpes
        Syphilis
        Arachnoiditis
    Trauma
        Fracture-dislocation
        Epidural hematoma
    Miscellaneous
        Subarachnoid hemorrhage
        Aneurysm
        Perineural root cyst
        Extradural meningeal root cyst
PLEXUS
    Abdominal Tumor
    Endometriosis
    Appendiceal abscess/retroperitoneal infection
    Retroperitoneal hematoma
    Pelvic fracture
PERIPHERAL
    Diabetes mellitus
    Trauma
        IM Injection
        Posterior dislocated femur
        Inferior gluteal artery aneurysm
    Entrapment
        Meralgia paresthetica
        Obturator
        Pyriformis
        Common peroneal
        Tarsal tunnel
    Wartenberg's neuritis
    Tumor
MISCELLANEOUS
    Primary sciatica

The more common L5–S1 herniation classically produces buttock pain with radiation down the posterolateral aspect of the thigh and calf into the lateral foot and small toe. This description refers to a classic S1 radiculopathy produced by impingement of the S1 root by the herniated fragment during its intraspinal descent (Fig. 1). Paresthesias, if present, are considered to be superior to pain radiation in subjective localization of root level involvement. On physical examination one may find loss of lumbar lordosis, focal tenderness at the level of vertebral involvement or along the course of the sciatic nerve, atrophy or weakness of gastrocnemius and soleus, and sensory deficit in the S1 dermatomal pattern. In cases of early neurologic impairment, the ankle jerk may be lost first. An important clinical point in establishing the differential is that radicular pain from disc herniation is almost always associated with limited straight leg raising (SLR), usually worse on the involved side. Crossed SLR and Lasegue's sign are less consistently present but provide additional confirmatory evidence.

L4–L5 herniation, on the other hand, is most commonly associated with L5 root involvement and produces buttock pain radiating to the anterolateral aspect of the lower leg to the dorsum of the foot and great toe. There may be L5 dermatomal sensory loss and associated foot drop (extensor hallucis longus weakness first).

The much less common upper lumbar disc herniation is associated with anterior femoral or crural pain. There may be attendant diminution of knee jerk and quadriceps weakness. SLR in these cases is usually negative, but of potential benefit is the presence of the femoral stretch sign (extension of the hip in the lateral or prone position reproducing femoral radicular pain).

The rare central disc herniation may occur at any level from the conus medullaris to the lumbosacral junction and, in contradistinction to lateral protrusions, may have catastrophic functional consequences. It is uncommon, as the annulus is supported in its central portion by the posterior longitudinal ligament; however, in its most fulminant form, it may result in the cauda equina syndrome, with saddle anesthesia, a patulous anus, bowel/bladder and sexual dysfunction, and as such is considered a surgical emergency.

While the above discussion pertains to the common syndromes associated with disc herniation, a large lateral herniation may impact on more than one root by simultaneously affecting the root exiting the neural foramen (Fig. 1). In addition, conjoined nerve roots may produce multi-level root involvement with a singular level of disc protrusion.

Radiographic evaluation of the patient with suspected disc protrusion should commence with plain lumbosacral spine roentgenograms, which may reveal partial loss of the intervertebral space at the affected level. More importantly, however, they may disclose evidence of other pathology (metastases, osteophytes, etc.) simulating disc disease. The radiographic alternatives for the definitive diagnosis and surgical decision making include CT, myelography, and MRI. It is beyond the scope of this chapter to discuss in detail their individual merits. The favorable predictive value of myelography has been discussed extensively elsewhere.[11] Nerve root injection,[25] epidural venography,[45] and discography as diagnostic modalities have in general been superceded by present-day CT (plain or post-myelography) and MRI. Both CT and MRI have the inherent benefit of being noninvasive; CT is generally superior to MRI in defining associated bone-related pathology (e.g., foraminal stenosis), but MRI with the use of surface coils is rapidly advancing in this area and offers the advantages of direct sagittal imaging without radiation.

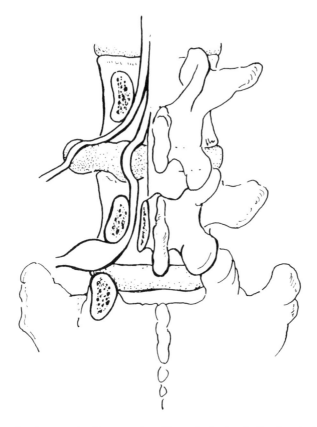

FIGURE 1.   Impingement of two roots with a single level disc herniation occurring laterally.

LUMBAR SPONDYLOSIS

Lumbar spondylosis is a general term that refers to the osteophytic formation and disc degeneration commonly seen in the elderly population.[49] It is usually pronounced at the L3–L4, L4–L5, and L5–S1 interspaces. A significant amount of disc resorption occurs with age, especially at L5–S1, and this finding in isolation may not be pathological. Typical radiographic appearances include hypertrophic changes in the posterior joints with facet enlargement, increased thickness of laminae and ligamentum flavum, and osteophyte formation, often anterior and lateral to the vertebral body. Lumbar spondylosis *per se* has no characteristic symptomatic consequences; it is the encroachment on intervertebral foramen or the spinal canal which produces symptoms. In this light, it is a confusing and ill-defined term in the literature. Root symptoms are multifactorial; mechanisms include hypertrophic osteoarthropathy or telescoping of posterior diarthrodial joints producing a decreased foraminal aperture, degenerative spondylolisthesis, and hypertrophic changes resulting in a stenotic spinal canal that causes direct cauda equina compression. Clinically the symptomatic spondylotic patient is older than the patient harboring a ruptured disc, often suffers multiple root involvement, and has *infrequent* discrete sensory, motor, or reflex changes. Attacks are more insidious in onset, often unrelenting, and of lower amplitude in severity.[15] We shall proceed with a discussion of the major coexistent symptomatic outcomes of lumbar spondylosis.

FORAMINAL ROOT COMPRESSION SYNDROME

The spondylotic spine is a major factor in the etiology of root compression at the intervertebral foramen. Anatomically the foramen size normally decreases with descent of the lumbar spine; this factor, in combination with larger size of the lower lumbar and upper sacral roots, accounts for the differential susceptibility to root compression with foraminal stenosis of the lower lumbar roots. Foraminal stenosis compresses the nerve root some distance below and lateral to the site of disc impingement (Fig. 2); an exception to this is the lateral extruded disc fragment impacting on the root at the foramen. For this reason the stenotic foramen at L5–S1 impinges on the exiting L5 root in contradistinction to the prolapsed disc which compresses the S1 root during its intraspinal descent (see Fig. 2). This is important clinically in determining the site of radicular compression, necessitating thorough radiographic evaluation at these two levels of possible involvement. The clinical history of insidious onset of multiple dermatomal levels in the spondylotic spine may suggest the syndrome. Definitive neurologic deficit is less frequent than with discogenic disease; physical examination may reveal painful lumbar torsion, extension, and lateral flexion. SLR is less consistently present than with disc herniation.

THE STENOTIC LUMBAR CANAL

There is a wide variation of spinal canal size among individuals. A congenitally narrow canal is considered to predispose to symptomatic stenosis with osteophytic compromise in aging. Spondyloarthrosis and degenerative disc disease reach maximum prevalence in the fifth and sixth decades, which accounts for the late onset of symptoms. The presence of a degenerative spondylolisthesis or a herniated disc may also exacerbate a marginal canal. The AP diameter is considered the most significant in producing symptoms. The radiographic measurement at the posterior margin of the intervertebral foramen from the posterior vertebral body to the inner border of the lamina on the lateral lumbosacral film of < 13 mm is considered to be significant for possibly symptomatic stenosis. This anatomic canal compromise is felt to potentiate ischemia of the cauda equina, thus producing symptoms. The lumbar canal diameter is reduced in extension, which causes increased protrusion of disc spaces, decreasing length of the spinal canal, infolding of the ligamentum flavum, and shortening and increased bulk of the cauda equina roots, the net effect of which is increasing bulk of the roots in combination with decreasing diameter of the canal, thus exacerbating symptoms.[15] The clinical corollary commonly ascribed to the stenotic lumbar canal is one of intermittent low back pain with "cauda equina claudication," to be differentiated from the more common vascular origin of leg pain with exercise. Symptoms of cauda equina claudication are invariably sensory at onset (paresthesias, burning pain), usually commencing in the lumbosacral region and descending (the so-called "sensory march"). Vascular insufficiency sensory deficits *per se* are rare; pain begins in the calf, and motor dysfunction is a common early symptom. During symptomatic exercise in the patient with neurogenic claudication, one may elicit sensory, motor or reflex changes in *multiple roots,* which are usually absent in true vascular intermittent claudication.

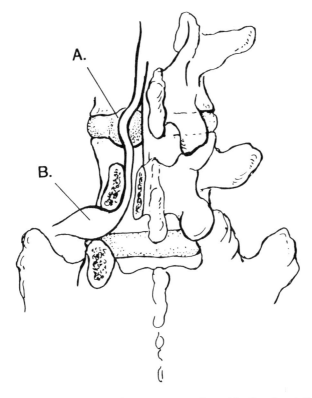

FIGURE 2. Comparison of sites of root compromise with disc herniation (*A*) and foraminal stenosis (*B*).

Symptoms of patients with a stenotic canal are alleviated with flexion of the spine (the patient may be unable to sleep in the prone position, which increases lumbar lordosis), and as such is an important differential point.

Achondroplastic dwarfism is archetypical of congenital spinal stenosis. The underlying mechanism in this familial disorder is aberrant endochondral ossification, resulting in hypoplasia of pedicles and a sagittally narrow canal. There is coexistent decreased vertebral body height and increased lumbar lordosis. In contrast to the norm, the lumbar canal is progressively stenotic in descent.[7] The adult with achondroplasia (usually > 40 years) is commonly symptomatic with LBP, paresthesias on standing, radicular pain, and myelopathy from upper lumbar involvement (especially at the dorsal-lumbar junction).

Lateral recess narrowing and foraminal stenosis may often accompany stenosis of the lumbar canal as a result of shortened, thick pedicles and enlarged articular facets; thus radicular symptoms in these patients are multifactorial. While plain spine radiographs are useful for evaluation of general osteophyte formation, stability, and foraminal compromise, axial CT is exceptionally useful in demonstrating detailed osseous information with relevance to spinal canal dimensions, lateral recess, and foraminal narrowing.[6,8,42] MRI presently offers less detailed bony resolution but, as with water-soluble contrast myelography, is valuable in the diagnosis of spinal stenosis.

SPONDYLOLISTHESIS

Spondylolisthesis or vertebral body subluxation is important when considering spondylogenic causes of radicular disturbances of the leg. The most common manifestation of symptomatic spondylolisthesis of any etiology is LBP. However, lateral recess syndrome[31] or foraminal stenosis may occur secondary to increased fibrotic tissue formation around posterior articular surfaces. With subluxation there is often coexistent "pedicular kinking" of the exiting nerve root causing irritation.[30] Isthmic spondylolisthesis may produce root symptoms by mere fibrous hyperplasia surrounding the isthmic defect. The clinical presentation is that of LBP with possible unilateral or bilateral radiculopathy. Physical examination often reveals tenderness of the affected interspace (commonly L5–S1 or L4–L5) and exaggerated lumbar lordosis; SLR is less reliably present. The incidence of spondylolysis (i.e., the presence of a defect in the pars interarticularis) is 7% in the general population, and radicular pain is sometimes wrongly attributed to this entity. It is generally agreed that subluxation of greater than 25% of the vertebral body may contribute to symptoms of spinal stenosis (vis à vis above).

PAGET'S DISEASE

Osteitis deformans is a relatively common entity that afflicts 3% of the population over 40 years of age, and predisposes to radicular and myelopathic symptoms.[3] Paget's disease is characterized by anomalous bone metabolism—resorption followed by osteoblastic activity. The usual spine-related clinical history is the insidious onset of LBP preceding radicular pain. Radiographic features include hyperostotic vertebrae (multiple area involvement with coarse trabeculations). Oblique lumbar films may document foraminal encroachment. Patients with advanced cases may develop thoracic kyphosis with subsequent stenosis and myelopathy. Of clinical importance is that neurological symptoms are usually present in the more advanced polyostotic cases with their concordant characteristic features: tibial bowing, waddling gait, and increased head size. Sciatic nerve impingement has been reported in cases of extensive pelvic and long bone involvement[9] (pelvic outlet syndrome, see later).

ANKYLOSING SPONDYLITIS

Ankylosing spondylitis (Marie Strumpell's disease) is a probable immunologically mediated spondylitis predominantly afflicting young men. The spondylitis commences in early adulthood (25–30 years) and manifests as insidious LBP with radiation down the buttocks, and the later development of true sciatica in 75% of patients. Sacroiliac joints are involved early. With progression of the disease, fusion and narrowing of vertebral apophysial joints occur which culminate in the classic "bamboo spine" seen radiographically. Early cases with LBP and sciatica may be difficult to differentiate from other spondylogenic causes, but in progressive disease there is spinal rigidity which, if it involves thoracic segments, will limit chest wall expansion. The history may be helpful. In contrast to other arthropathies, pain is often worse upon arising in the morning and improves with activity. Physical examination may reveal loss of lumbar lordosis, sacroiliac joints that are painful to palpation, and decreased mobility of the spine in all planes of motion. Radiographic sacroileitis, family history, the presence of other systemic manifestations of the syndrome (e.g., iritis, aortic insufficiency), and histocompatibility antigen testing (+ HLA B27 in 63–96% of cases[5,18]) should secure the diagnosis.

BONE LESIONS

Other important bony sources of radicular disturbances that must be included in the differential diagnosis are primary and secondary vertebral tumors. Metastases represent the largest group in the adult, and in a reported series this was diagnosed as the source of sciatica in 7% of patients over 50 years of age.[13] The most common tumors metastatic to spine include those affecting the breast, bronchi, prostate, and thyroid. Routine breast and rectal examination, chest radiograph, and biochemical evaluation (including calcium and serum alkaline phosphatase) should adequately screen the majority of these. Less commonly renal cell carcinoma or multiple myeloma may involve the spine; when these tumors are suspected, careful urine analysis and serum protein electrophoresis may be fruitful. The hallmark of metastatic vertebral disease is back pain, usually continuous, and less amenable to alleviation with bedrest than other more benign forms of pathology. Back pain may be associated with radicular symptoms by direct compression of nerve roots by tumor, or pathologic fractures and subsequent instability of the spine. In these cases plain radiographs are invaluable both in the diagnosis of the metastatic lesion and in the determination of stability. Roentgenograms may miss tumor, however, if less than 30% of the vertebral body is involved;[27] thus radioisotopic bone scan or CT are more sensitive in this regard. However, the bone scan may be positive in disc disease, facet joint arthritides, and nonpathologic vertebral body fracture; thus correlation with plain x-ray films or CT is imperative.

Much less commonly primary bone lesions may present with root symptoms; in younger patients, Ewing's sarcoma or osteogenic sarcoma must be considered. In the patient with Paget's disease, rapid progression of symptoms may herald the onset of an osteogenic sarcoma. Other bone lesions such as eosinophilic granuloma, aneurysmal bone cyst, and osteoid osteoma must be excluded. Specific radiographic appearance may aid in this differentiation. Chordoma, a tumor postulated to originate from notochordal remnants, has a predilection for the sacrum and has little rival in its radiographic appearance (bony erosion by an ossified mass). The rare sacral cyst of unknown etiology has been reported to cause radicular symptoms[22] and sexual or bladder dysfunction.[15]

Rarely extramedullary hematopoiesis associated with congenitally inherited anemias may involve the vertebral column and, as such, contribute to radicular involvement in producing foraminal encroachment and spinal stenosis.

INTRASPINAL PATHOLOGY

Tumors / Demyelinating Disease

From a therapeutic standpoint, one of the most important diagnoses to consider in the patient with low back pain with or without sciatica is the presence of an intraspinal tumor. Back pain is common and spinal tumors are rare.[12] Pain is an early manifestation of all spinal cord tumors, either intramedullary or extramedullary, and may be local or have segmental radiation. In defining the segmental level of involvement, one must consider the anatomic discrepancy between vertebral body and spinal cord level, as well as the crossing of the anterolateral spinothalamic fibers subserving pain modalities occurring over 2–3 segmental levels.[49] Conus involvement invariably impairs parasympathetic innervation (bowel, bladder, and sexual dysfunction), and an appropriate history must be pursued. While in theory there is an increased incidence of Brown-Sequard syndrome with extramedullary tumors, and intramedullary lesions classically have been associated with dissociated sensory loss (relative sparing of dorsal column mediated modalities), in practice this anatomic differentiation is often difficult. Both intramedullary and extramedullary tumors involving the conus or higher should be associated with upper motor neuron signs; this is useful in differentiation from cauda pathology. Sharp, burning pain in a segmental distribution is secondary to dorsal root entry zone involvement by the tumor or possible demyelinating disease. The history of rapid onset, other anatomically located deficits (e.g., ocular involvement), possible Lhermitte's sign, and CSF immunoglobulin profile should aid in the differentiation of MS from an intramedullary tumor or syrinx. Occasionally MS may be associated with a polyneuropathy multiplex, confusing the diagnosis.[2] Spinal cord tumors in children, in addition to back pain, often cause insidious scoliosis and lower extremity deformities, illustrating the necessity of normal motor function for skeletal development.

Tumors of the cauda equina often represent more of a diagnostic dilemma; while back pain with or without sciatica is the primary mode of presentation, there are *no* characteristic signs or symptoms.[12] Less common presentations include painless weakness, sphincteric disturbances, or painless sensory deficit. As with cord tumors, a protracted history (> 2 years) commonly precedes the diagnosis. One celebrated clinical criterion for differentiation of spinal cord or cauda tumors is the exacerbation of pain in recumbancy, even compelling some patients to sleep in a chair;[38] the exact mechanism is poorly understood but is believed to be partially attributable to the decreased lordosis and increased length of the spinal canal in recumbancy, causing traction on nerve roots, or a possible ball-valve effect with tumor being forced caudally with dynamic changes in CSF pressure.[38] Pain may also be markedly exacerbated by a jolt or jar; however this phenomenon is shared with other sources of back pain, including disc space infections. The histologic nature of the cauda tumor may sometimes be anticipated clinically. Neurofibromas and meningiomas are well recognized as causes of radicular pain; signs such as a positive SLR or Lasegue's sign may be present. Myxopapillary ependymomas and neurofibromas have been noted by several authors to be associated with early sphincteric disturbance, and should be considered in a patient with a patulous anus and saddle anesthesia.[16] In addition to the above, the much less common teratoma, lipoma and dermoid tumors should be included in the category of cauda lesions that produce radicular disturbance. Diagnostic evaluation includes plain roentgenograms of the lumbosacral spine, which may show enlargement of the neural foramen in cases of a neurofibroma, or increased interpedicular distance from an intraspinal mass. Note that mere scalloping of the posterior vertebral bodies in itself is not considered pathological. MRI or water-soluble contrast myelography are the modalities of choice for defining intraspinal pathology. New generation MRI is superior in visualizing intramedullary tumors and demyelinating disease and is noninvasive. Myelography, however, allows CSF sampling at the time of the procedure (cytology, protein, immunoglobulins, etc.).

Other Intraspinal Etiologies

A host of other much less common intraspinal sources of radicular pain must be considered:

1. *Perineural cysts,* first described by Tarlov (1938), typically involve the sacral roots and are usually incidental findings on imaging studies. In general they are *not* considered to be causally related to neurologic symptoms; however,

in some reported cases, symptoms have abated following surgical drainage.[48] In a similar fashion meningeal diverticulae, which freely communicate with CSF and thus fill during myelographic studies, are rarely attributed to radicular symptoms. These cysts predominate in adults and are to be distinguished from extradural spinal cysts of congenital origin found in younger patients, which are more frequently symptomatic. They have inconsistent communication with CSF pathways and are hypothesized to enlarge by a one-way ball-valve phenomenon and as such produce mass effect. In the thoracic region they may be associated with progressive spastic paraparesis, whereas in lumbar cysts the usual presentation is radicular pain.[49] Rarely, intradural extramedullary arachnoid cysts producing sciatica have been reported.[28]

2. *Subarachnoid hemorrhage* (SAH) has been well described as a source of radicular pain.[12,22] An apoplectic history, headache, and meningeal signs may intimate aneurysmal or vascular malformation rupture. Unruptured aneurysms by virtue of mass alone may cause root irritation in the absence of SAH. SAH associated with a cauda tumor has been reported as the initial mode of presentation.[12]

3. *Inflammation of lumbosacral roots,* producing dermatomal pain and sensory loss, may follow herpes zoster or rarely herpes simplex infection.[2] Careful history of previous attacks of shingles, a dermatomal distribution, and preceding or ensuing skin lesions with a characteristic temporal pattern of evolution are confirmatory. Diagnosis is secured by biopsy of the lesions and by demonstration of varicella-zoster virus by direct immunofluorescence technique. Lumbosacral radiculitis with sensory and bladder deficit has been rarely described following genital HSV (type II) infection. Again, a thorough sexual history and careful examination for genital lesions are mandatory. Direct culture or immunofluorescence of the skin lesions will demonstrate virus.

4. *Adhesive arachnoiditis* is primarily a radiographic diagnosis, and may be a consequence of antecedent meningitis, SAH, or intrathecal administration of antibiotics or anesthetics. In the majority of cases there is no discernable predisposing factor.[2] It may generate bilateral radicular pain and neurologic deficit (both motor and sensory). Diagnosis is made with typical myelographic appearance ("candle gutters")[44] or MRI demonstrating clumping of nerve roots.

PLEXUS ORIGINS

After exiting the neural foramen, the lumbar and sacral roots merge to form the lumbosacral plexus in the retroperitoneal space. In this region they are prone to exposure to mass lesions, trauma, and infection associated with abdominal and pelvic viscera. Abdominal masses of any source (ovarian; uterine, including pregnancy; colon; renal; etc.) may impinge on the plexus, causing pain and neurologic deficit. *Mixed* dermatomal and nerve involvement and careful abdominal and/or pelvic examination should help to clarify the source. Of note is that retroperitoneal involvement *may* cause LBP; thus differentiation from a cauda lesion may be difficult. However, adequate imaging of the spinal canal (MRI or myelography) should exclude this. Another interesting cause of plexus involvement is so-called "cyclic sciatica" from endometriosis of the pelvis.[17] This "catamenial" may affect femoral or sciatic nerve distribution. The history will be remarkable for the repetitive temporal sequence of pain, which correlates with histologic changes in ectopic endometrium associated with the changing endocrinologic milieu preceding and during menses.

Trauma to the abdomen (blunt or open) may affect the plexus by a variety of mechanisms. In addition to direct trauma, pelvic fracture may interrupt the plexus or cause vascular injury, resulting in a compressive retroperitoneal hematoma or aneurysms of the hypogastric and common iliac arteries, in turn causing compression and radicular pain.[26,32] Of consideration is that retroperitoneal hemorrhage may occur spontaneously in patients receiving anticoagulants. Open trauma will require direct surgical exploration; in blunt trauma the CT scan of the abdomen and plain films of the lumbosacral spine and pelvis may be invaluable for demonstrating bony injury or a retroperitoneal collection.

PERIPHERAL CAUSES

Statistically one of the most common causes of segmental sensory loss from a peripheral cause is diabetic neuropathy. It is estimated that 15% of patients with diabetes mellitus will manifest signs and symptoms of neuropathy during the course of their illness. Clinically the presentation takes several forms, the most common being a symmetrical, distal (leg > arm) *insidious* sensory loss, along with leg paresthesias, trophic skin ulcers, and neuropathic joints. Muscle weakness is less prominent. Less common presentations include acute mononeuropathy, and rapidly progressive, painful, primary motor involvement (mononeuropathy multiplex), presumably caused by microvascular infarctions in the vasa vasorum of peripheral nerves. In addition to fasting hyperglycemia, diagnostic clues include multiple root involvement and electrodiagnostic evidence (up to 50% of patients will have EMG or nerve conduction velocity abnormalities).[2]

Extrapelvic trauma may be associated with both sciatic and femoral involvement. One of the most common mechanisms of sciatic injury is a gluteal intramuscular injection that is placed too far medially or inferiorly in the buttock, resulting in pain, dysesthesias, and motor and sensory deficits in those regions subserved by the sciatic nerve. Posterior dislocation of the femur also is potentially injurious to the sciatic nerve; this is usually a neuropraxic injury that results in partial deficit (especially peroneal involvement).[23,38] Prognosis for recovery is good. Rarely, myositis ossificans (i.e., juxta-articular ossification secondary to traumatic fracture-dislocation of the hip) has been reported with late sciatic compression following injury.[23] Traumatic aneurysms of the inferior gluteal artery are well documented.[26,32,39] These are usually pseudoaneurysms associated with blunt trauma to the buttock and produce *late* symptoms of sciatica, with corresponding motor, sensory, and vasomotor changes in the lower limb. They are often palpable with an attendant audible bruit. Rarely a primitive sciatic artery may be subject to traumatic aneurysmal formation.[19] Angiography is the diagnostic study of choice in suspected vascular injury.

ENTRAPMENT NEUROPATHIES

There exist several potential sites for peripheral nerve entrapment in the lower extremity. The cardinal feature that differentiates these entities from more proximal sources of pathology is the presence of pain and neurologic dysfunction in the limb *without coexistent back pain*. The causes of compression neuropathies of the lower limb include space-occupying lesions (ganglia, local tumors), fibrous bands (idiopathic or postsurgical), and fibrous arches at the origins of muscles.[24] There are six common locations of involvement:

  1. *The obturator nerve may be compromised* by an inelastic fibrous sheath

during its passage through the obturator fascia in the obturator foramen, usually secondary to local inflammation (e.g., osteitis pubis or inguinal adenitis).[26] The clinical manifestation is groin pain with radiation down the inner thigh, with possible adductor spasm and weakness. Pelvic x-ray or groin examination may disclose the pathology; however osteitis may not become evident radiographically for 3–6 weeks.

2. *Meralgia paresthetica (Bernhardt-Roth syndrome):* The lateral femoral cutaneous nerve (LCFN) of the thigh may become entrapped while traversing the fascia lata adjacent to the anterior superior iliac spine. The LFCN comprises the ventral divisions of L2 and L3, and supplies sensory distribution to the anterolateral surface of the thigh as far as the knee. This is a rather common entrapment neuropathy and constitutes the cause of leg pain in 6.7 to 35% of cases in some series.[21] Dull ache with paresthesias/dysesthesias in the antero-lateral thigh is common. There is *often* associated referred pain to the gluteal area, thus posing some difficulty in differentiating this entity from an upper lumbar disc herniation. The entrapment is exacerbated by a pendulous abdomen, corsets, trusses, pregnancy, or an intrapelvic tumor. Pain is worse with ambu-lation and men may experience discomfort from hyperesthesia in the involved area while wearing tight trousers. In differentiating meralgia paresthetica from root pathology, it is important to search for other evidence of root involvement (motor or reflex changes). In equivocal cases diagnostic nerve block may be of benefit.[15]

3. *Common peroneal nerve:* Either the common peroneal or the anterior tibial branch may be compressed in its juxta-fibular course. The peroneus longus muscle itself may have a compressive arch[14] or post-traumatic or surgical fibrosis may be the offender. One interesting etiology seen in the Far East is stretching of the lateral compartmental musculature from extended periods of crossed-leg sitting.[26] If the main trunk of the nerve is compressed, the primary clinical deficit is motor loss in both the extensor and peroneal group, resulting in foot drop *and* eversion weakness (in contrast to the L5 root weakness, causing foot drop). Sensory loss from the musculocutaneous branch produces hypesthesia in the outer surface of the leg and foot in addition to a small area of skin in the dorsal first web space. Sometimes of diagnostic help is palpable tenderness at the fibular head in the region of compression.

4. *Pyriformis (pelvic outlet) syndrome:* The sciatic nerve may become com-promised at its emergence from the pelvis at the greater sciatic notch;[34] it passes below the pyriformis muscle and may be compressed between the base of the sciatic notch and the muscle or the muscle and the sacrospinous ligament. This irritation may produce sciatica, however, again with no concordant low back pain. As the impingement is increased by pronounced lumbar lordosis, symptoms are exacerbated by walking or standing. A useful clinical sign is the mitigation of pain during SLR by external rotation of the leg. The latter should have no effect on discogenic sources but relaxes the pyriformis, thereby relieving compres-sion at the sciatic notch.[26] Also helpful in the clinical differentiation is preferential sparing of the gluteal muscle groups from wasting (see disc disease).

5. *Tarsal tunnel syndrome:* Compression of the posterior tibial nerve below the medial malleolus produces a syndrome analogous to median nerve compres-sion at the carpal tunnel in the forearm, with pain radiation and sensory deficit in the plantar aspect of the foot. In a similar fashion to the carpal tunnel syndrome, the pain may radiate proximally into the calf.

6. *Morton's metatarsalgia:* Pain and paresthesias along opposing surfaces of two adjacent toes are caused by compression of plantar digital nerves between metatarsal heads.

Other infrequent peripheral causes of leg sensory disturbances include the rare neurogenic schwannoma or neurofibroma,[1,37] and the migrant sensory neuritis of Wartenberg. The latter is a clinically benign relapsing-remitting condition that causes searing pain in multiple cutaneous sensory nerves. It is considered to be secondary to an innate sensitivity of peripheral nerves to stretch, which induces pain.[29] The pain is brief in duration and may be followed by sensory deficit with multiple areas of involvement;[46] improvement in deficit is the rule. Subacute trochanteric bursitis in the elderly patient may present with pseudo-radicular pain radiating down the lateral thigh.[43] Local point tenderness at the superolateral femur which responds to injection of local anesthetic may aid in confirming the diagnosis.

Primary sciatica is a rare, idiopathic entity that at present is poorly understood. The spectrum of pain may vary from a dull ache to a lancinating, tic-like pain along the distribution of the sciatic nerve. It is a diagnosis of exclusion; phenytoin has been used by some authors with success.[15]

CONCLUSION

While the list of potential causes of radicular symptoms is long and diverse, a small number of common etiologies are culpable in the majority of cases. Of paramount importance in the differential diagnosis is a thorough history and physical examination, with careful consideration of the anatomical location of the lesion and exclusion of metabolic sources of sensory impairment. Appropriately utilized modern imaging modalities (especially present generation CT and MRI) should confirm the diagnosis in all but the most obscure presentations.

REFERENCES

1. Abernathey CD, Onofrio BM, et al: Surgical management of giant sacral schwannomas. J Neurosurg 65:286–295, 1986.
2. Adams RD, Victor M: Principles of Neurology, 3rd ed. New York, McGraw Hill, 1985, pp 703–708, 684–685.
3. Amyes EW, Vogel PN: Osteitis deformans (Paget's disease) of the spine with compression of the spinal cord: report of three cases and discussion of the surgical problems. Bull LA Neurol Soc 19:18, 1954.
4. Bartlett J: The problem of sciatica. Practitioner 204:529–537, 1970.
5. Bingham WF: The role of HLA B27 in the diagnosis and management of low-back pain and sciatica. J Neurosurg 47:561–566, 1977.
6. Buirski G: The investigation of sciatica and low back pain syndromes: current trends. Clin Radiol 38:151–155, 1987.
7. Caffey J: Achondroplasia of the pelvis and lumbo-sacral spine: some roentgenographic features. Am J Roentgenol 80:449, 1958.
8. Carrera GF, Williams AL, Haughton VM: Computed tomography in Sciatica. Radiology 137:433–437, 1980.
9. Chrisman OD, Snook GA, Walker HR: Paget's disease as differential diagnosis in sciatica. Clin Orthop 37:154–159, 1964.
10. Eisenberg D, Gomori JM, Findler G, et al: Symptomatic diverticulum of the sacral nerve root sheath. Neuroradiology 27:183, 1985.
11. Espersen JO, Kosteljanetz M, Halaburt H, Miletic T: Predictive value of radiculography in patients with lumbago-sciatica: a prospective study. (part II). Acta Neurochir 73:213–221, 1984.

12. Fearnside MR, Adams CBT: Tumours of the cauda equina. J Neurol Neurosurg Psychiatry 41:24–31, 1978.
13. Fernbach JC, Langer F, Gross AE: The significance of low back pain in older adults. Can Med Assoc J 115:898–901, 1976.
14. Fettweis E: A cause of sciatic pain: non-traumatic peroneal nerve compression. Germ Med Mon 13:535–536, 1968.
15. Finneson BE: Low Back Pain. Philadelphia, J.B. Lippincott Co., 1980, pp 427–554.
16. Garfield T, Lyth SN: Urinary presentation of cauda equina lesions without neurological symptoms. Br J Urol 42:551–554, 1970.
17. Head HB, Welch JS, Mussey E, et al: Cyclic sciatica. Report of a case with introduction of a new clinical sign. JAMA 180:521–524, 1962.
18. Hudgkins WR: Ankylosing spondylitis and sciatica (letter). J Neurosurg 48:668–669, 1978.
19. Hutchinson JE, Candice JWV Jr, McAllister FF: The surgical management of an aneurysm of the primitive sciatic artery. Ann Surg 167:277–281, 1968.
20. Johnson EW, Melvin JL: Value of electromyography in lumbar radiculopathy. Arch Phys Med Rehab 52:239–243, 1971.
21. Jones RK: Meralgia paresthetica as a cause of leg discomfort. Can Med Assoc J 111:541–542, 1974.
22. Keet PC: The lumbar disc and its imitators. S Afr Med J 49:1169–1176, 1975.
23. Kleiman SG, Stevens J, et al: Late sciatic-nerve palsy following posterior fracture-dislocation of the hip. J Bone Joint Surg 53A:781–782, 1971.
24. Kopell HP, Thompson WAL: Peripheral Entrapment Neuropathies. Baltimore, Williams and Wilkins, 1963.
25. Krempen JF, Smith BS: Nerve root injection. A method for evaluating the etiology of sciatica. J Bone Joint Surg 56A:1435–1444, 1974.
26. Lam SJS: Peripheral nerve compression syndromes in the lower limb. Guy Hosp Rep 117:49–61, 1968.
27. Lewinnek, GE: Management of low back pain and sciatica. Int Anesthesiol Clin 21:61–78, 1983.
28. Maroun FB, Jacob JC: Uncommon causes of sciatica. Can Med Assoc J 103:1292–1295, 1970.
29. Matthews WB, Esiri M: The migrant sensory neuritis of Wartenberg. J Neurol Neurosurg Psychiatry 46:1–4, 1983.
30. McNab I: Negative disc exploration. An analysis of the causes of nerve root involvement in 68 patients. J Bone Joint Surg 53A:891–903, 1971.
31. McNab I: The management of spondylolisthesis. Prog Neurol Surg 4:246, 1971.
32. Miller JW, Stuart WE, Tytus JS, et al: Gluteal Artery Aneurysm. A Case Report. J Bone Joint Surg 56A:620–622, 1974.
33. Mixter WJ, Barr JS: Rupture of the intervertebral disc with involvement of the spinal canal. N Engl J Med 211:210, 1934.
34. Mizuguchi T: Division of the pyriformis muscle for the treatment of sciatica. Arch Surg 111:719–720, 1976.
35. Negrin P, Fardin P: Clinical and electromyographical course of sciatica. Prognostic study of 41 cases. Electromyogr Clin Neurophysiol 27:125–127, 1987.
36. Ober FR: The Classic. Back strain and sciatica. Clin Orthop 219:4–7, 1987.
37. Prusick VR, Herkowitz HN, et al: Sciatica from a sciatic neurolemmoma. A case report and review of the literature. J Bone Joint Surg 68A:1456–1457, 1986.
38. Rasmussen TB, Kernohan JW, Adson AW: Pathological classification with surgical consideration of intraspinal tumors. Ann Surg 3:513–31, 1940.
39. Rinaldi I, Fitzer PM, et al: Aneurysm of the inferior gluteal artery causing sciatic pain. J Neurosurg 44:100–104, 1976.
40. Robinson JS: Sciatica and the lumbar disk syndrome. A historic perspective. South Med J 76:232–238, 1983.
41. Rothman RH, Simeone FA: The Spine, 2nd ed. Philadelphia, W.B. Saunders, 1982, pp 508–645.
42. Rosa M, Capellini C, et al: CT in low back and sciatic pain due to lumbar canal osseous changes. Neuroradiology 28:237–240, 1986.
43. Swezey RL: Pseudo-radiculopathy in subacute trochanteric bursitis of the subgluteus maximus bursa. Arch Phys Med Rehab 57:387–390, 1976.
44. Teng P, Papatheodorou C: Myelographic findings in adhesive spinal arachnoiditis. Br J Radiol 40:201, 1967.
45. Van Damme W, Hessels G, et al: Relative efficacy of clinical examination, electromyography, plain film radiography, myelography, and lumbar phlebography in the diagnosis of low back pain and sciatica. Neuroradiology 18:109–118, 1979.

46. Wartenberg R: Neuritis. Sensory Neuritis. Neuralgia. New York, Oxford University Press, 1958, pp 233–247.
47. Weber H: Lumbar disc herniation. A prospective study of prognosticating factors including a controlled trial. J Oslo City Hosp 28:33–64; 89–103, 1978.
48. Wilkins RH: Intraspinal cysts. In Wilkins RH, Rengachary SS: Neurosurgery, Vol III. New York, McGraw-Hill, 1985, pp 2061–2069.
49. Wilkins RH, Odam SL: Spinal extradural cysts. In Vinken PJ, Bruyn GW: Handbook of Clinical Neurology, Vol. 20. Tumors of the Spine and Spinal Cord. Part II. Amsterdam, Elsevier, 1976, pp 137–175.

PHILLIP H. OMOHUNDRO, MD
RICHARD PAYNE, MD

REFLEX SYMPATHETIC DYSTROPHY

Phillip H. Omohundro, MD
Cincinnati Sportsmedicine and The
Midwest Institute for Orthopedics,
Cincinnati, Ohio

Richard Payne, MD
Associate Professor of Neurology
University of Cincinnati Medical
Center
Cincinnati, Ohio

Reprint requests to:
Richard Payne, MD
Department of Neurology (ML 525)
Univ. Cincinnati Medical Center
4010 Medical Sciences Bldg.
231 Bethesda Ave.
Cincinnati, OH 45267

INTRODUCTION AND CLINICAL FEATURES

The term reflex sympathetic dystrophy (RSD) refers to a constellation of symptoms and signs following injury to bone, nerve and soft tissue.[8,9,18,19,29,30,32,34-36,57-59,62,67,69,70,83-86,89,91,93] Typically, the patient will report pain and hyperpathia within hours (or less commonly days) following a variety of causes of tissue injury, especially blunt trauma, inflammatory disorders, myocardial and cerebral infarction, and peripheral nerve injury. Clinical syndromes identical to RSD have historically been called by a variety of names such as minor causalgia, post-traumatic dystrophy, mimocausalgia, reflex algodystrophy, among others. All of these syndromes likely have a common (but currently poorly understood) pathophysiology, and little is to be gained by the proliferation of synonyms. Arguably, (major) causalgia may be viewed as a special case of RSD in which there is major injury to peripheral nerve.[47]

Management of the patient with RSD can prove to be difficult and frustrating for both the physician and patient. The orthopedist is often the primary treating physician, as many of the cases complicate trauma to the extremities. There have been reports of RSD following failed lumbar spinal surgery, but this syndrome is not well defined.[10,44] Additionally, RSD following cervical spondylosis accounts for less than 5% of cases in a large series.[35,36] Thus the primary focus of this discussion is on RSD syndromes in the extremities, since these are much more common.

The clinical syndrome can have a variable presentation. Casten and Betcher divided the syndrome into three grades.[9] The classic presentation of a swollen, immobile painful limb that is hypersensitive to touch is easily recognized by most clinicians.[8,34,47] The spectrum, however, ranges from subtle swelling and persistent pain without clear evidence of vasoconstriction to cases resembling the classic descriptions cited above. One must be alert to the possibility of RSD when evaluating any patient whose course following injury or surgery is a departure from the expected result, especially if the pain appears to be out of proportion to radiographic or physical signs of underlying pathology or ongoing tissue injury.

Trophic changes such as subcutaneous atrophy and osteoporosis generally occur late in the course. The pathogenesis of these trophic changes are problematic—they may be secondary to a prolonged increase in sympathetic "tone"[76] but more likely are related to disuse of the painful extremity.[46]

Extra-articular soft tissue swelling may be evident. Many patients report inability to tolerate changes in the weather, especially cold,[6] and pain that is exacerbated by stress, fear or excitement.[8,47,39] Often, patients note a feeling of cold in the involved extremity or the recent need to wear socks to bed because of (painful) cold feet. Hypersensitivity to light touch (hyperpathia) is a very frequent finding and is a cardinal feature of the disorder.[46,76] The region of hypersensitivity may correspond to a peripheral nerve distribution, i.e., the infrapatellar branch of the saphenous nerve in RSD complicating trauma to the lower extremity,[49a] but is often wider than the area of sensory loss or initial trauma.

PATHOPHYSIOLOGY OF PAIN IN REFLEX SYMPATHETIC DYSTROPHY

Reflex sympathetic dystrophy is associated with pain and presumed sympathetic nervous system dysfunction. The sympathetic nervous system is implicated in RSD because many features of the syndrome, especially pain, improve after sympathetic blockade, particularly when it is performed early in the course of the disorder.[8,47,76] In addition, recent experimental observations[60] in animals provide strong evidence for somatic afferent-sympathetic efferent interactions that may be important in the pathogenesis of pain and hyperpathia following trauma.

Several theories have been proposed to explain the pain and the involvement of the sympathetic nervous system in the reflex sympathetic dystrophies, especially causalgia, and can be grouped along four lines:

1. Nerve injury produces abnormal discharges in sympathetic "afferents."[76]
2. Sensitization of peripheral sensory receptors (mechanoreceptors and/or nociceptors) by sympathetic activity.[3,61]
3. The formation of ephapses (artificial synapses) as a consequence of nerve injury, which allows shunting of current from sympathetic efferent fibers to somatic afferent fibers at the site of injury.[33]
4. Spontaneous ectopic discharges may develop at the site of nerve injury either in areas of focal demyelination or at the site of neuroma formation.[13]

None of the above hypotheses accounts for all of the clinical features of RSD. For example, with the exception of sympathetic afferents in visceral nerves which mediate autonomic reflexes (i.e., splanchnic nerve afferents), sympathetic afferents have not been convincingly demonstrated.[76] In addition, sympathetic *efferent* activity is obviously at least as important as afferent activity in the production of this clinical syndrome, and abnormal activity in afferent fibers does not account for the effects of sympathetic outflow. Although mechano-receptors (such as pacinian corpuscles) are innervated by sympathetic efferent fibers, and sympathetic stimulation may sensitize mechanoreceptors (and no-ciceptors, albeit only transiently),[61] sympathectomy is not 100% effective in abolishing pain and hyperpathia in causalgia,[41] so sympathetic-somatic afferent interactions cannot be the only mechanism. Although ephapses have been dem-onstrated at the site of nerve injury in experimental animal models of peripheral nerve injury,[33] they tend to occur late in the course of nerve injury and tend to effect large myelinated rather than unmyelinated (i.e., nociceptive or sympa-thetic) fibers. Thus it is not likely that the formation of ephapses, alone, could account for pain and hyperpathia in RSD. Finally, spontaneous ectopic dis-charges also occur relatively late in experimental peripheral nerve injury models.[13] Thus this phenomenon would not likely account for the immediate presence of burning pain, but might account for delayed paroxysmal, lancinating pain, which is not uncommonly encountered in RSD and causalgia.

A recent hypothesis emphasizes the relationship between *normal* sympa-thetic efferent activity and activity in low threshold mechanoreceptors in the pathogenesis of pain in causalgia.[60] Experimental animal data suggest that trauma, with activation of C-nociceptive fibers, may *sensitize* wide dynamic range (WDR) neurons in the spinal cord. These neurons receive input from peripheral nociceptors and non-nociceptive (i.e., thermoreceptors and mechanoreceptors) sensory units, and are important for signalling the presence of potentially tissue-damaging stimuli applied to the skin. Sensitization of WDR neurons may produce spontaneous activity and a lower threshold for repetitive firing, such that (pre-viously) innocuous manipulation of the skin, or normal or increased levels of sympathetic efferent activity may produce pain and hyperpathia by activating mechanoreceptors in the skin, thereby promoting an increase in the firing rate of WDR neurons.[60]

As emphasized by Roberts,[60] this hypothesis is consistent with the following experimental and clinical facts: (1) persistent sensitization of WDR neurons may occur in animal models of chronic pain following trauma and activity in C-nociceptors;[60] (2) low-threshold mechanoreceptors may be sensitized via sym-pathetic stimulation.[61] (Note: Nociceptors do not develop long-lasting sensiti-zation after sympathetic stimulation[60]); (3) normal levels of sympathetic activity in the extremity are apparently sufficient to cause pain in man,[82] and (4) sym-pathetic blocks are more likely to be successful for management of pain in RSD or causalgia in man when allodynia (or hyperpathia) is a prominent feature.[41]

In addition, this hypothesis would explain several important clinical features of RSD such as persistent pain after (even trivial) trauma; the association between pain and hyperpathia in RSD; the appearance of RSD with apparently normal levels of peripheral sympathetic tone; and the efficacy of sympathetic block in most patients. It does not clearly explain the appearance of so-called trophic changes such as edema, subcutaneous atrophy, osteoporosis, etc., nor does it explain the lack of efficacy of sympathetic blockade in rare patients. It is currently suggested that some of the trophic changes (i.e., osteoporosis) are secondary to disuse.[46] In some patients the lack of efficacy of sympathetic blockade may be related to incorrect diagnosis (as there are several syndromes that superficially mimic RSD but do not respond to sympathetic blockade—see reference 41), and to delay in treatment of RSD, such that permanent changes in the central nervous system have occurred which cannot be reversed by peripheral sympathetic blockade.[76]

DIAGNOSTIC STUDIES

The presence of reflex sympathetic dystrophy must be established on clinical grounds, based on the criteria listed above (Fig. 1).[47] Laboratory data may be confirmatory or may indicate other disorders that may superficially mimic RSD. For example, blood studies such as a CBC, erythrocyte sedimentation rate, or antinuclear antibody titers, when abnormal, may direct attention to an alternate diagnosis such as inflammatory arthropathy and vasculitis. Plain roentgenograms,[29,36] bone scans,[11a,19,30a] and thermograms[18,28,52,63,71,88] have all been used to corroborate a diagnosis of RSD, but none of these studies demonstrates pathognomonic features.

Plain x-rays may show osteopenia, which is usually seen in the later stages of RSD.[29] In the early stages of RSD, the x-rays are usually normal and provide few clues as to diagnosis. Kozin reports a high percentage (80–90%) of changes in fine-detailed roentgenograms viewed at 4- to 8-fold magnification, but these are generally not available for routine evaluations.[36]

Bone scans are positive in 49–92% of cases, showing increased uptake at the site of the involved bone.[10,11a,19,24,30a,36,72] Recent reports emphasize the use of three-phase bone scanning in RSD involving the hand.[11a,24,30a] Radionuclide angiography is performed for immediate bone imaging after the intravenous injection of technetium methylene diphosphonate to determine hemovelocity and blood pool data (Phase I). Static images are obtained 3–5 minutes after injection (Phase II). Finally, a delayed high-resolution image is obtained 2–3 hours after injection (Phase III). Demangeat et al.[11a] demonstrated that the imaging patterns in the three phases were dependent on the timing of the bone scan in relationship to the time after trauma (i.e., the stage of RSD). Therefore a negative bone scan does not exclude the diagnosis of RSD, since delayed images may show normal or hypofixation of technetium in late stages of RSD.[11a,24]

Thermograms have also proved helpful but are not diagnostic.[28,71,88] Temperature changes of 2 degrees Centigrade or greater are highly suggestive of RSD but must be interpreted in the overall clinical context. Lack of availability and specificity of technology has limited the usefulness of thermography for the routine assessment of patients with RSD.[71]

THERAPY OF REFLEX SYMPATHETIC DYSTROPHY

Sympathetic blockade

Ancillary testing may prove helpful, but the physician must have a high index of suspicion to proceed with the diagnostic workup of the patient (Fig. 1).[85,86] Sympathetic blockade remains the standard for establishing the diagnosis of RSD and for initiating treatment.[37,47,80,94] Sympathetic blockade may be accomplished by a variety of means, and selection of a specific type of sympathetic block depends on the clinical situation and the expertise of the physician.

Evaluation of the completeness of sympathetic blockade can be judged by several techniques. Skin temperature can be measured by a variety of commercial thermistors; a rise in skin temperature of 2–3°C should be observed.[90] Thermography may also be used as a non-invasive, easily repeatable measure of skin temperature asymmetry after a sympathetic block.[28,88] Skin galvanic response,[15] blood flow,[82] and sweat response in the extremity are additional methods that may be employed to assess the adequacy of a sympathetic block.

Chemical sympathetic blocks can be performed by four different methods:

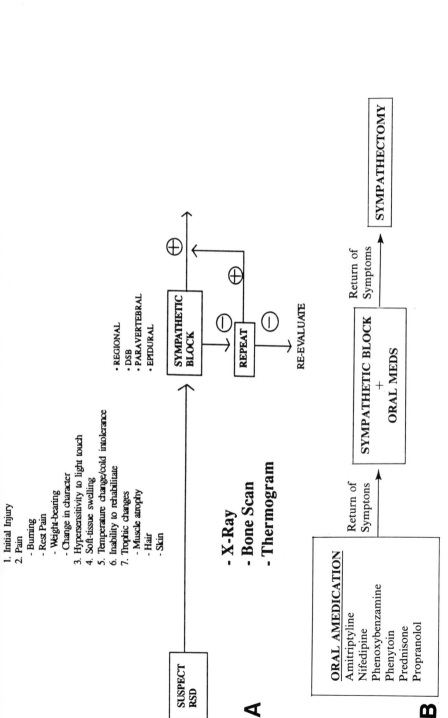

1. Initial Injury
2. Pain
   - Burning
   - Rest Pain
   - Weight-bearing
   - Change in character
3. Hypersensitivity to light touch
4. Soft-tissue swelling
5. Temperature change/cold intolerance
6. Inability to rehabilitate
7. Trophic changes
   - Muscle atrophy
   - Hair
   - Skin

- X-Ray
- Bone Scan
- Thermogram

SUSPECT RSD

SYMPATHETIC BLOCK

• REGIONAL
• DSB
• PARAVERTEBRAL
• EPIDURAL

⊕

⊕

REPEAT

⊖

⊖

RE-EVALUATE

A

ORAL AMEDICATION
Amitriptyline
Nifedipine
Phenoxybenzamine
Phenytoin
Prednisone
Propranolol

Return of Symptons

SYMPATHETIC BLOCK
+
ORAL MEDS

Return of Symptons

SYMPATHECTOMY

B

FIGURE 1. *A,* Algorithm for diagnosis and treatment of RSD. *B,* Algorithm for treatment of RSD after return of pain following sympathetic block.

TABLE 1. Sensitivity of Nerve Fibers to Local Anesthetics*

Group	Modality Subserved	Sensitivity to Local Anesthetics
A (myelinated) alpha	Large motor, proprioception (reflex activity)	1%
Beta	Small motor, touch and pressure	1%
Gamma	Muscle spindle fibers (muscle tone)	1%
Delta	Temperature and sharp pain, possibly touch	0.5%
B (myelinated)	Preganglionic autonomic fibers	0.25%
C (unmyelinated)	Dull pain, temperature, touch (like delta, but slower)	0.5%

*Modified from Ramamurthy and Winnie.[53]

(1) intravenous or intra-arterial regional blockade, (2) differential spinal block (DSB), (3) paravertebral, and (4) epidural.[12,42,92] Regional blocks are performed with either reserpine[5] or guanethidine.[7,23,25–27,31,81] However, guanethidine is not available in the United States for routine clinical use.

Differential spinal block (DSB) involves a progressive blockade of sympathetic, sensory and motor nerve fibers. This may be done by sequential 5 cc injections of 0.25%, 0.50%, and 1.0% procaine into the subarachnoid space (Table 1).[53] Following each injection, the patient is evaluated by measuring vital signs, skin temperature, level of analgesia to pinprick, motor response, and pain relief. The injections are spaced at least 10–15 minutes apart in order to allow the full effect to be determined. Pain relief of 80% or greater with sympathetic blockade alone usually indicates a positive response and strongly suggests the presence of sympathetically maintained pain. Pain relief is reevaluated at 2 hours, 24 hours, and 48 hours following completion of the block. Headaches from dural leaks are not uncommon, and although they are usually self-limited, they may occasionally require an epidural blood patch.

Paravertebral sympathetic block may be performed by the injection of local anesthetics (2–5 cc, 2% xylocaine or 0.5–0.75% bupivacaine) in the region of the (lumbar) sympathetic ganglion. This block may be performed by either a single injection or the insertion of a catheter for continuous infusion. Continuous paravertebral infusion has been reported for periods of 14–21 days.[6,12]

Epidural sympathetic block may be performed by the insertion of a catheter at cervical, thoracic, or lumbar levels for intermittent injection or continuous infusion of a local anesthetic.[38] After a loading dose of 10 cc of 0.25% bupivacaine, sympathetic blockade is maintained by either continuous infusion of 6–10 cc per hour of 0.125% to 0.25% bupivacaine. The catheter can be left in place for up to 6 days.[53]

Thus sympathetic blockade may provide diagnostic information and is useful in the therapy of RSD. The initial block may provide pain relief lasting only a few hours (paravertebral) to several days (intravenous guanethidine).[17] If sympathetic blockade corroborates the clinical diagnosis, there are several options for long-term management. These include some combination of repeated sympathetic blocks, physical therapy, oral medications (Table 2) (sympatholytics, calcium channel blockers, steroids, and nonsteroidal anti-inflammatory analgesics and rarely narcotics), and surgical or neurolytic sympathectomy. Typi-

TABLE 2. Commonly Used Drugs and Doses for the Management of RSD.

Amitriptyline
    Dose: 25 mg po tid
Nifedipine
    Dose: 10 mg po tid up to a maximum of 30 mg po tid
Phenoxybenzamine
    Dose: 10 mg po tid up to 40 mg po tid
Phenytoin
    Dose: 200–300 mg po daily in divided doses
Prednisone
    Dose: 20 mg po daily up to 70 weeks *or* 100–200 mg daily for 2–3 weeks then taper dose
Propranolol
    Dose: 40 mg po daily up to 320 mg po daily in divided doses

cally, paravertebral sympathetic blocks are repeated weekly or bimonthly until the beneficial effects plateau.[90]

Permanent sympathectomy (via surgical interruption or the injection of neurolytic agents such as 6% phenol in water in 10–20 cc volume into the lumbar paravertebral space) should be done only when there is unequivocal but transient benefit from sympathetic blockade.[4,48,66–68,74] With few exceptions, permanent sympathectomy should not be first-line treatment because there is a small but definite recurrence rate of pain after sympathectomy;[8,47] in addition sympathectomy may also be complicated by the development of post-sympathectomy pain.[40,54,65,87] Surgical or neurolytic sympathectomy may be considered early in the course of therapy for patients with relative contraindications to repeated exposure to local anesthetics or drugs. This is often an issue in young women of child-bearing age who have developed RSD with intractable pain related to sports injuries.

Post-sympathectomy neuralgia must be distinguished from recurrent RSD pain.[40,45,87] Following the initial (usually dramatic) pain relief, the patient develops a *new* pain syndrome. This pain typically occurs abruptly and is often described as a deep muscle ache of the entire extremity. Treatment with mild analgesics and anticonvulsant drugs such as phenytoin and carbamazepine have been reported to be effective[54] but the process is usually self-limited and resolves in 2–3 months. The pathogenesis of post-sympathectomy pain is obscure, although an animal model of this disorder has been described recently.[65]

Return of the *original* RSD pain after sympathectomy may occur as well. Although the pathophysiology of this phenomenon is not clear, cross innervation from the contralateral sympathetic chain has been proposed.[45,55,87] This has led to contralateral sympathectomy with improvement in pain in some instances.[45] However, bilateral sympathectomies may interfere with bladder, bowel, and ejaculatory function, and, the patient must be fully informed of these possible complications. Adequate pain relief may not be obtained if the original sympathectomy was performed at an inadequate spinal level. Proper determination of the level of planned sympathectomy is essential to success.[16]

Drug Therapy

A variety of pharmacologic agents have been used to manage pain associated with RSD.[47] Table 2 lists some of the more commonly used drugs. Drugs that are useful in RSD may be grouped as follows: (1) oral sympatholytic drugs, (2) anti-inflammatory drugs, (3) tricyclic drugs, (4) anticonvulsants, (5) calcium-channel blockers, and (6) narcotic analgesics. In selected patients these agents may be useful as adjuncts or as primary therapy in the management of RSD.

Both alpha- and beta-adrenergic antagonist drugs have been used in RSD.[47] Prazosin, an alpha-1 adrenergic antagonist, has been reported to be effective for the management of causalgia in doses of 2 mg po bid.[1] Phenoxybenzamine, which has both alpha-1 and alpha-2 adrenergic antagonist effects, was reportedly successful in doses ranging from 40–120 mg/day in the management of 40 soldiers with causalgia associated with gunshot wounds to major peripheral nerve trunks.[21] Neither of these studies reported controlled, blinded observations, and thus cannot be construed as definitive. In the authors' experience, these agents may be useful in the short term, but their use is often limited by side effects, particularly orthostatic hypotension in normotensive individuals.

The use of beta-adrenergic antagonist drugs such as propranolol (in divided doses of up to 320 mg/day) has also been reported to be useful in the management of post-traumatic neuralgia in an open trial,[49,73] although a controlled study showed no benefit.[64] This is of interest, because unlike alpha-adrenergic blockers, beta blockers do not suppress sympathetically induced neural activity in experimental models of peripheral nerve injury.[14]

Prednisone in doses of 60–80 mg/day has been reported helpful in the management of RSD, particularly when joint involvement is marked, and when shoulder-hand syndrome exists.[11,22,35,77,78] Nonsteroidal anti-inflammatory agents such as ibuprofen, naproxen, and diflunisal are commonly used as "general purpose" analgesics in RSD, although to our knowledge there have not been any controlled trials documenting their efficacy in this disorder.

Tricyclic antidepressant drugs such as amitriptyline, desipramine, doxepin, and imipramine are commonly used for management of chronic pain,[20] especially neuropathic pain.[43] Amitriptyline is perhaps the most commonly used tricyclic for this indication, and is typically given in doses starting at 10–25 mg at bedtime, and ranging from 75–150 mg day.

Anticonvulsant drugs such as phenytoin and carbamazepine are often helpful in causalgia and RSD, particularly when paroxysmal, lancinating pain is a prominent feature.[2,47,75] Carbamazepine (200 mg po tid) and phenytoin (100 mg po qid) have been reported to be effective in 3 of 4 patients treated for causalgia complicating sciatic nerve injury.[2] Experimental models of peripheral nerve injury have demonstrated spontaneous discharges at the site of nerve damage and in the central nervous system,[76] and it is hypothesized that anticonvulsant drugs may be effective by suppressing these discharges.[75]

Calcium channel blockers have also been used in the management of causalgia and RSD.[51] Nifedepine, in doses of 10 mg po tid, has been reported to alleviate pain in open trials of RSD, but controlled studies of its efficacy or of the efficacy of other calcium channel blockers have not been performed. Of note, Devor[13,14] has reported that regenerating nerve sprouts in experimentally induced neuromas may synthesize new calcium channel protein, and blockade of this ionophore may, in theory, reduce spontaneous and sympathetically evoked discharges in axons.

Narcotic analgesics have been reported to be ineffective[47] or relatively contraindicated for long-term management of patients with causalgia complicating iatrogenic nerve injuries because of the development of "addiction."[32] However, a controlled trial designed to assess the efficacy and adverse effects of narcotic analgesics in the management of causalgia and RSD has not been done.

Non-drug Therapy

The role of physical therapy is critical in the treatment of RSD.[47,50,67] The physical therapist is very helpful in maintaining maximum possible motion in affected joints, thereby minimizing dystrophic changes in muscles and connective tissues. It is often necessary to perform sympathetic blocks and to initiate other therapies to control pain (e.g., triggerpoint injections, ultrasound treatments, and transcutaneous electrical nerve stimulation [TENS] therapy) so that the patient will achieve enough pain relief to participate actively in physical therapy.[47,50,79] In fact, failure of the patient to respond to usual postoperative physical therapy regimens because of pain may lead the therapist to suspect RSD. Standardized and repeated assessments of muscle strength and range of motion are important to document and quantitate responses to therapy. All patients with the diagnosis of RSD should have an initial consultation with a physiatrist or physical therapist, and almost without exception should be followed by a rehabilitation specialist. Patients may be taught exercises and range of motion techniques to use at home; this has a secondary benefit in allowing the patient to be more actively involved in his care.

Psychological Therapy

Many patients with chronic pain develop changes in personality and lifestyle that compound their management. In fact, many reports have emphasized the association between increased levels of stress and anxiety and exacerbations of pain in RSD, including Weir Mitchell's classic descriptions of causalgia complicating nerve injuries during the Civil War.[39,47,76] In addition, there have been suggestions that certain personality types may be predisposed to development of causalgia after (iatrogenic) nerve injuries.[32] Therefore in addition to the usual psychological support offered by the physician, one must consider a variety of specific, psychologically based therapies in the management of RSD, including behavioral relaxation, hypnosis, and biofeedback.[47] Often consultation with a psychiatrist or clinical psychologist with expertise in chronic pain management is helpful, and is usually recommended to assist in the evaluation of the psychological status of the patient, and to execute the above therapies.

Figure 1 summarizes an approach to the management of patients with known or suspected RSD. Essential to the care of patients with RSD is early, aggressive management of pain, especially the use of sympathetic blockade. For patients who refuse or who have a contraindication to sympathetic block (e.g., hypersensitivity to local anesthetics, baseline systemic hypotension, coagulopathy or systemic anticoagulation), one might begin therapy with tricyclic drugs, an alpha- or beta-adrenergic blocker, or a calcium channel blocker (Fig. 1B), which are not usually recommended. It is our impression that the effectiveness of drug therapy may be enhanced by sympathetic blockade. One must emphasize the need for early diagnosis and aggressive treatment early in the course of suspected RSD, and therapy (especially sympathetic blockade) is often more beneficial when initiated within the first 3–6 months following injury.[90]

Case Reports

The following cases illustrate principles in the management of RSD complicating trauma and orthopedic surgery.

CASE 1.   A 41-year old woman sustained an injury to her left knee while skiing. She developed an acute hemarthrosis and her examination revealed a grade 3 Lachman and grade 3 opening to valgus stress. Arthroscopic examination confirmed a complete disruption of the anterior cruciate ligament (ACL) and medial collateral ligament (MCL). Additionally, a central ulceration was located on the patella, and a cartilaginous lesion of the medial femoral condyle was graded as 2B. The patient opted for conservative treatment and was placed in a cast for 4 weeks followed by a brace. She did well in a rehabilitation program, regaining full motion and excellent muscle tone. Five and one-half months after her injury, she began to experience anterior and medial knee pain and swelling after increasing the tension on her stationary bike. The swelling responded to a short course of oral steroids, but the pain persisted. A bone scan showed slightly increased uptake over the lateral femoral condyle but was otherwise normal. The patient continued with oral anti-inflammatory agents and rehabilitation, but the pain persisted and became burning in nature. Pain began in the right knee with hypersensitivity to a light touch in both knees. A bone scan was repeated (2 months after the first scan), which was unchanged from the previous study. A continuous epidural block was performed (using 0.025% bupivicaine infused at 10 cc/hr at the L2–3 spinal level) for 3 days with complete relief of pain. Nifedipine, 10 mg po tid, was continued for 4 months after the sympathetic block with satisfactory pain relief. The patient has been unable to resume skiing because of orthopedic instability of the knee, but is actively participating in a rehabilitation program.

CASE 2.   A 17-year-old girl had a 6-year history of retropatellar pain of the left knee that had been diagnosed as "chondromalacia." The pain was unresponsive to conservative treatment and ultimately prevented recreational activity such as ice skating. After many small injuries over five years, both from falls and twists and the persistence of the retropatellar pain, the patient underwent arthroscopy. At surgery she had softening

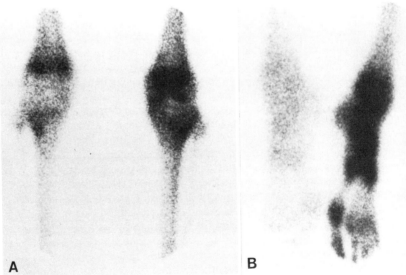

A   **B**

FIGURE 2.   Case 2: Bone scan showing increased uptake in left knee (*A*) and distal left lower extremity (*B*) in a case of RSD complicating multiple knee trauma and arthroscopy.

of the articular cartilage of the patella and lateral patella tracking. Arthroscopic chondroplasty as well as a lateral retinacular release was performed. The postoperative course was prolonged; the patient experienced difficulty regaining motion in the knee, and her ability to bear weight on the knee without pain limited rehabilitation. Hyperpathia to light touch around the knee, burning pain in the knee, and increased pain to cold exposure developed. Slow progress occurred over the next year. Plain x-rays revealed diffuse osteoporosis, and a bone scan showed increased uptake in the entire extremity (Fig. 2). A sympathetic block was performed (using 0.20% bupivicaine infused at 10 cc/hr at the L2–3 spinal level) after placement of an epidural catheter; this produced complete relief of symptoms. Pain relief continued for 1 week when recurrent trauma from a fall precipitated return of symptoms. Repeat epidural blockade was performed, again with complete relief of symptoms. Oral medications were added: nifedipine, 10 mg po tid; phenytoin, 100 mg bid; and amitriptyline, 25 mg po QHS. A physical therapy program emphasizing quadriceps rehabilitation with isometric exercises, electrical muscle stimulation, and a TENS unit was initiated. The patient continues to make good progress, both in terms of her RSD symptoms and underlying knee problems.

ACKNOWLEDGMENTS

The authors wish to thank Diane Longest and Susan Owens for assistance in preparation of this manuscript. Dr. Payne is a recipient of a Robert Wood Johnson Minority Faculty Development Award.

REFERENCES

1. Abram SE, Lightfoot RW: Treatment of longstanding causalgia with prazocin. Reg Anaesth 6:79–81, 1981.
2. Albert ML: Carbamazepine for painful post-traumatic paraesthesiae. N Engl J Med 290:693, 1974.
3. Barasi S, Lynn B: Effects of sympathetic stimulation on mechanoreceptor and nociceptor afferent units with small myelinated (A-delta) and unmyelinated (C) axons innervating the rabbit pinna. J Physiol (London) 341:51P, 1983.
4. Barnes R: The role of sympathectomy in the treatment of causalgia. J Bone Joint Surg 35B:172–180, 1953.
5. Benzon HT, Chomka CM, Brunner EA: Treatment of reflex sympathetic dystrophy with regional intravenous reserpine. Anesth Anal 59:500–502, 1980.
6. Betcher A, Bean G, Casten D: Continuous procaine block of paravertebral sympathetic ganglions. JAMA 151:288–292, 1953.
7. Bonelli S, Conosente F, Movilia PG, et al: Regional intravenous guanethidine vs. stellate ganglion block in reflex sympathetic dystrophies: a randomized trial. Pain 16:297–307, 1983.
8. Bonica J: Causalgia and other reflex sympathetic dystrophies. In Bonica J (ed): Advances in Pain Research and Therapy, Vol. 3. New York, Raven Press, 1979, pp 141–166.
9. Casten D, Betcher A: Reflex sympathetic dystrophy. Surg Gynecol Obstet 99–101, 1955.
10. Carlson DH, Simon H, Wegner W: Bone scanning and diagnosis of reflex sympathetic dystrophy secondary to herniated lumbar discs. Neurology 27:791–793, 1977.
11. Christensen K, Lensen EM, Abee I: The reflex dystrophy syndrome response to treatment with systemic corticosteroids. Arch Chir Scand 148:653–655, 1982.
11a. Demangeat J-L, Constantinesco A, Brunot B, et al: Three phase bone scanning in reflex sympathetic dystrophy of the hand. J Nucl Med 29:26–32, 1988.
12. Denson D, Raj P, Saldahna F, et al: Continuous perineural infusion of bupivacaine for prolonged analgesia; pharmacokinetic considerations. Int J Clin Pharmacol Ther 21:591–599, 1983.
13. Devor M. Nerve pathophysiology and mechanisms of pain in causalgia. J Auton Nerv Sys 7:371–84, 1983.
14. Devor M, Janig LW: Activation of myelinated afferents ending in a neuroma by stimulation of the sympathetic supply in the rat. Neurosci Lett 24:43–47, 1981.
15. Drocacci P, Francini F, Maresca M, Zoppi M: Skin potential and EMG changes induced by cutaneous electrical stimulation. II. Subjects with reflex sympathetic dystrophies. Appl Neurophysiol 42:125–134, 1979.

16. Erdemir H, Gelman S, Galbraith JG: Prediction of the needed level of sympathectomy for post-traumatic reflex sympathetic dystrophy. Surg Neurol 17:353–354, 1982.
17. Eriksen S: Duration of sympathetic blockage. Anesthesia 36:768–771, 1981.
18. Ficat P, Hungerford D: Reflex sympathetic dystrophy. In Disorders of the Patello-Femoral Joint. Baltimore, Williams and Wilkins, 1977, pp 149–169.
19. Genant H, Kozin F, Bekerman C, et al: The reflex sympathetic dystrophy syndromes. Diagn Radiol 117:21–31, 1975.
20. Getto CJ, Sorkness CA, Howell T: Antidepressants and chronic nonmalignant pain: a review. J Pain Sympt Manag 2:9–18, 1987.
21. Ghostine SY, Comair YG, Turner DM, et al: Phenoxybenzamine in the treatment of causalgia: report of 40 cases. J Neurosurg 60:1263–1268, 1984.
22. Glick EN: Reflex dystrophy (algoneurodystrophy): results of treatment by corticosteroids. Rheumat Rehab 12:84–88, 1973.
23. Glynn CJ, Basedow RW, Walsh JA: Pain relief following post-ganglionic sympathetic blockade with IV guanethidine. Br J Anaesth 53:1297–1301, 1981.
24. Greyson ND, Tepperman PS: Three-phase bone studies in hemiplegia with reflex sympathetic dystrophy and the effect of disuse. J Nucl Med 25:423–429, 1984.
25. Hannington-Kiff J: Relief of Sudeck's atrophy by regional intravenous guanethidine. Lancet 2:1132–1133, 1977.
26. Hannington-Kiff J: Intravenous regional sympathetic block with guanethidine. Lancet 1:1019–1020, 1974.
27. Hannington-Kiff J: Relief of causalgia in links by regional intravenous guanethidine. Br Med J 367–368, 1979.
28. Hendler N, Uematesu S, Long DS: Thermographic validation of physical complaints in "psychogenic" pain patients. Thermography 23:283–287, 1982.
29. Herrmann L, Roineke H, Caldwell J: Post-traumatic painful osteoporosis. Am J Roentgenol Rad Ther 47:1353–1361, 1947.
30. Holden WD: Sympathetic dystrophy. Arch Surg 57:373–384, 1948.
30a. Holden LE, Mackinnon SE: Reflex sympathetic dystrophy in the hands: clinical and scintigraphic criteria. Radiology 146:761–775, 1981.
31. Holland A, Davies K, Wallace D: Sympathetic blockade of isolated limbs by intravenous guanethidine. Can Anaesth Soc J 24:597–602, 1977.
32. Horowitz SH: Iatrogenic causalgia: classification, clinical findings, and legal ramifications. Arch Neurol 41:821–824, 1984.
33. Janig W. Causalgia and reflex sympathetic dystrophy: in what way is the sympathetic nervous system involved? Trends Neurosci 8:471–477, 1985.
34. Kleinert H, Cole N, Wayne L, et al: Post-traumatic sympathetic dystrophy. Orthop Clin North Am 4:917–927, 1973.
35. Kozin F, McCarthy D, Sims J, Genant H: The reflex sympathetic dystrophy syndrome. I. Clinical and histologic studies: evidence for bilaterality response to corticosteroids and articular involvement. Am J Med 60:321–331, 1976.
36. Kozin F, McCarthy D, Sims J, Genant H: The reflex sympathetic dystrophy syndrome. II. Roentgenographic and scintigraphic evidence of bilaterally and periventricular accentuation. Am J Med 60:332–338, 1976.
37. Leipzig TJ, Mullan SF: Causalgic pain relieved by prolonged procaine amide sympathetic blockade. J Neurosurg 60:1095–1096, 1984.
38. Linson MA, Leflert R, Todd DP: The treatment of upper extremity reflex sympathetic dystrophy with prolonged continuous stellate ganglion blockade. J Hand Surg 8:153–159, 1983.
39. Lioz T, Payne RC: Causalgia: report of recovery following relief of emotional stress. Arch Neurol Psych 53:222–225, 1945.
40. Litwin M: Post-sympathectomy neuralgia. Arch Surg 84:121–125, 1982.
41. Loh L, Nathan PW: Painful peripheral states and sympathetic blocks. J Neurol Neurosurg Psychiatry 41:664–671, 1978.
42. Lofstrom JB, Lloyd JW, Cousins MJ. Sympathetic neural blockade of the upper and lower extremity. In Cousins MJ, Bridenbaugh PO (eds): Neural Blockade in Clinical Anesthesia and Management of Pain. Philadelphia, J.B. Lippincott, 1980, pp 574–620.
43. Maciewicz R, Bouckoms A, Martin JB: Drug therapy of neuropathic pain. Clin J Pain 1:39–49, 1985.
44. Mockus M, Rutherford R, Rosales C, Pearce W: Sympathectomy for causalgia. Arch Surg 122:668–672, 1987.
45. Munn JS, Baker WH: Recurrent sympathetic dystrophy: successful treatment by contralateral sympathectomy. Surgery 102:102–103, 1987.

46. Ochoa JL, Torebjork E, Marchettini P, Sibak M: Mechanisms of neuropathic pain: cumulative observations, new experiments, and further speculation. In Fields HL, Dubner R, Cervero F, (eds): Advances in Pain Research and Therapy, Vol. 9. New York, Raven Press, 1985, pp. 431–450.

47. Payne R: Neuropathic pain syndromes with special reference to causalgia and RSD. Clin J Pain 2:59–73, 1986.

48. Persson AV, Anderson LA, Padberg FT: Selection of patients for lumbar sympathectomy. Surg Clin North Amer 65:393–403, 1985.

49. Pleet AB, Tahmous AJ, Jennings JR: Causalgia: treatment with propranolol. Neurology 26:375, 1976.

49a. Pollock KE, Poehling GG, Kosman AG: Reflex sympathetic dystrophy of the knee. Presented at the Arthroscopy Association of North America. Houston, Texas, May 1987.

50. Portwood M, Lieberman J, Taylor R: Ultrasound treatment of reflex sympathetic dystrophy. Arch Phys Med Rehab 68:116–118, 1987.

51. Prough D, McCooky C, Poehling G, et al: Efficacy of oral nifedipine in treatment of reflex sympathetic dystrophy. Anesthesiology 62:796–799, 1985.

52. Rajapakse C, Grennan DM, Jones C, et al: Thermography in the assessment of peripheral joint inflammation—a re-evaluation. Rheum Rehab 20:81–87, 1981.

53. Ramamurthy S, Winnie M: Regional anesthetic technique for pain relief. Semin Anesthesiol 4:237–249, 1985.

54. Raskin N, Leuinson S, Hoffman P, et al: Post-sympathetectomy neuralgia: amelioration with diphenyhydration or carbamazepine. Am J Surg 128:75–78, 1974.

55. Ray B, Console D: Residual sympathetic pathways of the paravertebral sympathectomy. J Neurosurg 5:23–50, 1948.

56. Richlin D, Carron H, Rowlingson S, et al: Reflex sympathetic dystrophy: successful treatment by transcutaneous neural stimulation. J Pediatr 84–86, 1978.

57. Rosen PS, Graham W: The shoulder-hand syndrome: historical review with observations on seventy-three patients. Can Med Assoc J 77:86–91, 1987.

58. Rowlingson S: The sympathetic dystrophies. Int Anesthesiol Clin 21:117–129, 1983.

59. Richards RL: Causalgia: a centennial review. Arch Neurol 16:339–350, 1967.

60. Roberts W: A hypothesis on the physiological basis for causalgia and related pains. Pain 24:257–311, 1986.

61. Roberts WJ, Elardo SM. Sympathetic activation of A-delta nociceptors. Somatosensory Res 3:33–44, 1985.

62. Russek HI: Shoulder-hand syndrome following myocardial infarction. Med Clin North Am 42:1555–1562, 1958.

63. Salisbury RS, Parr G, DeSilva M, et al: Heat distribution over normal and abnormal joints: thermal pattern and quantification. Ann Rheum Dis 42:494–499, 1983.

64. Scadding JW, Wall PD, Parry CBW, et al: Clinical trial of propranolol in post-traumatic neuralgia. Pain 14:283–292, 1982.

65. Schon F: Postsympathectomy pain and changes in sensory neuropeptides: towards an animal model. Lancet 1:1158–1160, 1985.

66. Schutzer S, Gosslig H: The treatment of reflex sympathetic dystrophy syndrome. J Bone Joint Surg 66A:526–629, 1984.

67. Shumacker H: A personal overview of causalgia and other reflex sympathetic dystrophies. Ann Surg 201:278–289, 1985.

68. Shumacker HB, Spiegel IJ, Upjohn RH: Causalgia. I. The role of sympathetic interruption in treatment. Surg Gynecol Obstet 86:76–86, 1948.

69. Shumacker HB, Spiegel IJ, Upjohn RH: Causalgia. II. The signs and symptoms with particular reference to vasomotor disturbance. Surg Gynecol Obstet 86:452–460, 1948.

70. Shumacker HB: Causalgia III. A general discussion. Surgery 24:485–503, 1948.

71. Siegel MG, Siqueland KA, Noyes FR: The use of computerized thermography in the evaluation of non-traumatic anterior knee pain. Orthopedics 10:825–883, 1987.

72. Simon H, Carlson D: The use of bone scanning in the diagnosis of reflex sympathetic dystrophy. Clin Nucl Med 5:116–121, 1980.

73. Simson G: Propanolol for causalgia and Sudek atrophy. Lancet 1:227, 1974.

74. Spurling RG: Causalgia of the upper extremity treatment by dorsal sympathetic ganglionectomy. Arch Neurol Psychiat 23:784–788, 1930.

75. Swerdlow M: Anticonvulsant drugs and chronic pain. Clin Neuropharmacol 7:51–82, 1985.

76. Sunderland S: Nerves and Nerve Injuries, 2nd ed. Edinburgh, Churchill Livingstone, 1978, pp 377–472.

77. Steinbrocker O, Neustadt D, Lapin L: Shoulder-hand syndrome. Sympathetic block compared with corticotropins and corticosone therapy. JAMA 9:788–791, 1953.
78. Steinbrocker O: The shoulder-hand syndromes present perspective. Arch Phys Med Rehab 49:384–395, 1968.
79. Subbarao J, Stillwell GK: Reflex sympathetic dystrophy syndrome of the upper extremity: analysis of total outcome of management of 125 cases. Arch Phys Med Rehab 62:549–554, 1981.
80. Szeinfeld M, Pallares VS: Considerations in the treatment of causalgia. Anesthesiology 58:294–296, 1983.
81. Tabira T, Shibasaki H, Kurdiwa Y: Reflex sympathetic dystrophy (causalgia) treatment with guanethidine. Arch Neurol 40:430–432, 1983.
82. Tahmoush A, Mally J, Innings JR: Skin conductance temperature and blood flow in causalgia. Neurology 33:1483–1486, 1983.
83. Tahmoush AJ: Causalgia: redefinition as a clinical pain syndrome. Pain 10:187–199, 1981.
84. Takats G: Reflex dystrophy of the extremities. Arch Surg 34:939–956, 1937.
85. Thurber CM, Benjamin KJ, Harber GR, et al: Post-traumatic reflex sympathetic dystrophy. J Foot Surg 22:349–352, 1983.
86. Tietjen R: Reflex sympathetic dystrophy of the knee. Clin Orthop 209:234–247, 1986.
87. Tracy GD, Syndney MS, Cockett FB, Lond MS: Pain in the lower limb after sympathectomy. Lancet 1:12–14, 1957.
88. Uematsu S, Hendler N, Hungerford D, Long D, Ono N: Thermography and electromyography in the differential diagnosis of chronic pain syndromes and reflex sympathetic dystrophy. Electromyogr Clin Neurophysiol 21:165–182, 1981.
89. Vasudevan SV, Myers B: Reflex sympathetic dystrophy syndrome; importance of early diagnosis and appropriate management. Wisc Med J 84:24–28, 1985.
90. Wang JK, Johnson KA, Ilstrup D: Sympathetic blocks for reflex sympathetic dystrophy. Pain 23:13–17, 1985.
91. Warfield CD: The sympathetic dystrophies. Hosp Pract 5:52C–52J, 1984.
92. Weber M, Drayer J: Central and peripheral blockade of the sympathetic nervous system. Am J Med 110–118, 1984.
93. Wieth FD, Rutherford RB: A civilian experience with causalgia. Arch Surg 100:623–638, 1970.
94. Wittmoser R: Possibilities of using sympathectomy for treatment of pain syndromes. Appl Neurophysiol 47:203–207, 1984.

JOHN J. KELLY, JR, MD

FOCAL NEUROPATHIES OF THE LEG

Associate Professor of Neurology,
Tufts-New England Medical Center,
Boston, Massachusetts

Focal neuropathies affecting the leg are commonly encountered in orthopedic and neurosurgical practices. Patients may present with spontaneous or post-traumatic neuropathies as the primary complaint, or nerve damage may occur as a complication of surgery or other treatment for spine or joint problems. In addition, such practitioners, by nature of their knowledge and interest in bone and muscle anatomy and function, are often consulted about patients with medical or surgical problems complicated by focal nerve damage. Thus, it is important that all orthopedists and neurosurgeons have a thorough knowledge of the principles of focal peripheral nerve injury and be acquainted with specific focal neuropathies that affect the leg.

GENERAL COMMENTS

Patients with focal nerve damage generally present with some combination of pain and neurologic deficit. Pain, of course, is common in the setting of orthopedic or neurosurgical disease. Without neurologic deficit, the presence of nerve damage is often difficult to determine unless the pain itself is highly specific and characteristic of neurologic disease, as in root pain due to a herniated lumbar disc. Although pain is the commonest manifestation of focal nerve damage, neurologic deficit is frequently present, so that recognition of nerve damage is generally readily accomplished.

Focal nerve injury generally causes acute pain that is maximal at the site of the nerve injury. Such pain, likely due to injury to the nervi nervorum, is most often localized deep in the tissues and is aching in quality. From this site, the pain may radiate more distally in the distribution of the nerve. Radiating pain may also have a deep and aching character but, in the acute or subacute setting, is more commonly sharp and shooting, often provoked by movement of the affected part with traction of the compressed or inflamed nerve. With time, however, proximal symptoms abate and distal radiating pain changes in quality, becoming more persistent, pervasive, and dysesthetic, and often attains qualities akin to causalgia and reflex sympathetic dystrophy (see the next chapter). Such pain is less clearly related to movement or traction of the affected part but is more spontaneous in nature. Elements of burning, gnawing, and deep aching pain are intermixed, often precipitated by seemingly trivial stimuli such as gentle contact (by bed clothes or a breeze) to the affected area or a change in atmospheric pressure. Such patients guard and protect the affected part, which develops secondary cutaneous, muscular, bony, and autonomic trophic changes. The patient in turn becomes a tormented wreck of his former self, unable to eat or sleep or enjoy life's pleasures.

Focal or multifocal nerve damage should not be confused with the asymmetric onset of a generalized polyneuropathy, as may occur in diabetes, toxin exposure (alcohol), or other systemic disorders such as uremia or hepatic insufficiency. These patients may also develop disturbing dysesthesias and paresthesias of one or both legs with hypersensitivity to soles and feet and secondary trophic changes. However, except very early in the course, the symptoms and signs, although asymmetric, are bilateral. Thus, there is distal weakness and wasting of both legs, ankle jerks are absent bilaterally, knee jerks are both depressed or absent, and sensory impairment is present in both feet. However, a patient with a mild, underlying subclinical polyneuropathy (diabetes, alcohol) can develop a superimposed entrapment neuropathy because the metabolically more vulnerable nerves are more susceptible to trauma. Such a situation should always be suspected in a seemingly healthy, young patient who develops a focal neuropathy spontaneously or for trivial reasons. If careful examination does not reveal evidence for more generalized involvement, nerve conduction velocities and EMG are essential tools in searching for more widespread involvement. This is important since, even though these patients may recover fully, they are at risk for developing further episodes and surgical procedures may be riskier in these patients, since these nerves are more vulnerable and less tolerant of the retraction and relative ischemia that occur during nerve surgery. Also, such a discovery may alert the physician and the patient to the presence of a previously unsuspected or concealed medical problem, such as subclinical diabetes or occult alcoholism.

In addition, widespread evidence of subclinical polyneuropathy on EMG with features of segmental demyelination without evidence for underlying toxic or metabolic disease raises the question of a polyneuropathy with hereditary abnormalities of myelin sheaths rendering nerves more susceptible to compression. Such a neuropathy, the so-called "polyneuropathy with hereditary predisposition to pressure palsies" or "tomaculous neuropathy" after the peculiar and highly characteristic sausage-like (tomacle) swellings of myelin sheaths observed on nerve biopsy, is common, passed on from one generation to another, becomes symptomatic in the teens or twenties, and renders those it affects peculiarly susceptible to neuropathies due to nerve compression at common sites (ulnar-elbow, peroneal-knee, nerve root-disc) following minor trauma. Recognition of these patients is also important, since surgery is almost never indicated and further episodes can be prevented or ameliorated by avoiding provocative positions and activities.

Focal mononeuropathies or plexopathies occurring in the legs for no apparent reason, especially if sudden and painful, should always excite the interest and suspicion of the clinician. Most commonly, as mentioned above, diabetes or some toxic process is the culprit, and these can be readily detected by careful history (from the spouse if necessary) and examination and a minimum of laboratory tests, including careful nerve conduction velocities and EMG of both legs. However, if one of these conditions is not found, other systemic conditions should be considered. In older patients, particularly men, vasculitis due to periarteritis nodosa or the other vasculitides should be considered. Although this disease often appears in the setting of a systemic illness with weight loss, anemia, fever, arthralgies, myalgias and renal involvement with hypertension, a primary or initial neurologic presentation is also common. Despite the apparent mononeuritic quality of the involvement, nerve conduction velocities and EMG always demonstrate more widespread, subclinical involvement of multiple nerves in the extremities with a distal predominance and features of asymmetric axonal degeneration rather than demyelination. This makes distinction from benign, focal, compressive neuropathies easy because, unless the patient has an underlying diabetic or other polyneuropathy, other nerves are typically completely normal in these cases and the affected nerve usually, at least in the subacute phase, demonstrates evidence of focal demyelination with focal slowing of conduction and conduction block across the compression site. The finding of an unexplained focal neuropathy with features of axonal degeneration in the setting of more widespread, distal axonal damage mandates a workup for systemic disease, even if the patient at that moment appears relatively well.

Treatment of focal nerve damage in the legs varies with the individual syndromes, which will be discussed below, but some general rules apply. Nerve conduction velocities and EMG are invaluable not only in localizing the process but in predicting the pathology (demyelination or axonal degeneration) and pathophysiology (compression, vasculitis) and in guiding therapy. Thus, the discovery of an isolated, focal, demyelinative lesion suggests an excellent prognosis. Little more than protection of the affected part and nerve need be accomplished and recovery is usually quick and complete. Surgery is almost never indicated in this setting unless persistent compression and damage to the nerve is unavoidable by virtue of anatomic abnormalities or vocation. In this setting, surgery is almost invariably successful. Nerves with primarily axonal injuries with little evidence of demyelination are more difficult. These nerves can be the subject of chronic and recurrent trauma, which eventually turns an initially demyelinative lesion into one with predominantly axonal damage. In addition, processes such as ischemia, severe trauma, diabetes with infarction, inflammation, and similar disorders can focally damage nerves and cause an axonal lesion. When nerves are so damaged, the results of treatment are generally less satisfactory. Nerve conduction velocities and EMG are less useful in localizing the process to a distinct segment, since the hallmarks of focal demyelination are now absent. However, nerve conduction velocities and EMG are excellent at detecting axonal damage and thus predicting which patients will do poorly, no matter the treatment. Surgery should be approached carefully in these patients, since the result is seldom satisfactory. Only if damage is progressive and unavoidable should surgery be attempted. These patients either fail to recover or recover slowly after such surgery, since regeneration is slow (about 1 mm per day). Often, patients present with a mixture of axonal and demyelinative nerve damage. These patients are most difficult and often require careful consideration by both the surgeon and a neurologist experienced in peripheral nerve pathology

TABLE 1. Major Focal Neuropathies of the Leg

Buttock and Posterior Thigh	Medial Leg
Sciatic neuropathy	Saphenous neuropathy
Sacral plexopathy	Anterior Shin and Dorsum of Foot
Anterior and Lateral Thigh	Peroneal neuropathy
Lateral femoral cutaneous neuropathy	Posterior Calf and Sole
Femoral neuropathy	Tibial neuropathy
Lumbar plexopathy	Sole of Foot and Toes
Medial Thigh	Tarsal tunnel syndrome
Obturator neuropathy	Plantar neuropathy

and electrophysiology. Patients with underlying polyneuropathies with super-imposed focal neuropathies are also difficult problems. These polyneuropathies, and diabetes in particular, render nerves more susceptible to trauma and manipulation. Thus, seemingly successful, uncomplicated surgery can end disastrously with a nonfunctional, infarcted nerve and an angry, litigious patient. The surgeon, in general, should avoid the temptation to surgically attack these problems.

SPECIFIC SYNDROMES (Table 1)

Since patients present with complaints of pain and neurological dysfunction related to anatomic regions, focal neuropathies are best approached from this perspective.

Posterior Hip and Thigh Pain

Posterior hip and thigh pain caused by focal neuropathies is most commonly due to lumbosacral radiculopathies affecting the L4, L5, or S1 roots due to degenerative disease of the spine with lumbar stenosis, herniated lumbar discs or, less commonly, neoplastic involvement of the lumbar spine. These radiculopathies and polyradiculopathies are discussed in the first chapter of this monograph.

Sciatic Neuropathies.   The term sciatica, although commonly used, is a misnomer, since pain in the sciatic nerve distribution is almost always due to radicular disease, even in the absence of back pain when pain is localized to the sciatic notch and distally. True sciatic neuropathy due to compression of the sciatic nerve at the sciatic notch (Fig. 1) or distally deep within the thigh is rare in clinical practice. However, tumors or tight fascial bands can affect the sciatic nerve at the notch and can mimic root diseases. In addition, surgical hip repair can damage the sciatic nerve because of the proximity of the hip joint to the course of the nerve. Other causes include trauma to the pelvic area, external compression of the nerve in the buttocks, injection injury into the sciatic nerve in the region of the gluteus maximus, infiltration by tumors, and injury following

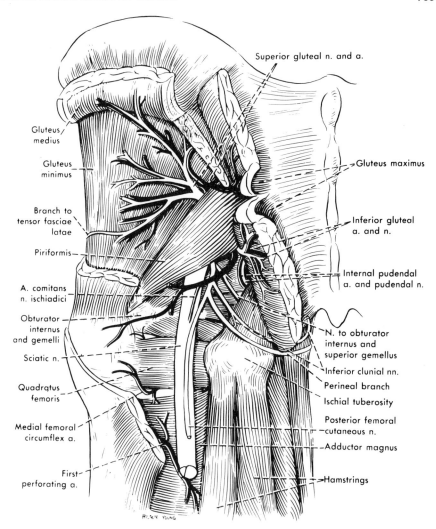

Superior gluteal n. and a.

Gluteus
medius

Gluteus
minimus

Branch to
tensor fasciae
latae

Piriformis

A. comitans
n. ischiadici

Obturator
internus
and gemelli

Sciatic n.

Quadratus
femoris

Medial femoral
circumflex a.

First
perforating a.

Gluteus maximus

Inferior gluteal
a. and n.

Internal pudendal
a. and pudendal n.

N. to obturator
internus and
superior gemellus

Inferior clunial nn.

Perineal branch

Ischial tuberosity

Posterior femoral
cutaneous n.

Adductor magnus

Hamstrings

FIGURE 1. Sciatic nerve as it exits from the sciatic notch deep within the buttocks. It is covered here by the piriformis muscles and is generally well protected by overlying adipose and muscular tissue. (Reproduced from Hollinshead WH, Jenkins DB: Functional Anatomy of the Limbs and Back, 5th ed. Philadelphia, W.B. Saunders, 1981, with permission).

pelvic or hip fractures. Sciatica is sometimes ascribed to a controversial disorder called the piriformis syndrome, in which the sciatic nerve, as it exits from the sciatic notch, is said to be compressed by the piriformis muscle. However, upon careful study, most of these patients have radiculopathies or other problems, and the actual piriformis syndrome, if it occurs, is quite rare. More distally in the thigh, trauma and benign nerve tumors such as schwannomas and neurofibromas cause progressive sciatic neuropathy.

EMG and radiologic studies are essential for differentiation and localization of these problems. In addition, CT and MRI of the buttock and thigh region will detect neoplastic involvement. This is especially true in slow-growing schwannomas or neurofibromas, which can present with distal pain and paresthesias provoked by compression of the involved segment (sitting on a firm object). EMG usually demonstrates axonal damage distally. The diagnosis can often be by deep palpation of the upper thigh or buttock region and confirmed by CT or MRI of the affected region. Prolonged compression of the buttock and thigh region due to coma, often associated with drug and alcohol abuse, or anesthesia, especially in thin individuals, can cause serious axonal damage to the sciatic nerve. Swelling, discoloration, and cutaneous and subcutaneous necrosis of the compressed area with an increased CK level and myoglobinuria are telltale signs. Rare causes of sciatica neuropathy include herpes simplex, herpes zoster, AIDS, and Lyme disease. Vasculitis can also preferentially infarct the sciatic nerve in the upper thigh, which is the vascular watershed area, resulting in semiselective involvement of the peroneal nerve.

Sacral Plexopathy. Plexopathies less commonly affect the sacral than the lumbar plexus (Fig. 2). However, infiltrative lesions due to pelvic malignancies (uterine, rectal, lymphoma) can infiltrate the sacral plexus, causing progressive buttock, posterior thigh, and distal leg symptoms and signs. The key to diagnosis is the history of progressive, localized disease, suggesting the presence of a slow-growing neoplasm. Also, aneurysm surgery and intraarterial chemotherapy can result in ischemia and infarction of the sacral plexus. Retroperitoneal hemorrhage can compress the plexus. Herpes zoster may also cause a subacute plexopathy. Trauma uncommonly affects the sacral plexus and only in the setting of extensive pelvic fractures. EMG and CT scan are invaluable in discovering the etiology of sacral plexopathies.

Lateral and Anterior Hip and Knee Pain

Neurologic pain in this region is not as common as posterior hip and thigh pain but still occurs frequently enough to be a neurologic problem. The most common cause is lateral femoral cutaneous neuropathy or meralgia paresthetica (Fig. 2). This neuropathy results from compression of the lateral femoral cutaneous nerve as it passes through its foramen in the lateral inguinal ligament just medial to the anterior superior iliac spine. Such compression often is due to a change in posture or gait occasioned by orthopedic disease of back, hip, knee, or foot, and can be a source of considerable confusion to clinician. Also, sudden weight gain or loss with a change of a relation of the abdominal wall to the thigh results in altered angulation of the nerve with nerve compression. This neuropathy can also be due to retroperitoneal disease such as benign and malignant tumors. These patients report pain and altered sensation in an elliptical area over the lateral thigh region. They often grip the lateral thigh with their hand to indicate the affected area. The pain is provoked by walking, standing, or prolonged sitting. The pain is rarely shooting in quality but is often burning, dysesthetic, or hyperesthetic. Examination reveals no weakness or reflex loss but decreased pinprick, temperature, and light touch in the area involved. Sensory loss is usually only partial unless the neuropathy is severe and long-standing, but the border is generally fairly well-defined. Occasionally, there is a tender area medial to the anterior superior iliac spine where the nerve leaves the foramen. Straight leg raising and reverse straight leg raising tests are negative

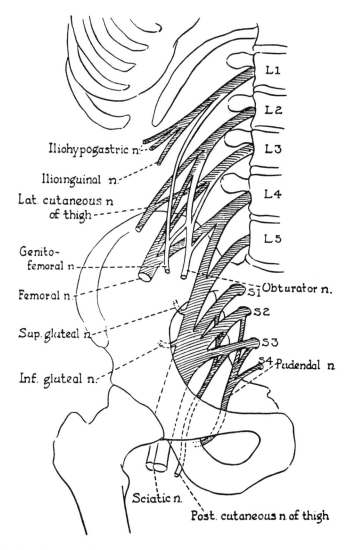

FIGURE 2. Lumbosacral plexus and origin of major nerves from the plexus. (Reproduced from Hollinshead WH, Jenkins DB: Functional Anatomy of the Limbs and Back, 5th ed. Philadelphia, W.B. Saunders, 1981, with permission).

but the hip rotation and abduction test may produce pain radiating into the lateral thigh. Treatment involves correction of the underlying abnormality such as improvement of gait and posture or weight loss. Rarely, injection of depot steroids into the area of the foramen can be tried. Surgical decompression or neurectomy is almost never indicated except in especially severe and refractory cases.

The next most common cause of hip and thigh pain is so-called *femoral neuropathy* (Fig. 3), which is almost never purely femoral nerve in nature but almost always represents either a radiculopathy, polyradiculopathy, or a lumbar plexopathy. In order of decreasing frequency, most common causes include

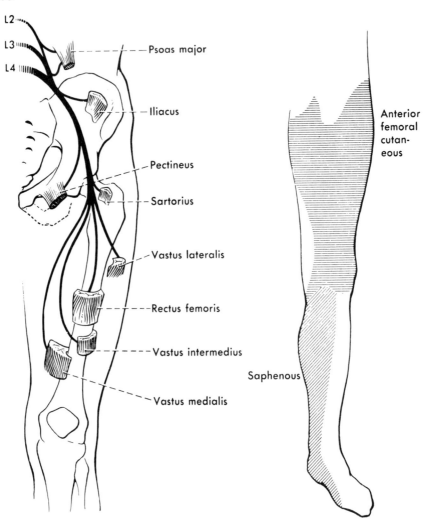

FIGURE 3. Motor and sensory distribution of the femoral nerve, including the saphenous branch. (Reproduced from Hollinshead WH, Jenkins DB: Functional Anatomy of the Limbs and Back, 5th ed. Philadelphia, W.B. Saunders, 1981, with permission).

diabetes, radiculopathy, and cancer. Diabetes is by far the commonest cause of apparent femoral neuropathy, also referred to as diabetic amyotrophy of Garland or diabetic polyradiculopathy. More recently, the non-committal term "proximal diabetic neuropathy" is preferred, since the site of pathology is in the plexus, roots, or both. Patients typically have maturity-onset diabetes and present spontaneously or following some precipitating event such as surgery (often orthopedic) with severe pain in the groin and anterior thigh, rapid progressive weakness and atrophy of the anterior thigh muscles, and loss of the knee jerk. Sensory loss is often minimal in the anterior thigh or absent altogether. Although superficially localized to the femoral nerve distribution, and hence the reason for the popular name, careful clinical examination and EMG demonstrate almost invariable involvement of obturator-innervated muscles and occasionally other proximal and distal leg muscles. Characteristically the lumbosacral nerve roots show profuse, widespread evidence of denervation (thus suggesting the term diabetic polyradiculopathy to some). Occasionally, bilateral involvement occurs. Patients are often diagnostic puzzles. They lose weight, are depressed, and are thought to have a malignancy. Often, no serious diabetic neuropathy is present prior to onset and glucose intolerance is mild. Though they generally are extensively evaluated, nothing is found. Patients almost invariably improve spontaneously with decreased pain, weight gain, and a gradual increase in strength and muscle bulk. By one to two years after onset, recovery is often good and fairly complete. The cause is unknown but most evidence points to a vasculopathy with infarction of nerves and roots. Since these patients are often elderly and have degenerative disease of the spine, avoidance of surgery for presumed disc or spinal stenosis is important. The EMG, which shows widespread nonlocalized denervation, and clinical acumen are the keys to recognition.

Mid-lumbar discs (or lumbar metastases) can also cause radicular pain and deficit in the anterior thigh region. Presence of back pain and associated findings, EMG, and imaging studies allow differentiation. Tumors of the abdomen and upper pelvis can infiltrate the lumbar plexus with resultant symptoms in the anterior thigh. It is sometimes difficult to distinguish this syndrome from discogenic radiculopathy or, in diabetics, from proximal diabetic neuropathy. Here again, EMG and CT scan are essential. Other uncommon causes of femoral neuropathy or lumbar plexopathy include aneurysms, iliacus hematomas or abscesses, herpes zoster, hip surgery or trauma with fractures of the proximal femur or pelvis, and inadvertent femoral nerve injury during femoral vein or artery procedures.

Medial Thigh and Leg Pain

Obturator neuropathies (Fig. 4) are rare and more or less restricted to lesions in the region of the obturator foramen with pain in the medial thigh and weakness of hip adduction. The adductor reflex of the thigh, which is difficult to elicit, will be asymmetrically reduced. Passive hip abduction (obturator stretch test) can produce pain in the medial leg. Occasionally, tumors in the lower pelvis in the region of the obturator foramen can infiltrate the nerve. Saphenous neuropathies are also rare. They are usually due to direct trauma, often after surgery on saphenous veins (varicose vein surgery or arterial grafting). The infrapatellar branch of the saphenous nerve can also be injured during knee surgery or trauma with numbness and pain inferior to the patella. Nerve conduction velocities and EMG can help in recognizing obturator and saphenous neuropathies and in separating them from other causes of medial leg and thigh pain.

Anterior Tibial Pain

Focal neuropathies affecting the anterior tibial region and dorsum of the foot are the most common variety of focal neuropathies of the leg, and peroneal neuropathy at the knee due to compression at the head of the fibula is the most frequent in this group. The peroneal nerve (Fig. 5) departs from the sciatic in the mid to lower posterior thigh, travels in the lateral popliteal fossa, and winds

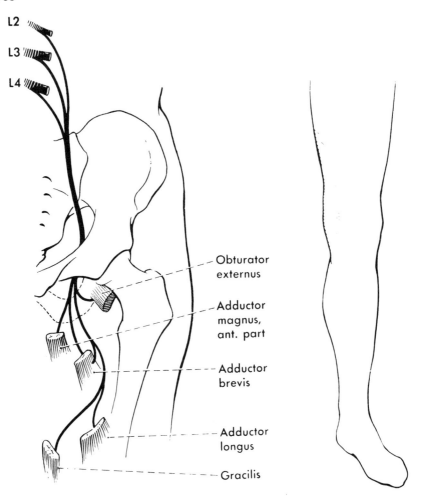

FIGURE 4. Motor and sensory distribution of the obturator nerve. (Reproduced from Hollinshead WH, Jenkins DB: Functional Anatomy of the Limbs and Back, 5th ed. Philadelphia, W.B. Saunders, 1981, with permission).

around the neck of the fibula. Here, habitual leg crossing, especially in thin patients or patients with underlying mild peripheral nerve diseases, like diabetes, makes the nerve particularly susceptible to compression. Patients present with foot drop and weakness of foot eversion and toe dorsiflexion. Numbness in the anterior tibial region and dorsum of the foot occurs. Pain is less common. Peroneal compression usually comes on gradually and is the result of recurrent compression. Also, trauma in the region of the knee with or without fracture of the fibula can also damage the peroneal nerve. Sudden adduction and flexion injuries of the ankle and prolonged squatting or knee bending can stretch and damage the nerve. A rare syndrome of fibula tunnel entrapment has also been reported. In the hospital setting, a common cause of peroneal neuropathy is prolonged bed rest, often after surgery, with compression of the nerve between

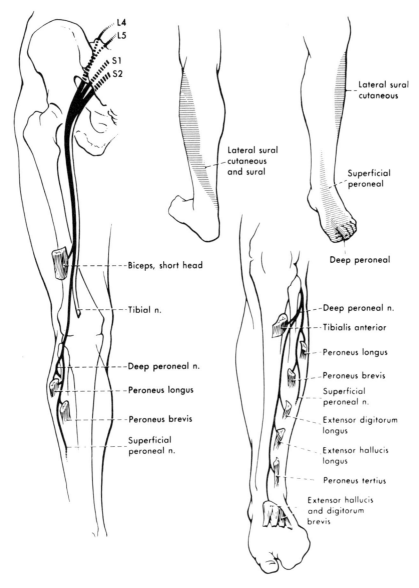

FIGURE 5. Distribution of the peroneal nerve. Note the biceps femoris, the only muscle innervated by the peroneal nerve above the knee. (Reproduced from Hollinshead WH, Jenkins DB: Functional Anatomy of the Limbs and Back, 5th ed. Philadelphia, W.B. Saunders, 1981, with permission).

the bed and the fibula head. This should be watched for carefully and prevented by keeping the legs from turning out, and by using sheep-skin padding or a water bed.

Although usually due to compression at the fibula head, peroneal neuropathies can also occur more proximally. Lesions of the proximal sciatic nerve in the upper thigh due to trauma, tumors, or nerve infarcts can cause a relatively

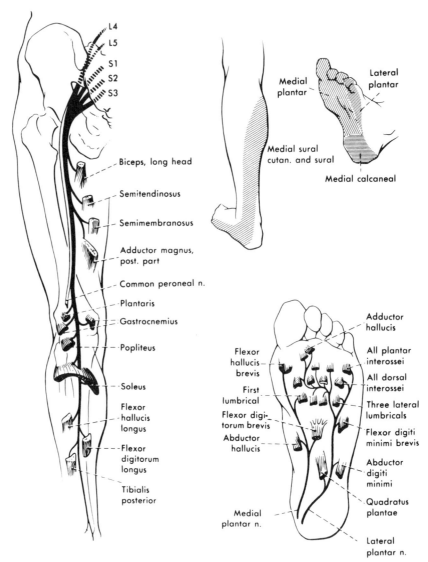

FIGURE 6. Tibial nerve motor and sensory branches. The distal tibial nerve gives off the sural, calcaneal and plantar nerves. (Reproduced from Hollinshead WH, Jenkins DB: Functional Anatomy of the Limbs and Back. 5th ed. Philadelphia, W.B. Saunders, 1981, with permission).

selective peroneal neuropathy. Vascular infarcts are likely in this region since this is the watershed area of vascular supply to the sciatic nerve. The peroneal branch is lateral and less well vascularized than the tibial, and thus is especially susceptible to infarction or compression. Hip replacement surgery can also selectively injure the peroneal branch of the sciatic nerve at this level, and since the symptoms and signs are the same as for a peroneal lesion at the fibula head, EMG is necessary to distinguish between the two. Lack of slowing of conduction or absence of conduction block at the fibula head on nerve stimulation and involvement of the short head of biceps femoris (the only peroneal-innervated muscle above the knee) on needle EMG point to more proximal involvement. L-5 radiculopathies occasionally cause relatively isolated foot drop. The key to diagnosis is recognition of weakness of foot inversion, which is a function primarily of the tibialis posterior muscle innervated by the tibial nerve below the knee. Rarely, peroneal neuropathies at the fibula head can selectively affect the superficial or deep branch of the peroneal nerve, with weakness restricted to foot drop and numbness of the web-space between toes 1 and 2 in the case of deep peroneal palsies, or weakness of eversion and numbness of the lateral calf and dorsum of the foot (except the web-space) in the case of superficial peroneal palsies. Also rare is distal peroneal neuropathy in the region of the bimalleolar line. Here, the deep peroneal nerve travels underneath the bimalleolar fascia, the so-called *anterior tarsal tunnel.* Compression causes pain with atrophy of the EDB and numbness of the web-space between digits one and two.

Posterior Calf Pain

Pain in the posterior calf can be due to nerve lesions restricted to this area or can radiate from more proximal lesions as in radiculopathies or sciatic neuropathies. Occasionally, radiculopathies can present with pain restricted to the calf region. In such cases, however, accompanying features, such as back or hip pain or provocation by certain postures or positions, suggest more proximal origin. Patients with sciatic or tibial nerve lesions (Fig. 6) may present with pain in the calf and numbness of the calf and sole. Most common causes are local lesions such as Baker's cyst, ganglion or trauma at the knee which results in compression of the tibial nerve in the popliteal fossa. Isolated tibial neuropathies are actually rare. Sural neuropathies are also rare and direct trauma is usually the cause. Occasionally, sural involvement can occur as part of a tibial neuropathy at the knee.

Heel and Sole Pain

The distal tibial nerve (Fig. 6) supplies branches to the heel (calcaneal branches) and then passes through the tarsal tunnel to supply intrinsic muscles of the foot and cutaneous innervation to the sole (medial and lateral plantar nerves). The branches can be injured by trauma at or just below the knee, sparing branches to the gastrocnemius and posterior tibilias muscles, which are usually given off in the region of the popliteal fossa. Thus, the ankle jerk and foot inversion will be spared but numbness and weakness of heel and sole, atrophy of toe flexors, and intrinsic foot weakness/atrophy will be present. EMG is usually necessary to localize these lesions. Rarely, injury restricted to the calcaneal branch of the tibial nerve or to the sural nerve occurs.

The so-called tarsal tunnel syndrome is a controversial disorder. The classical description is pain over the tarsal tunnel and into the sole in the distribution of the medial or lateral plantar nerves (or both) provoked by weight bearing, walking, or pressure over the tarsal tunnel area and relieved by leg elevation. Although commonly diagnosed by foot specialists, electrophysiologic verification is required. True neurogenic tarsal tunnel syndrome is actually quite rare. The vast majority of cases prove to be foot, bony, ligamentous, tendinous, or articular disease or the asymmetric onset of a painful polyneuropathy. Nerve conduction velocities and EMG are either normal, with lack of selective slowing of conduction of motor and sensory fibers of the plantar nerves across the tarsal tunnel, or show more widespread abnormalities. Since the diagnosis is often difficult, electrophysiologic verification of motor and sensory nerve conduction across the tarsal tunnel for both branches of the plantar nerves and evaluation of other distal nerves and muscles to exclude polyneuropathy is essential.

In the foot, plantar neuropathies can occur. The most common is Morton's neuroma, which causes pain in the forefoot which radiates to the toes. Morton's neuroma typically occurs between the metatarsal heads of digits three and four, with pain radiating into the web-space between these toes. However, plantar nerves can also be injured in other regions by fibrous bands or scars. Treatment by padding of this area and change in shoes is often satisfactory. If necessary, surgery can be performed to remove scar tissue compressing the nerve. Electrophysiological demonstration of abnormality is generally desirable before such surgery is performed.

CONCLUSION

Peripheral nerve injuries are common in orthopedic and neurosurgical practice. Knowledge of peripheral nerve anatomy, physiology, and pathology is essential for proper management of these patients. Such neuropathies can occur spontaneously as a result of trauma or may be caused by a surgical procedure. Early recognition and prompt management lessen disability. Management by a physician (orthopedist, neurosurgeon, or neurologist) expert in dealing with these lesions and early, careful nerve conduction velocities and EMG are essential, since the examination can be difficult acutely and information gained by these studies is often important in prognosis and management. In addition, anticipation of the potential for nerve injuries is important in certain situations, as in sciatic or femoral nerve injuries in hip surgery, or peroneal neuropathy at the fibula head after prolonged bed rest in asthenic patients. Fortunately, most focal neuropathies in otherwise healthy people resolve satisfactorily with prompt recognition and proper treatment.

REFERENCES

1. Dawson DM, Hallett M, Millender LH: Entrapment Neuropathies. Boston, Little, Brown, 1983.
2. Hollinshead WH, Jenkins DB: Functional Anatomy of the Limbs and Back, 5th ed. Philadelphia, W.B. Saunders, 1981.
3. Kelly JJ Jr: Electromyography for the Clinician. In Spitell JA Jr (ed): Clinical Medicine, Philadelphia, Harper & Row, 1981, ch. 28.
4. Stewart JD: Focal peripheral neuropathies. New York, Elsevier, 1987.

INDEX

Entries in **boldface type** indicate complete chapters